MEN, BIRDS,
AND ADVENTURE

OTHER BOOKS BY
VIRGINIA S. EIFERT

LOUIS JOLLIET
Explorer of Rivers

LAND OF THE SNOWSHOE HARE

MISSISSIPPI CALLING

RIVER WORLD
Wildlife of the Mississippi

THE BUFFALO TRACE
The Story of Abraham Lincoln's Ancestors

OUT OF THE WILDERNESS
Young Abe Lincoln Grows Up

THREE RIVERS SOUTH
A Story of Young Abe Lincoln

WITH A TASK BEFORE ME
Abraham Lincoln Leaves Springfield

NEW BIRTH OF FREEDOM
Abraham Lincoln in the White House

DELTA QUEEN
The Story of a Steamboat

Men, Birds, and Adventure

THE THRILLING STORY OF THE DISCOVERY OF AMERICAN BIRDS

Virginia S. Eifert

ILLUSTRATED

DODD, MEAD & COMPANY, NEW YORK

PRINTED IN THE UNITED STATES OF AMERICA

BY VAIL-BALLOU PRESS, INC., BINGHAMTON, N. Y.

This book is dedicated to the Illinois State Museum which, since my early childhood, has played a vital and inseparable part in my life, my interests, and my work. It is also dedicated to Thorne Deuel, Museum Director, for his friendship and encouragement over many years.

ACKNOWLEDGMENTS

FOR their help in locating the numerous old and almost forgotten books which formed the nucleus of much of my material, I am deeply indebted to a number of people and to several libraries—to Lincoln Library, Springfield, Illinois; to Illinois State Library, especially to Esther Hunn, Patricia Ourth, and Louise B. Nantz; to Milner Library at Illinois State Normal University, and to Eleanor W. Welch, Clara Guthrie, Margaret Lawrence, and William Nye of that staff; and to the library of the University of Illinois. I offer my thanks to Dr. William J. Beecher, of the Chicago Academy of Sciences, for his help.

I am extremely grateful for the use of the Illinois State Museum's library facilities and particularly for the opportunity to use the splendid Barnes Collection of Ornithological Literature, as well as for the unending help, interest, and perseverance of Orvetta Robinson in finding material for me. I wish also to thank Ruth Kerr, Frances S. Ridgely, Roy McClanahan, and Milton D. Thompson of the Museum staff for their aid. The interested and careful work by Charles W. Hodge in photographing old bird portraits to illustrate this book has been of tremendous value to me and was an indispensable part of its completion.

I am privileged to have had the help of Herman D. Eifert, Thorne Deuel, and Raymond T. Bond in editing the material; and the assistance of Larry N. Eifert and David F. Childs, who carried hundreds of pounds of old and very heavy books to and from libraries for me.

The picture of the raven and falcon pipes is used by courtesy of the Illinois State Museum. Material quoted in the chapter entitled "Goose Chase," originally appearing in Sutton's *Birds in the Wilderness*, is used through the courtesy of the Macmillan Company.

VIRGINIA S. EIFERT

FOREWORD

T HEY were the men who discovered America and all its parts, and, in the exploring, they found America's birds. The often incredible hardship and hunger, the punishment of weather and of terrain, and the ultimate triumph of truth, all played their part in man's ornithological adventures, from the shores of the Atlantic to the waters of the Pacific, from Mexico to the Arctic Ocean. These stories are not fiction; they are all facts, many of them obtained from the journals of the adventurers, who could be astonishingly calm about their near brushes with disaster.

John Burroughs wrote: "What I offer . . . is a careful and conscientious record of actual observations and experiences, and it is true as it stands written, every word of it."

The adventurers after birds were really the ones who wrote this book . . . true, every word of it.

V. S. E.

CONTENTS

FOREWORD ix

1. FIFTEEN HUNDRED YEARS AGO THERE
   WAS A RAVEN 1
2. COLUMBUS 10
3. MARK CATESBY 20
4. THE LURE OF LOUISIANA 30
5. GEORG WILHELM STELLER 39
6. WILLIAM BARTRAM 53
7. CAPTAIN COOK, JOHN LEDYARD, AND
   THE THRUSH OF NOOTKA SOUND 63
8. LEWIS AND CLARK 74
9. THE YELLOWSTONE EXPEDITION 91
10. ALEXANDER WILSON 107
11. JOHN JAMES AUDUBON 119
12. PRINCE MAXIMILIAN OF WIED 136
13. TOWNSEND, NUTTALL, AND THE
    WESTWARD TRAIL 146
14. RAILROADS, BIRDS, AND BOUNDARIES 159
15. BIRDS AND THE ARMY 175
16. FRANKLIN, RICHARDSON, AND THE
    CALL OF THE NORTH 190
17. THE TELEGRAPH TRAIL 205
18. THE CRUISE OF THE CORWIN 217

xi

CONTENTS

19. GOOSE CHASE   231
20. THE LAST NEW BIRD   241
    BIBLIOGRAPHY   259
    INDEX   267

ILLUSTRATIONS

FOLLOWING PAGE 34

Falcon and raven pipes from the Hopewellian era

Yellow-breasted chat by Mark Catesby

Ruffed grouse by Mark Catesby

Georg Steller's jay

Spectacled cormorants, now extinct

The varied thrush by William Swainson

The Cock of the Plains or sage grouse

Lewis and Clark's magpie by Alexander Wilson

FOLLOWING PAGE 130

The red-headed woodpecker; with yellow-bellied sapsucker, hairy and downy woodpeckers

Scissor-tailed flycatcher; golden-crowned kinglet; western kingbird and Say's phoebe

The burrowing owl by Peale, with cliff swallow

Alexander Wilson's favorite woodpeckers

Audubon's first bird portrait: the belted kingfisher

Carolina paroquets by Audubon

Maximilian's Jay by John Cassin

Collie's magpie-jay

xiii

ILLUSTRATIONS

FOLLOWING PAGE 226

Black-capped vireo

The phainopepla by John Cassin

Ross's gull and Gambel's quail

Richardson's owl by William Swainson

Franklin's and Richardson's grouse by William Swainson

Kennicott's owl

Crested shrike by Robert Ridgway

Young auk by Robert Ridgway

CHAPTER ONE

FIFTEEN HUNDRED YEARS AGO THERE WAS A RAVEN

THE man sat on a river bank and watched a raven tearing apart a dead fish. He gazed for a time and then bent over the thing he held in his hands. He was using flint and abrasive sand to shape a piece of stone, and now and again he glanced back at the hunched dark bird on the shore.

The man was a Hopewellian who belonged to one of the prehistoric communities which, about 2,500 years ago, settled along the rivers of the Middle West. He and his tribe lived at a little distance from the Ohio River in southern Illinois. The forests round about were deep and full of game; pecan trees grew in the bottomlands; the river provided fish and clams; and there were salt springs along the Saline River nearby. The Hopewellian cornfields and squash vines bore well, and there was enough leisure for some men so that they might sit on a river bank and look at a bird.

To many early people, there was a significance in the raven. The Pacific Coast Tlingits and the New York Iroquois depicted this bird in exaggerated forms as enormous masks and totems, but the man on the river shore was carving one accurately and carefully from a small piece of stone. It was slow and exacting work, and it was a long time before it was finished. He had had to look at a raven many times before he had it right.

There must be a certain characteristic stance of the shoulders, the right way in which the bird held its head, the correct slant to the big beak, with some long scratches carefully incised on either side to show the whisker-bristles. He made the tail wedge-shaped so that anyone would know it was different from the squared-off tail of the crow. Then, with infinite labor and care so as not to crack the stone, he made a hollow in the figure's back to hold tobacco, and drilled a lateral hollow in the base as a tube through which the breath was sucked when the raven pipe was smoked in the ceremonial circle. When it was completed, the raven effigy was $4^{13}/_{16}$ inches long and $2^{7}/_{16}$ inches high at the bowl, which came on the highest part of the bird's back. The platform on which it stood was beautifully shaped and curved. The whole piece was then polished to a high gloss.

The Hopewellian had carved an accurate portrait of the northern raven. His name is unknown, his language unknown, his way of life largely unguessed; but the raven pipe which this man created more than fifteen hundred years ago is as distinctively the portrait of the raven, *Corvus corax,* as if he had painted and described it yesterday.

It is only known of him that his ancestors lived along the Mississippi about 500 B.C. and that, a thousand years later, the Hopewellians had grown decadent and become absorbed by other groups. Yet the art of this man and of others like him, scattered among the prehistoric peoples of America, who were keen observers of nature, illustrates some of the wildlife of this continent long before any white man saw it. The kinship of prehistoric observation bridges the great gap between him and us, and between then and now, which is not so great a gap after all if he can communicate with us through his art and his experiences with birds. In the common tongue of art and nature, there is really no gap at all.

This man told us about his raven as concisely as Audubon described and painted the birds which, hundreds of years later, he also saw along the Ohio. Audubon, in fact, camped not many miles from the place where the raven pipe may have been made. Other men before and after Audubon commented on that wildlife along the river; many mentioned birds and adventured among them; but perhaps the first was that unknown artist of a lost tribe, centuries ago on the lower Ohio River, when ravens still lived along its shores.

The prehistoric people—the Early Archaic Hunters, the Woodland People, the Hopewellians, and the Mississippians who, in that order, one giving to another in culture (or taking in conquest), preceded the later Indians—could not escape seeing birds. Like the deer and buffalo and rabbits, birds were food; but they also had an artistic and pleasurable value, and this very recognition among early people was an indication of their developing mental growth, awareness, and stability.

The earliest people in America were wanderers. Their Siberian ancestors, refugees of the Ice Age, moved into northwestern America, evidently by way of Bering Strait or the Aleutians, and then migrated with the birds and mammoths down certain open corridors left by the advancing ice sheets in the central valley of the United States to the warmer, wetter, more food-filled areas. Some descendants of these people, at least eleven thousand years ago, had come to the upper valley of the Mississippi at the time when the last ice sheet was not many miles away to the north. The thawing ice was sending down torrents of melt-water which swelled the Mississippi and all its tributaries to greater proportions than today's high water ever knows.

The Early Archaic Hunters lived a nomadic life in trying to kill enough game to support themselves, for one family needed an area of about two hundred square miles on which to subsist. They ate birds, mammals, clams, fish, fruits, nuts, seeds, but they did not know how to plant gardens so that families might stay in one place, or how to build houses and live in communities. If they had a culture, and an awareness of nature aside from eating it, they left no record of the fact. Only their flints, food bones, and primitive tools were found where ancient fires had been regularly made in camping places under overhanging cliffs.

In these camping spots, some of which have been lately discovered, the remains of bird bones are prominent. Many are nicely polished and of great variety—the bones of birds that lived eleven thousand years ago. Some bones were cut and smoothed to a point for use as awls in punching holes in deerskin to make garments and moccasins. Evidences of meals were abundant in ashes of long-extinct fires—remains of Canada goose, mallard, wild turkey, snow goose, wood duck, blue-winged teal, ruddy duck, ring-necked duck, pintail, bobwhite, whistling swan, passenger pigeon, Hudsonian curlew, bald eagle, little brown crane, and red-winged blackbird. These were the birds the Early Archaic Hunters knew.

But except for eating them and using the leg-bones for tools, these early people did not see birds as did the later ones, the Hopewellians. The latter had a knowledge of agriculture, lived in settled communities in houses of log and thatch and matting, and had time for religion, art, and for an observation of birds which included a study of the raven.

About 500 A.D., the warring Mississippians came up the valley and wiped out the pleasant Hopewellian communities, most of which had grown decadent with soft living and had forgotten to be watchful of enemies. Since ability in the arts had declined some time before the conquest, the raven pipe may have been made a good while before the tentative date given for it. At the height of Hopewellian power, it was customary to embody the figure of a bird or mammal on the bowl of a pipe because this was a ceremonial object which was used only on special occasions, and great art could therefore be lavished upon it. The bird pipes became outstanding examples of America's first bird art, the work of prehistoric ornithologists who knew what they were seeing.

For this art they obtained fine pieces of stone and often went long distances to find it. The river valleys had little that could be used except chunks of igneous rock that had been dropped by the glaciers. The rest were obtained in the Hopewellians' various trading operations, which often took them hundreds of miles from home. And the pieces of stone were carefully chosen by the artist himself to suit the bird he was about to carve. Dark conglomerate was used for the raven, red sandstone for the cardinal, gray-green pipestone for the Carolina parakeet, red-brown Ohio pipestone for the falcon. Any naturalist, in recognizing these charming Hopewellian birds, would applaud the suitability of the medium.

When the raven pipe was completed, it was used for a time; no one can know for how long, or where, or by whom. But eventually it came into possession of a man in the village along the lower Ohio. On a red clay hilltop that overlooked the Saline River and its valley and across the treetops to the shining breadth of the Ohio not far away, a burial space had been cleared, seventy-five feet long and about sixty feet wide. This area was then covered with a layer of white sandy clay. Because there was none situated naturally on the hilltop, the women and slaves had had to go some distance with their grass baskets to dig the white stuff with their clam-shell scoops, load the baskets, and trudge back up the hill, over and over again. They spread the clay over the cleared area and tramped it down with their feet. When a basket broke in the emptying, it was left where it fell, and fifteen centuries later the impressions of the weaving were still plain in the earth.

Fifteen bodies were laid in various graves through the mound, and with some of them were placed cherished or symbolic possessions or offerings. On one side of a forty-foot circle lay a man who may have held high rank and wealth; it had evidently been he who owned the raven pipe, for it was placed at his side. On the far side of the circle a woman was placed with her shell beads around her neck, and a young child beside her. An effigy pipe in the shape of a falcon was laid with the child.

It was a very exact little falcon, less than three inches long. Its

5

head was exaggerated in size, but it had a notched beak characteristic of falcons and was probably meant to be a sparrow hawk. The wings were carved as they naturally cross over each other on the tail. But the lower part of the pipe's base had been broken some time before. When it was laid with the child, the rough break had been smoothed as if by much handling, and the markings of the bird itself showed wear and a certain blurring. Perhaps when the pipe was broken it was no longer useful to the child's father, so he had given it to him to play with, and the toy bird had thus become smoothed by much handling. And when death had come to him and his mother, the little falcon had been buried with them in the mound. No one can be sure of the reason, of course; the bird may have been part of a medicine bundle and left with the child for safe conduct on his journey to the land of the dead. Whatever the reason, the raven pipe and the falcon pipe were left in the growing mound.

The slaves and women brought innumerable basket-loads of earth from the woods and heaped it over the burials. When it was almost three feet high and tamped down well by moccasined feet, more people had died and were laid on this second level. Then more earth, laboriously brought in baskets, covered them as the mound grew. When it became a little more than ten feet high, it was finished.

The mound was perched on top of the hill. Trees grew upon it. Clumps of orange turkey-foot grass in winter waved tall plumes in the wind. The Hopewellians were gone. The Mississippians were gone. The Shawnees and Chickasaws who had come to make salt were gone, too. So were the French who had come to carry on the salt business at the saline springs. So were the American pioneers who had broken ground for farms on the hills and river bottoms; Black John who had once owned part of the hill was gone. The ravens were all gone, too. The mound with its secrets stood on the top of the hill and was now scarcely to be distinguished from the hill itself.

In 1954, the young men of a summer's archaeological expedition began to work here, cautiously, slowly, and with great care laying open the old mound in order to learn its story. One day when the heat bore down on the bare, brown, perspiring backs of the student archaeologists, and the cicadas shrilled their buzz-saw cries, and even the oak leaves looked dusty and wilted, they reached the level of the mound floor. Everything they had found thus far, down to the last bead, shell, tooth, bone, and fragment of pottery, had been carefully removed, numbered, wrapped, and boxed for the winter's study. Now with soft brushes and small spoons they patiently cleared away the earth around the burials they were finding. On one side of a circle they came upon a raven pipe and, on the other side, a brown pipestone falcon, both dim with earth, yet, when washed, as unchanged as when they had been interred. Their owners had been long since reduced to crumbling bones, but the raven and the falcon were timeless.

The archaeologists were excited. They had found effigy pipes before—not many, for they were always rare—and had examined splendid depictions of birds on pipes. There had been the Carolina parakeet's head carved on a green pipestone bowl; the full figure of a cardinal; a truly beautiful owl; as well as the crow, ivory-billed woodpecker, various ducks, ravens, and eagles. The archaeologists recognized them as plainly as they might recognize bird portraits by modern painters. But they had never seen a raven like this one, this link between a bird and a man who had lived long ago, with the men and birds of today.

It was easy to understand the Hopewellians' interpretation of the raven, the falcon, the parakeet, but it was quite another matter for men to comprehend the picture that had been painted on a gray limestone cliff above the Mississippi. When the strange prehistoric depictions of a creature called the Piasa Bird were discovered, it could not be related to any known bird, mammal, or reptile, and it was therefore somehow horrible. It was called a bird, but it didn't

7

look like one. It had neither reason nor explanation, and perhaps because of that there were men who refused to believe that the paintings had been there at all, even after they had themselves seen them. When the pictures disappeared, the mystery and the arguments deepened.

The Piasa may always remain a mystery. Legends related that this creature, whose portraits were on the bluffs above Alton, Illinois, twenty miles northeast of St. Louis, represented a monster bird which had ravaged the valley. It had been destroyed by a self-sacrificial chief who offered himself to the thing and, as it swooped to carry him off, it had been filled with poisoned arrows shot by concealed warriors. The Piasa Bird had fallen, flapping and smoking and writhing, into the river and had never been seen again. To commemorate the event, so the legends explained, two pictures of the creature had been painted high on the river cliffs.

That there really were early paintings on the cliffs, and that they showed some sort of winged monster of quite inconceivable design are acknowledged in fact. Jolliet and Marquette saw them; later explorers reported them. But not until they were destroyed by weather and falling rock did most of the legends come to light. Most or all were figments of modern imagination based on typical Indian legends of monsters and heroes.

Still, no one could say who had painted the pictures of a strange bird-creature high on the limestone, of such great size and with such skill that Marquette in astonishment declared that French artists would have had a hard time doing as well. Yet no Frenchmen and no other white men were believed to have come here before Marquette and Jolliet in 1673. Besides, stubborn people insisted, there had been no such monster. But the Piasa Bird *had* been painted on the bluffs; there was no escaping that fact.

Great wings, serpent-like tail, horns above a tigerish face, four feet with claws—bird, reptile, myth, no one knows what it represented. Then in the late 1940's a piece of Hopewellian pottery, catalogued as Late Woodland Ware, was found not far south of the Piasa cliffs. Men who had dismissed the fanciful legend of the Piasa Bird swallowed hard and examined more closely the strange figure incised on the neck of what had been a well-formed oval bowl. Here was a design which had been impressed with cording to make four repeated patterns—designs representing a creature with great angular wings, long neck and small head (no horns, however), and forked tail. It depicted no known creature, yet the Hopewellians had been noted for realism in art. The design was basically so much like what had been recalled of the Piasa paintings that the mystery of the creature rose again.

The mystery no doubt will never be solved. Bird, reptile, but perhaps not a myth—it is part of those days before white men came to America, when there may have been birds and adventures which the white man would never see and never know.

CHAPTER TWO

COLUMBUS

THE centuries passed, and still only the native Americans knew our birds. In the year 986 A.D. Bjarni Herulfson became lost in a North Atlantic fog while seeking Greenland. He was blown off course and evidently sighted the coast of North America, but he refused to land. He had a single-minded purpose and that was to find Greenland, to which his father had rashly accompanied Eric the Red.

Not until fourteen years later, in 1000 A.D., when Leif Ericson set out to find that land which the uncurious Bjarni had sighted, did any European set foot upon North America or see its wildlife. Leif Ericson and those who followed him—his brother Thorvald and Thorfinn Karlsevni—mentioned few specific creatures, but they did see eider ducks on the northern coasts and landed long enough to collect fresh eggs to add welcome supplies to the food brought from Greenland. Partridges, wild turkeys, and eider ducks were the birds mentioned in the old sagas, but they were only incidental to the coming and going of the Norsemen.

Not until Columbus headed westward to seek a way to India did the birds finally have a vital role in man's adventuring in the New World. It was the birds that led Columbus across the Atlantic and directed him to the West Indies rather than to the mainland of a new continent which would later be called America, after another voyager. Columbus knew birds; he relied upon their instincts and altered his course again and again in order to follow them. At many a moment of low courage, they sustained him.

In his letter to the King and Queen of Spain, he said:

I left the city of Granada on the twelfth of May, in the year 1492, being Saturday, and came to the town of Palos, which is a sea-port; where I equipped three vessels well suited for such service, and departed from that port, well supplied with provisions and with many sailors, on the 3rd day of August of the same year, being Friday, half an hour before sunrise, taking the route to the islands of Canaria, belonging to your Highnesses, which are in the said Ocean Sea, that I might hence take my departure for navigating until I should arrive at the Indies, and give the letters of your Highnesses to those princes so as to comply with my orders. . . .

And so Christopher Columbus set forth with his three small ships to the west. By September 9, when they had lost all sight of land, and there was no real prospect of any view of Japan and the Indies rising before them, the men grew more and more filled with fear and misgivings. They knelt often to pray, and between prayers they cast angry looks at the Admiral and muttered among themselves.

Columbus could see what he was in for, so he practiced a little deception upon his crew. In setting down in the log the number of leagues traversed in a day, he always wrote down fewer than they actually had gone, so that the crew would not think they were quite so far away from Spain as he knew they were. For a while it had a good effect.

Then in a few days a cheering incident occurred. Two birds flew past, a royal tern with bright carmine beak, black cap, and white wings and body, and a boatswain bird or tropic-bird, beautifully marked with black on its white wings and two extremely long, flowing, white tail feathers. It was like seeing familiar faces from home. The men brightened immediately. They talked about the birds all day; there was a wonderful lift to the spirits. Columbus did not disillusion his men, perhaps because even he did not know, when they declared to each other that such birds never went more than twenty-five leagues from land and that surely land must now be very near, just over the horizon. The birds could not lie.

But day after day the horizon in all directions remained empty. Daily the men watched for that ever-imminent land. Night after night the stars went over in a bright-dark sky, while the sea endlessly slapped at the three little Spanish hulls pushing westward in a fair wind, and there was no land in sight. No land. But the birds, disconcertingly, were seen almost every day. For a long time they kept up the courage of the men on the *Niña*, the *Pinta*, and the *Santa Maria*, and if they were worth nothing more, that was enough.

Fortunately, the weather was fine during the entire outbound voyage. Foul weather would have made the journey too much for any man to bear. Mornings were beautiful, and the Admiral commented in his journal that all they needed were the songs of nightingales to feel that it was indeed April in Andalusia—instead of September in the middle of the unknown Atlantic Ocean.

September 18: Martin Alonso Pinzon of the *Pinta* saw great multitudes of birds flying westward, and he hoped to see land that night. A great cloud appeared in the north, which is a sign of land.

A booby, called *alcatraz* by the Spaniards, came down and rested for a while on a mast, and in the afternoon another arrived; they both sat there looking down at the men. Now, surely, thought the Admiral of the Ocean Sea, praying, land cannot be much farther away.

At dawn on September 20 the men caught a bird that was like a tern, they declared. But it was a river bird, they amended, and not a sea bird at all, because the feet were webbed like those of a gull. This was odd reasoning; perhaps they had never seen a petrel, which ranges far at sea, is tern-like, and has webbed feet like a gull. Then at dawn something wonderful happened. Three land birds came singing to the ship. They disappeared before sunset, after resting all day in the rigging. The men yearned after their little visitors, wishing they knew where they themselves were going with as much assurance as the birds seemed to know in the trackless waste of sea and sky.

On September 25 the day began with a calm, and afterward a fair breeze pushed out the sails to the west. At sunset Martin Alonso Pinzon went upon the poop of his ship for an observation. They heard his yells below, heard him as far away as the other ships. He shouted to the Admiral, claiming the reward which had been offered to the man who first sighted land—because there was land ahead, land at last. He could see it!

"Land! Land!" cried the men, and the Admiral made them get down on their knees with him to thank God for His goodness.

But it was not land. Not yet. It was only a low dark cloud that looked like a line of distant hills. The high spirits of the men on the three ships sank to a new low of desperation. In spite of the birds, which were still seen every day, discontent and mutiny were boiling up in the crew. They had been sailing west for two months and had not reached land. Was there really no end to this ocean, as some declared? No land . . . there *must* be land.

On October 7 the crew of the *Niña* saw great numbers of birds flying from north to southwest. The flights appeared, were gone, and were followed by more. Either the birds were going to sleep on land, or they were flying from the winter which might be supposed to be near in the land from which they were coming; in either case, land should not be too far. The Admiral was aware that most of the islands held by the Portuguese had been discovered by following the flights of birds, so now he resolved to give up the due western course to which he had held so faithfully and shaped a course west-southwest for the two following days.

It was the birds of America, migrating in October, that now led and directed Columbus. They determined where he eventually landed and thus set much of the course of history, for if he had gone on his original course he might have found a less hospitable land and the less friendly natives of the palmetto flats and Everglades of Florida. The birds guided him, and he turned southwest. But he is not there yet; it is only October 9.

Throughout the night of October 9 they heard birds passing overhead, for the season was reaching the peak of migration and their high-flung voices passed across the stars and above the creaking masts. If he could only be as sure as the birds were, only knew where he was going, or if he would ever come back to tell of his experiences. . . .

On October 10 the men on the three ships had reached the breaking point. They could not endure the suspense any longer. Endlessly they had been seeing birds, always with the promise that they never went far from land, had been seeing these creatures since the ships had left the Canary Islands, and it had all come to nothing, nothing. They wanted to go back. Columbus made a speech on each ship and told them that, much as they might complain, he was going to reach the Indies or die in the attempt. He would not go back to Spain without finding them or knowing the route so that other ships could follow.

The men and the captains complained and muttered privately among themselves. Then the captains presented an ultimatum to the Admiral: They would continue on the course for three days longer, they said, and no more. Then, whether the Admiral wished to do so or not, they would turn about and sail back to Spain. They could not endure this torment any longer. Fresh water was getting low, food was molding, worms were gnawing holes in the hulls. They must go back.

With bitter counter-arguments, Columbus held his ground. He reminded them that for the very reason that their water was low, the food bad, and the hulls leaking, they must continue. How, he asked scornfully, his gray eyes cold, could they expect to survive another two months' voyage back to Spain? It was impossible without time in a port in which to refit the ships and stock fresh supplies.

The captains had no answer. They looked down at their shoes. They insisted on their ultimatum: three days more, and then they would turn back. But the men among themselves plotted to kill Columbus and throw his body overboard. The captains would not know what had become of him, and would then have full command.

Three days. It was October 10. Three more days. The Admiral did not sleep much that night. He could not sleep in the day. He paced the deck, paced his small, stuffy cabin. He gazed endlessly with eyes red-rimmed and burning with weariness. He turned a tanned face to the dark blue tossing waves and the bright, warm sky. Two days. . . .

On Octboer 11 the sea was running more heavily than before. Petrels skimmed by, low over the waves, their little feet kicking up flecks of foam as they flashed in the troughs and up over the crests. The men on the *Pinta* in sudden excitement and renewed hope saw a green reed and a pole, which they hauled aboard and examined incredulously; it appeared to have been worked with iron. They scooped up a branch of a wild rose bush with red berries— *Escaramojos*, the men called them, with joy at seeing something familiar. Everyone breathed afresh and rejoiced at these most favorable signs.

After sunset, the Admiral returned to his original western course and they proceeded briskly. It was night, and the *Pinta* was ahead because she sailed faster. So it was the *Pinta* that sighted land. Land? At ten o'clock at night, how could anyone be sure? Yet there was a spark of light, light where there would be none on the ocean, like a candle flame, rising and falling, then vanishing. The Admiral admonished his men to keep a close watch, but they did not need to be told that. No one, very likely, slept on that palpitant October night. Whether it was his turn or not, every man was on watch.

On Friday, October 12, the three ships came to a small island. The natives called it Guadahani. It did not look like Cipango, the island of Japan, nor even like one of the East Indies, but it was land. The Spanish saw naked brown people on the shore. The Admiral and some of his men and the captains went ashore; the captains carried two banners of the green cross and planted them in the sand. They found green trees and good fresh water, saw parrots, and saw fruits of kinds they had never known anywhere before. The Admiral of the Ocean Sea knelt and thanked God for their safe arrival in the Indies.

For nearly four months Columbus and his men explored the islands—the West Indies, not the East. In all his vain searching for Japan, he never forgot to enjoy the wild things that he found. He wrote of them, not as mere businesslike items in his journal, but with fervent expressions of his appreciation of beauty and his excitement at finding new birds, trees, flowers, people. He lived at a time in which there was no way to learn the names of new plants and animals; he knew only what was familiar in Spain and in the seas he had sailed earlier. He longed to know about the new things, but there was no way to find out.

Of one of the islands, he wrote:

The songs of the birds were so pleasant that it seemed as if a man could never wish to leave the place. The flocks of parrots concealed the sun; and the birds were so numerous, and of so many different kinds, that it was wonderful. There are trees of a thousand sorts, and all have their several fruits, and I feel the most unhappy man in the world not to know them, for I am well assured they are all valuable. I bring home specimens of them, and also of the land.

Again he said:

That I have no personal knowledge of these products causes me the greatest sorrow in the world, for I see a thousand kinds of trees, each one with its own special fruit, all green now as in Spain during the months of May and June, as well as a thousand kinds of herbs with their flowers, yet I know none of them except the aloe, of which I ordered a quantity to be brought on board.

Island after island the ships explored, looking for gold as well as for the more tangible and visible creatures native to the Indies.

It was gold, after all, which would make the best impression on their Highnesses. Columbus longed to find treasure to take back to his monarchs to prove that this wild voyage was of some use after all. But they found no gold. When they tried to describe it to the natives, they were smilingly told that this thing was surely on another island, always on another one some distance away, so that the ships kept chasing back and forth around the Caribbean without finding what they sought.

On Haiti, which Columbus called Española, the natives brought him a great many beautiful, gaudy parrots because he had expressed a wish to take back a present to the Queen. The birds of Haiti charmed him. He even heard certain kinds singing at night.

But Columbus had something more to think about than the birds. His ships were in trouble. The ship worms, the teredos, were eating large pieces of the hulls, and there was no way to stop them before they literally ate the vessels out from under the men. So Columbus ordered the three to keep moving, while water came into the bilges so fast that the crew was kept busy at the pumps both day and night.

The *Niña* was badly afflicted, and the *Santa Maria* was so leaky that at last, taking refuge in a harbor, she simply sank where she was moored. Now everyone must go back to Spain, if they got there at all, in the remaining two vessels. Columbus realized that he must get away from these warm seas where the worms were bad. He had heard another rumor of gold on Porto Rico and was heading there doggedly when they hit a wind which was just right for Spain. It fairly called to the little Spanish caravels to go along with it, and the Admiral relented. Gold was all very well, but he doubted if he would find any on this voyage. They had seen none at all so far, and he had begun to suspect the natives of sending them away on fabrications, just to get rid of them.

The wind called, the Admiral made up his mind, and he shouted his orders. The men cheered and leaped to the sails, and the fair wind took the tattered sails and bellied them out. The *Niña* and the *Pinta,* patched up and weak, but afloat, leaving the sunken *Santa Maria* on the bottom of the Caribbean for the teredos to finish off and for the corals to cover, started back toward Spain. With them went several natives whom Columbus wanted to present to the Queen, and a cage of parrots, as well as other souvenirs of the journey.

Storms struck the two ships on their way home. The rotted hulls leaked, and the men bailed and pumped furiously. They could almost smell Spain, could almost hear sheep bells on the Andalusian hills, could almost see the almond trees in bloom and hear the nightingales. Their homes called with a not-to-be-denied voice. Desperately they bailed, they prayed, they made vows to Our Lady of Guadalupe. The small ships slid down the vast green trough of a wave which seemed about to send them to the bottom of the sea while mountains of hissing water hung above the masts; then they slid up the vast glassy slope to the top again, with a sickening swoop. When the hulls leaked so fast that the men who pumped were up to their waists in water, Columbus knew that he had to get to Spain and report what he had found. There would be no other way for the King and Queen to know of his discoveries. Besides, if he did not come back, no one would know what had befallen the three ships and perhaps no other mariner would dare to venture into that unknown West which had slain them. He must get back.

When things looked most hopeless, Columbus wrote a letter explaining briefly where he had been and what he had found and enclosed it in a wine bottle so that if the ship went down, this at least might one day float to shore. Isabella and Ferdinand might therefore receive a watery message from the Ocean Sea, from the lost Admiral who lay among the corals.

But the *Niña* and the *Pinta* did not sink. They reached Madeira in the Azores. The storm calmed while the vessels were repaired and ballasted, yet as they proceeded there was more severe weather. To be so close—to be in danger of sinking almost within sight of home—yet, next day, through the blowing spume and rain, they sighted the dim rock of Cintra near the river of Lisbon, in Portugal. Columbus resolved in desperation to try to run the ships into the river out of the storm.

From the village of Cascaes, the people came out in the stinging wind and beating rain. With their faces lashed by the tempest of salt-spray, they knelt and prayed for the safety of the two ships battling in the great waves. The captive parrots from the Indies screeched and clung to their cage; many had already died. And the natives of the Indies lay sick and hopeless. The crew bailed and prayed, while all that wild morning the people of Cascaes remained on their knees on the beach. When, at last, the ships got into the river, everyone said that it was a true miracle.

Columbus carried his report and his parrots in person to their Majesties, along with his plant specimens and the Indians. He had made it, indeed. But always, in the quiet of nights on the solid land of Spain, he could hear once again the songs of birds in the Indies, could see the slim quills of the boatswain birds as they sailed around the ships, could hear the high-flung voices of migrating birds flying over the sea, sure of where they were going, could think back again to what he had written with such feeling:

Always the land was of the same beauty, and the fields very green and full of an infinity of fruits, as red as scarlet, and everywhere there was the perfume of flowers and the singing of birds, very sweet. Even the pigeons had their crops full of flowers which were sweeter than orange blossom.

CHAPTER THREE

MARK CATESBY

TWO hundred and twenty years lay between the coming of
Columbus to America and the coming of Mark Catesby. They
were years in which explorers sought out the mysteries of America,
men who were Spanish and Portuguese, French, Dutch, and English, who came to conquer, colonize, or convert. Not a great many
of them seemed to be more than ordinarily curious about the
American wildlife. They were aware of it because they could not
avoid it. The wildlife came out to meet them before their ships
landed, dogged their footsteps, beset their route, often stood in
the way of success, or aided it, or defeated life itself. The newcomers used birds and mammals for food or clothing, used vegetation for food or shelter or fuel. But not many were curious about
the names of things, or why and how they lived as they did. This
was not an unusual attitude for the times. It was characteristic of
the civilized countries in the seventeenth century, when natural
science was only slowly developing.

There were those who did see birds. Columbus had brought back
parrots from the Caribbean; Vizcaino in 1602 commented on the
cormorants of the Pacific Islands off California; Portolá named a
place in the Coast Range Gaviota Pass because a sailor had killed a
sea gull there; Don Ulloa explained in detail how vultures found
and ate the eggs of alligators. French priests described pelicans and

hummingbirds.

The English at times were more specific. George Percy, who came to Virginia in the first expedition in 1607 and was made president of the beset colony, told of wildlife in the area around Chesapeake Bay and the James River:

. . . black Birds with crimson wings, and divers other Fowles and Birds of divers and sundry collours of crimson, Watchet [pale blue], Yellow, Greene, Murry [dark red], and of divers other hewes naturally without any art using. We found store of Turkie nests and many Egges. If it had not been disliked, because the ship could not ride neere the shoare, we had settled there to all the Collonies contentment.

To this disaster-plagued settlement came Captain John Smith, who also had an eye to the wildlife and described it in detail for the King:

Of birds, the Eagle is the greatest devourer. Hawkes, there be of diverse sorts as our Falconers call them, Sparrow-hawkes, Lanarets, Goshawkes, Falcons, and Osperayes; but they all prey most upon fish. Partridges there are little bigger than our Quailes, wilde Turkies are as bigge as our tame. There are woosels or blackbirds with red shoulders, thrushes, and diverse sorts of small birds, some red, some blew, scarce so bigge as a wrenne, but few in Sommer. In winter there are greate plenty of Swans, Craynes gray and white with black wings, Herons, Geese, Brants, Ducks, Wigeon, Dotterell, Oxeies, Parrats, and Pigeons. Of all those sorts great abundance, and some other strange kinds, to us unknowne by name. But in sommer not any, or very few to be seene.

Not until the early eighteenth century did men begin to search out the birds of America in quest of knowledge, not meat. In Europe, men of wealth and of some scientific curiosity were collecting oddities of other lands, amassing private museums of shells and bird-skins and reptiles preserved in alcohol. The latter did not always arrive in good condition after the long voyage from America; crewmen aboard the vessels carrying them sometimes were so overcome by thirst that they drank the alcohol in which specimens were suspended. But those that did reach England and other European centers of culture and science were examined with vast interest. It was the dream of many a collector to go out to America and see for himself what was there; or, if he were too old, too indolent, or too fond of comfort to risk the difficulties and dangers of such a voyage, he sometimes could be persuaded to subsidize a young and eager naturalist to do it for him.

Young Mark Catesby, twenty-nine, first came to America in 1712 by financing his trip with the meager inheritance from his father, and while here he saved money by living with his sister Elizabeth, who had married a doctor and had come out to Virginia. He passed long, pleasant visits with friends in the Virginia Tidewater and in the quiet New World elegance of Williamsburg. He had spent much of his time in England as an eager student of botany and zoology. For some of his botanical friends and associates he planned to collect plants and seeds for their gardens and private botanical collections. This gave his visit a reason and special meaning.

With his American friends as guides, Catesby was shown about the countryside. He collected specimens wherever he went and delighted in the new, beautiful, unnamed species of wild flowers and trees which he found. He ventured into the deep, dark, echoing swamps of the James and the York and the Pamunkey, where the cypresses stood in still, brown water and where there were eerie voices that were like none he had ever heard in England. The voices stirred him as nothing else ever had. They were the cries of the wilderness, the voices of wild America, the call of excitement, the lure to adventure.

He stayed in Virginia for seven years; visits could be long in those days, and besides he loved the place and could not get enough of it. Yet, he had collected only plants, largely, for his friends; had observed and enjoyed, but done little else to mark his visit. He said:

I thought then so little of prosecuting a Design of the Nature of this Work, that in the Seven Years I resided in that Country (I am ashamed to own it) I chiefly gratified my Inclination in observing and admiring the various Productions of those Countries . . . only sending from thence some dried Specimens of Plants and some of the most Specious of them in Tubs of Earth, at the Request of some curious Friends, amongst whom was Mr. Dale of Braintree. . . .

But the natural history of a large, new country cannot be absorbed even in seven years—years which were the advance cultivation of his seed bed of future endeavor.

His friend, Dale, was impressed with his experiences. Mr. Dale felt that it was indeed a pity the wealthy gentlemen in England could not subscribe to the young man's work and support him during subsequent journeys to America for more purposeful collecting. The idea of a book to describe and illustrate the wildlife of America was already beginning to form in Mark Catesby's mind. It would give purpose to his explorations, a goal at which to aim.

Samuel Dale's plea fell on the right ears, and enough money was subscribed by men who were interested in adding to their own natural history collections to send him back to America. In 1722 he departed once more to the West.

With his subscribed funds, and not having to depend upon his relatives for support, he went this time to Charleston, South Carolina. Compared with the civilization of Virginia, Carolina was a raw frontier; wilderness lay close around it. The landscape offered tantalizing variation. Birds and plants differed from the shores to the hills some miles inland. He spent a blissful five days at Fort Moore, 140 miles up the Savannah River, where he exclaimed rapturously: "It is one of the Sweetest Countrys I ever saw." He wondered with mounting excitement what lay far up the Savannah and the Cooper and the Santee and the Edisto, whose mouths he explored and whose sea marshes he roamed in pirogue or high boots. Some day he would find a way to follow the rivers and see where they went, and what lived along them. Some said the rivers came from the mountains—a great range of mysterious mountains called Appalachians, or Smoky Mountains, so named because of their endless drifting fogs and clouds. The mountains, men said, formed a tremendous barrier to people wanting to travel west.

He set about making drawings of plants and birds, sometimes painting flowers or tree branch first and then, almost as an after-thought, adding a bird; or making the bird and then finding some plant that would look interesting with it.

. . . the Birds I painted when alive (except a few), and gave them their gestures peculiar to every kind of Birds, and where it could be admitted, I have added the Birds to those Plants on which they feed, or have any relation to. Very few of the Birds having names assigned them in the country, except some which were Indian names, I have called them after European birds of the same Genus, with an additional epithet to distinguish them.

However, he was endlessly puzzled with the kinds of birds he found, which he had never seen in England and to which he could give no accurate name. The New World warblers were indistinguishable as a family; he did not see the connections among them all, and thus called the myrtle warbler the yellow-rump, the hooded warbler a titmouse, the pine warbler a creeper, and the parula warbler a finch creeper.

In spite of his pardonable mistakes, Mark Catesby was America's first real ornithologist. Those who had come before him had largely looked at birds only when they had flown in front of them; he was the first to track them down and study them. Some had taken bird-skins to European collectors who had endeavored to give them names, but Catesby, on the scene, presented ideas on American birds which were new and unheard of at that time. He was two centuries ahead of most people with his theory that the chimney swifts flew to Brazil for the winter, instead of burying themselves in the mud, as the old books stated and most people still believed. He decided that "Birds of Passage," particularly swallows, "pass to the same latitude in the southern hemisphere as the nothern latitude from whence they came." He also believed that the American Indians had an Asiatic origin and had crossed from

Siberia by some land bridge at a remote time in history. In the eighteenth century, this was a startling idea.

In his bird paintings and their brief accounts—the book gives the latter in English and French—we can follow some of his adventures in the Carolina country. He must have ranged along the rivers and in the coastal marshes where the mud flats left twice a day by the tides were a gathering place for shore birds. He watched killdeers and saw how they rose in crying flocks to alarm other shore birds when hunters were near. He saw turnstones probing pebbles on the flats, and the oyster catcher with its startling red eye and red beak; watched black skimmers flying low over the surf with their long red scissor bills scooping up food from the water. Up to his knees in the salt marshes, he hunted out the secretive rails and bitterns and grebes, saw great blue herons, egrets, and cormorants. It was a bird-filled world, and he was part of it.

He went into the deep and mysterious lavender-blue light of the live oak forests hung with draperies of undulating Spanish moss, and felt the hush of strangeness and of the unseen eyes upon him. Everywhere he went he found new birds to paint and study as well as new plants to collect. Mark Catesby must have been a quiet man and a patient one to have seen so many birds and to have brought them down to paint while they were fresh. And when he found his own abilities unequal to the test of wits between man and bird, he had Indian friends upon whom to call. The Indians liked him. He was more fortunate than John Lawson, who came to America shortly before he did, and who had also been engaged in producing a book of American wildlife. Lawson, out hunting birds, was killed in the forest by the Tuscaroras. But the Indians with whom the amiable Mark Catesby came in contact evidently were his friends, and he relied upon them for help.

One was with him along a swamp edge where he heard the insane chattering and moonstruck madness of a yellow-breasted chat. He caught a glimpse of a mysterious gold-fronted bird as it leaped from a twig into the air and then turned and fell, twisting at a break-

neck angle, cackling and whistling and turning, down into the tree
again. It was so sudden that it had surprised him, and his fowling
piece wasn't ready. Then when he had it loaded and cocked, he
couldn't find the bird, though he could hear it still mocking him
and clucking and cheeping in the bushes. But the Indian crept close,
so still he might have been another tree, and shot the bird, snatching
the unwary singer out of tree and song and life.

In his hand Mark Catesby held his first yellow-breasted chat,
a creature of pure gilt throat and breast, large white-ringed eye
accented with black on the face, with smooth olive back and
wings and tail. He could not capture the unique song or the antics,
or even the unusual character of the chat, but he could at least
paint its portrait, in which he depicted it to show how the bird
held its legs in flight when it leaped upward, singing.

From the Indians he learned much. They often appeared at the
plantation where he was staying at the time, to present him with
something which they thought he might like. One day a Yuchi
brought him an enormous creature slung over his shoulder. It was
as tall as the man himself—a whooping crane with long white neck
and white body, and wings with broad black tips. It was the biggest
bird Mark Catesby had ever seen, and he longed to find these magnificent creatures alive in some sun-drenched swamp, as the Indian
described, where they did curious hopping dances and then rose,
trumpeting long, loud bugle-notes, in circling flocks to the sky.
He did not explore far enough, evidently, to see this sight; but he
did find the ivory-billed woodpecker in the old, moss-hung swamp
forests. He called it the Largest White Billed Woodpecker, and
painted it perched on a willow oak that grows in those swamps. The
big white chisel-beaks of these birds, he said, "are much valued by
Canada Indians, who make coronets of them for their Princes and
great Warriors by fixing them round a wreath, with their points
outward. Northern Indians having none, they buy them from
southern Indians at two or three buckskins a bill. . . . Nature having so formed their bills, that in an hour or two they can raise a

bushel of chips; for which the *Spaniards* call them *Carpenteros*."

When he felt he had exhausted the possibilities for new birds in the Carolina Low Country, he wanted to get away to another place, up into the hills and to the mountains, for he had heard that wildlife was much different there from that along the sea and in the swamps. His friends, the Yuchis and Catawbas, assured him they could take him wherever he wished to go, but they must go in spring when the freshets were coming down the streams so there would be easier canoeing. He did not say which route he took. He said only that he went with the Indians to the high country where he found many new things.

If he went into the Smokies or the Nantahala Mountains he would have had to go on foot, on the devious paths of the Cherokee or bear. Wherever it was, he did get to the high country, for there he found the painted trillium and the silverbell tree, the wild azalea called pinxter flower, the shooting star, and the ginseng. These are all characteristic of the deep, rich valleys of the Southern Appalachians where, particularly in the Smokies, the great forests have been little altered by time since they began over a hundred million years ago.

It was spring, and wild flowers and birds in the mountains were at their best. There he heard the strange throbbing concussions of sound which he had never heard before, and in a low tone he may have asked the Indians what it was. The Indian name meant nothing. Still the feathery drumming continued. An Indian motioned. They crept forward quietly through the ferns, avoiding the tangles of laurel thickets with their noisy leaves and whip-lash canes, until, in a beech forest of antiquity and majesty, they saw on a fallen log near a cluster of shooting stars a small, cock-like bird. Its wings were bowed, its tail was a fan, and it was drumming its springtime serenade. The ruffed grouse or partridge was another new bird for Catesby.

The Indians put up a bark hut as a shelter for him and his gear. They marveled at his ability to paint a picture on paper of something which they had themselves seen or had brought to him. When the sky looked like rain, they always put up a special house for him, their friend; they would not let him or his precious pictures and specimens get wet. There in the forest that afternoon, while the Indians worked, he must have painted the picture of the grouse among the pink and white blossoms of the shooting star.

There were other excursions with his Indians—hunting buffalo in the piedmont meadows, bears and panthers in the mountains, and always the birds. He painted 108 of them during his American years, a good many of them life-sized, though not always in good proportion to their setting. He also painted fishes, reptiles, and mammals.

Catesby went back to England in 1724, after a visit to the Bahamas where he collected more specimens, including the yellow-billed tropic bird which bears his name as discoverer. He never again returned to America. He spent his time finishing his paintings, writing his text, slowly and laboriously completing the monumental *Natural History of Carolina*. It had become an absorbing labor and his sole purpose in life.

Although the patrons who had financed his stay in America were very much pleased and impressed with his paintings, they had already invested so much money in him that they could not offer more at the moment. Financing a book or books of this sort was exorbitant. If he could not find a backer, he was determined to finance the thing himself. In order to cut his expenses, he went to an expert etcher for lessons in how to engrave copperplates. He thus engraved all of them himself, then filled in the colors on each one as well. This was a long and time-consuming business. Years were going by, and his volumes were far from ready to be printed. He still needed money. It was then that a scientific-minded friend, Peter Collinson, a Quaker merchant, stepped in and lent him what he needed, without interest, so that the books might be published and Catesby could thus earn a living by selling them.

The first section, containing twenty plates, was out in 1729. By 1746, when he was sixty-three, he was finished. In two huge volumes dedicated to Queen Caroline, the great work was done. Then Mark Catesby, unwell and with little money left, married. Thirty months later he died.

His adventuring into the back country of Carolina and Virginia had been an opening wedge in scientific knowledge of American natural history. He was the first to use any system and, more than anything, the first to paint large, lifelike portraits of birds and plants. Their names he carefully studied out, and it was from more than seventy of the names given by the pioneering Catesby that Karl Linnaeus formed the more polished Latin binomials which those birds bear today. For many years, Catesby's *Natural History of Carolina* guided young men into the fascinating fields of botany and ornithology. Those volumes have weathered the years with remarkable stamina, their heavy paper only a little speckled with brown, with their original plates which Catesby himself engraved and colored by hand.

CHAPTER FOUR

THE LURE OF LOUISIANA

IN 1718, while Mark Catesby was still having a delightful visit in the wilds of Virginia, young Antoine Simon Le Page Du Pratz, a Frenchman of Dutch parentage, came to Louisiana. He was one of many who bought land in John Law's Mississippi Bubble scheme, in which thousands were defrauded during one of the biggest swindles in history. Innumerable people had put their confidence in the wonders of Louisiana, had taken John Law's promises and descriptions as truth, had even believed in the beautifully designed street plan of that as yet unbuilt city, New Orleans, which would be the capital of the new country. Then the scheme blew up, and there were bankruptcy and howling in Europe.

Those who went to claim their land in America found wilderness and but little civilization. The New Orleans which Law had promised them—that beautiful city with its romantically-named streets—was a swamp, complete with Choctaws, alligators, mosquitoes, palmetto scrub, muddy water, and a great river writhing past the site. The place was less than nothing. There was only one structure there to identify it, a palmetto-thatched shack designated as the Commandant's house, but even he had not yet come, nor was he likely to do so if he valued his comfort.

Antoine Simon Le Page Du Pratz was one of those who bought land from the West India Company, in a tract along Bayou St.

John above New Orleans, and who came out in 1718 with eight hundred others to colonize. He had a great curiosity and interest in wildlife and had made a considerable study of it in Europe. He was twenty-three, rather gullible, and was ready to explore America. He looked eagerly toward a new life in this exciting land; after three long and rough months of sailing, it would be a paradise.

He was disillusioned, but not at all discouraged. He had expected to find a comfortable lodging, an inn, perhaps, in New Orleans, until his own house should be built, but except for that miserable hut which was humorously called the Commandant's Palace, there was nothing at all here to accommodate anyone. As a decided improvement over what he found, he took over the deserted hut of an Acolopissa Indian, which was situated on higher ground and was comparatively clean. Du Pratz got himself settled at once.

Then he looked about for some assistance with his housekeeping, someone to do his cooking and washing. He bought a pleasant Chitimacha Indian girl who seemed happy to come to the white man's service, even if neither one at first could understand the other. She was a sturdy, sensible girl with some initiative and personality, and with a good deal of energy in attacking problems. She thereafter devoted her life to the man who had bought her, and there was, perhaps, something more than a master-and-servant relationship.

The white man's inability to cope with Louisiana became her obligation. One day not long after settling in his hut near Bayou St. John, Du Pratz was startled by what looked like a horrible monster crawling toward him and his campfire. He ran for his gun but fumbled and dropped it in his flurry of trying to get it loaded before the creature attacked him. The Indian girl left her washing and, laughing indulgently like a mother with a beloved but rather silly child, waved him back. She took a large club and with little ado killed the alligator.

It was not long before the two could understand each other, he with enough words in Chitimacha to be intelligible, she with a growing French vocabulary, usually mixing the two incompatible tongues in a rapid-fire torrent when she was excited. She took it upon herself not only to work for young Antoine Du Pratz, but also to advise him. When he wondered if Fort Rosalie on the bluffs of the Natchez might not be a better place to live, with better air, cooler temperatures in summer, and more congenial people, she agreed that it would indeed be a very good idea. She set about packing at once, and went along with him when he departed.

It was while Antoine and the girl and two Negro slaves were bound upstream in a large pirogue that he became aware of the true magnificence of the wildlife he found everywhere, wildlife untouched and vastly abundant here in the Mississippi Valley. None of the books he had read in France had told him anything about what he might expect.

As the boat pushed up the river, skirting the great cypress swamps, crowds of gutturally squawking herons flew up. Hundreds of cormorants posed like gaunt black statues on all the dead trees; there was the hollow hammering of ivory-billed woodpeckers, the flash of small golden birds of which he caught only a brief glimpse before they were gone. It was a land of birds singing and flying or uttering sounds that seemed to him of prehistoric origin and somehow alarming, especially at night. He was glad when they could stay overnight or a few days with people who had built plantations along the river and who were already planting fields of indigo. To sleep in a house, away from the infernal nightly grunting and screaming and hallooing of the birds in the river swamps, was a relief. Yet they all fascinated him—the wood ibises mounting in widening circles into the warm blue sky; pelicans catching fish in their incredible basket-beaks; the laughing gulls coming upstream as far as the salt water went, and then turning back as if they knew it was all a fresh-water river northward. How far north went the river? He would like to explore it all.

They finally reached the two-hundred foot clay cliffs of the Natchez on which stood the palisaded fort called Rosalie, with the

French flag flying bravely over the wooden battlement. Around the fort ranged cabins of the settlers who had come here under French protection. There had been protests from the Natchez Indians who had owned that whole pre-empted area. The French had ignored the protests. There were many places along the Mississippi where a fort could have been built, but the French must have this spot.

When he found a cabin in which to live, the Indian girl immediately set about making it homelike while he went sight-seeing with an interpreter. This was all new country to see, quantities of birds to observe, new plants to collect and wonder about. He became friendly with some of the Natchez, who became his guides. Then, after six months at Fort Rosalie, he fell suddenly ill with a great pain in his leg which could not be cured. The doctor at the fort was certain that he must go to France and bathe in medicinal waters, but Antoine could not go. He would be dead before he could reach La Rochelle. He would have to cure himself here—or die.

His French friends tried to help, but he was suffering without any relief. The Indian girl in great concern applied some of her own remedies. When these did no good, she went out one day without telling him where she was going and sought out the Natchez town of White Apple. There she located one of Antoine's Indian friends, who came at once and applied a special poultice which, in eight days, miraculously took away all the pain. Cautiously he got to his feet; he was able to stand again, to walk! In joy he went outdoors and walked to the fort and to the bluffs' edge to look at the river and the birds, for the first time in four long and pain-filled months. Now he was again free, and life along the Mississippi was good—for a little while.

The French at Fort Rosalie had been assuming that because of their eminence and power in Europe they could occupy the Natchez territory with impunity. The Indians at their coming had been sullen, but not unruly. Suddenly in 1722 passion flared. There was an uprising, but it was quelled within three days of the outbreak, and it was assumed with arrogance that the Natchez had been put down forever. Yet anyone acquainted with these proud and splendid people should have realized that only extermination would quell them. Du Pratz, who did know them, was uneasy. He could not say what it was, but there was something—something that was wrong. It was in the air, among the moss-hung oaks, in the ravines; something.

He and the girl finally moved back to New Orleans. They had not been there many months before the terrible news came that the Natchez had at last attacked Fort Rosalie. The Commandant had refused to be warned. All the signs had been there. A Natchez woman had warned a soldier, had told him to go quickly and tell the Commandant that the Natchez had lost their senses, and for him to be on his guard night and day. But the Frenchman had refused to admit the danger; he would keep up the illusion of power, would not let the Indians see that he was possibly uneasy.

On a foggy, chill November night the Natchez came. They had planned for a long time with the Yazoos and Choctaws to attack the fort and New Orleans at the same time, but they now went ahead without their confederates and had the Fort Rosalie massacre all to themselves. They broke down the gates, swarmed the walls, burned the houses around the fort, killed in an orgy of death, set fire to the fort and its warehouses. As the flames scalded into the night, the glow could have been seen almost as far as the land of the Tonicas.

One man survived. Half dead, he made his way through the swamps and forests to New Orleans to warn the people there. Du Pratz knew with a shudder that although the Natchez had always been good to him, had cured his leg ailment, they would not have spared his life on that insane night of blood and fire.

In retaliation, the French set about to exterminate not only the Natchez but the Choctaws and the Yazoos. The war went on and on for months, with losses on both sides, until the French finally

The brown falcon pipe, above, and the raven pipe, below, represent birds known to the prehistoric Hopewellians, who lived along the rivers of the the Middle West from about 500 B.C. to 500 A.D. (*Photos courtesy of Illinois State Museum.*)

Œnanthe Americana.   Solanum &c fl: purpureo.

Mark Catesby watched the song-antics of the yellow-breasted chat and painted this picture to show how the legs were bent at a curious angle. With it is the red trillium (*Trillium cuneatum*). (*Natural History of Carolina*, Catesby, 1754.)

Somewhere in the southern mountains, Mark Catesby painted the ruffed
grouse with his newly-discovered shooting star (*Dodecatheon Meadia*).
When rain threatened, his Indian companions built a bark hut to shelter
him and his paintings. (*Natural History of Carolina*, Catesby, 1754.)

CARRULUS STELLERI.

London Printed for John Murray Bookseller to the Admiralty, January 1ˢᵗ 1829.

Georg Steller, on an Alaskan island in 1741, saw a flash of iridescent blue and black as a crested bird flew across a patch of sunlight . . . his discovery, Steller's jay. This portrait was painted in 1828 by William Swainson, from a specimen collected on the Franklin Expedition.

GRACULUS PERSPICILLATUS.

Spectacled cormorants, now extinct, were found by Steller, shipwrecked on Bering Island, and helped to keep the survivors from starvation. This portrait was painted in London by J. Wolf, from a specimen sent from Russia by Dr. Peter Simon Pallas, and it appeared in Daniel Giraud Elliot's *Birds of America, Discovered After Audubon and Wilson*, 1869.

ORPHEUS MERULOIDES.

London Printed for John Murray Bookseller to the Admiralty January 1st 1829

The varied thrush was discovered in 1778 by Captain Cook at Nootka Sound. The interior varied thrush was one of Lewis and Clark's discoveries, and it was seen again by John Richardson in 1819. His specimen was used as a model for this portrait by William Swainson.

The Cock of the Plains, or sage grouse, discovered by Lewis and Clark in Oregon, was sketched on a page of Clark's journal. Admittedly not an artist, he made numerous sketches of plants and animals found on the expedition. (*Original Journals of Lewis and Clark*.)

In 1808, Alexander Wilson painted Lewis and Clark's magpie, center: ". . . a very beautiful specimen sent from the Mandan nation, on the Missouri, to Mr. Jefferson, and by that gentleman to Mr. Peale . . . . where I had the opportunity of examining it." (*American Ornithology*, Wilson, 1808.) Includes also the winter hawk and crow.

won and the remaining Natchez were taken captive. The Yazoos and Choctaws had gone, vanished into the wilderness.

In all this trouble, M. Du Pratz set himself zealously to learn about and to write an account of this marvelous land of Louisiana —the Louisiana which extended so tremendously up the river and westward no one knew how far. He was delighted, endlessly charmed, with what he found. He had thought himself fairly knowledgeable about the birds of Europe, but these in America were somehow incomprehensibly different and he had to exert himself to give them names that were suitable.

He said: "Ever since my arrival in Louisiana, I made it my business to get information in whatever was new therein, and to make discoveries of such things as might be serviceable to society."

On his journeys into the interior, up to the Chickasaw country around Memphis, beyond to the Illinois country, and west through Louisiana, he remarked:

In such journeys as these we always take up our night's lodging near wood and water, where we put up in good time; then at sun-set, when every thing in nature is hushed, we were charmed with the enchanting warbling of different birds; so that one would be inclined to say, they reserved this favourable moment for the melody and harmony of their song, to celebrate undisturbed and at their ease, the benefits of the Creator. On the other hand, we are disturbed in the night, by the hideous noise of the numberless water-fowls that are to be seen on the Mississippi, and every river or lake near it, such as cranes, flamingo's, wild geese, herons, saw-bills, ducks, etc.

In all this wonderful and dangerous wilderness, where the Indians were apt to be peppery and frequently in revolt against the French, Du Pratz with his Chitimacha girl, sometimes with other companions or servants, roamed placidly about, ultimately covering thousands of miles of wild country, observing the wildlife and calmly writing about it in his journal.

In trying to learn what he could about the mammals and plants, the reptiles and insects and birds, he drew strange, crude pictures that were among the earliest natural history drawings to be made along the Mississippi. They were not at all the beautiful, recognizable paintings which Catesby at almost the same time was making a thousand miles to the east. Du Pratz's drawings had a primitive look, almost as if they had been done by a young child. His portraits of trees were two-dimensional, stylized, and about as unrecognizable as his birds, worms, and other animals. But they were his best, his desperate attempts to transmit to his kinsmen in France something of the wonder of the American wildlife. In his own way, he was as much impressed with the birds of Louisiana as another Frenchman, Audubon, was to be a hundred years later in these same swamps and forests. In those hundred years, hardly any other men looked at birds with a keen enough or discerning enough eye to write about them or paint their portraits.

He felt his own inadequacy. He said, "Birds are so very numerous in Louisiana, that if all the different kinds of them were known, which is far from being the case at present, the description of them alone would require an entire volume."

In winter, when hordes of migrant ducks and geese came south from some unknown nesting ground to spend months in the coastal marshes and along the bayous and swamps, he simply could not believe the numbers. "For one you see in France you may here count a thousand." He recognized, however, only three kinds—Indian ducks, wild ducks, and summer ducks. The latter (wood ducks) he greatly admired. "Their plumage is quite beautiful, and so changeable that no painting can imitate it. Upon their head they have a beautiful tuft of the most lively colours, and their red eyes appear like flames."

He especially admired the kingfisher. "This bird," he said, "it is well known, goes always against the wind; but perhaps few people know that it preserves the same property when it is dead. I myself hung a dead one by a silk thread directly over a sea-compass, and I can declare it as a fact, that the bill was always turned towards the wind."

He marveled at the immense flights of passenger pigeons. One day, on an excursion along the river, he had stopped on the bank when he heard a confused noise that seemed to be coming along the river from a distance below. He got into the canoe and paddled downstream, staying in the middle in case the noise meant danger. He could not think what it might be, this strange, rumbling, roaring racket. Then he saw a mass of wild pigeons flying close together, up and down into the live oaks, apparently beating down the acorns with their wings. The acorns showered down with a rattling to the ground, where the pigeons took turns eating, then beating, while the man, resting on his paddle, watched in amazement.

The hummingbird, as all visitors felt who saw it, was a most astonishing thing, a bird like nothing anyone in Europe had ever seen. He said:

The Humming-bird is not larger even with its feathers than a large beetle. The colour of its feathers is variable, according to the light they are exposed in; in the sun they appear like enamel upon a gold ground, which delights the eyes. The longest feathers of the wings of this bird are not much more than half an inch long; its bill is about the same length, and pointed like an awl; and its tongue resembles a sewing-needle; its flight is so rapid that it is always heard before it be seen. Although like the bee it sucks the flowers, it never rests upon them, but supports itself upon its wings, and passes from one flower to another with the rapidity of lightning. It is a rare thing to catch a Humming-Bird alive; one of my friends however had the happiness to catch one. He had observed it enter the flower of a convolvulus, and as it had quite buried itself to get at the bottom, he ran forwards, shut the flower, cut it from the stalk, and carried off the bird a prisoner. He could not however prevail upon it to eat, and it died four days later.

Antoine Du Pratz described fifty-seven kinds of American birds along the Mississippi, surely more than anyone else had done so early in our history. He was a good observer. But of all the birds he found and described, it was the Carolina parakeet, now extinct, that placed the name of Antoine Simon Le Page Du Pratz in orni-

thological books of today. In the earnest labor of the American
Ornithological Union to find the earliest accurate descriptions of
each American bird, it was to Du Pratz that they came for the
parakeet. Catesby's was only a few years later, but late enough not
to be given first credit for this delightful little bright bird which
Du Pratz named *Papagai à tête aurore*—the parrot with the sunrise
on his head.

With some humor and a good deal of perception he wrote:

The Parroquet of Louisiana is not quite so large as those that are usually brought to France. Its plumage is of a fine sea-green, with a pale
rose-coloured spot upon the crown, which brightens into red towards
the beak, and fades off into green towards the body. It is with difficulty
that it learns to speak, and even then it rarely practices it, resembling
in this the natives themselves, who speak little. As a silent parrot would
never make its fortune among our French ladies, it is doubtless on this
account that we see so few of these in France.

Between the efforts of Catesby and Du Pratz, by mid-eighteenth
century a large number of American birds had been discovered,
yet only a fraction of the total inhabiting the continent. Their work
was, however, the nucleus upon which grew the discoveries of the
great naturalists who were soon to follow.

CHAPTER FIVE

GEORG WILHELM STELLER

BRIEFLY and in heartbreak he watched the magnificence and the unexplored mystery of Alayashka, the Great Land, merge with the sea-fog as the ship, the *St. Peter,* headed westward toward disaster. For all of his life, it seemed, he had been waiting to come to this place, and now the surly Vitus Bering refused to linger more than a few hours at the new and unexplored shore. Captain Commander Bering had not even permitted him to reach the alluring mainland nearby.

Georg Wilhelm Steller stood by the rail and watched the land disappear into the mists. In his hand he held a dead bird of splendid shining blue and black, with a rakish black crest and a strong black beak. This was his trophy of the Great Land.

Steller was born in Germany in 1709, in the days when Peter the Great in Russia was endeavoring to drag his backward nation out of the category of Russian bears and uncultured peasants. While the boy was growing up with a fascination for nature in Windesheim, Germany, and poring over books of exploration, Peter was vigorously founding the Russian Academy of Science. He wanted to emulate the more advanced nations of Europe. He ordered beards shaved off and French spoken by people of education, and he insisted on hiring the best scientists to carry on research in order to bring honor to the Academy of Science and at the same time to himself and to Russia. His problem was that Russians had not yet come very far in science and he had therefore to go to European cities, chiefly to Germany, to find his scientists. Not many of these would consent to go to Russia for research, even at high pay; they had heard of the rigors of life away from Moscow and St. Petersburg. It was not worth it.

In his schooling, young Georg Steller followed his interest in zoology. He studied, however, in a three-way program, so that when he was finished with his education in Germany, he was a Lutheran minister, a physician, and a zoologist. His passion for the out-of-doors and his yearning for travel and exploration in far places, especially in North America, outweighed his duty to the other two professions. As a botanist he was making a name for himself in Windesheim, but not very much money to support himself. When he was suddenly invited to come as a botanical researcher to the Russian Academy of Science, he accepted.

It was 1734, and Czar Peter had recently died, when Georg Wilhelm Steller reached St. Petersburg. Peter's widow, Catherine, continued with his plans. To find out the secrets of the northern seas beyond Siberia, she gave the Danish navigator, Vitus Bering, orders that were so huge and so grandiose that he needed to be several men to accomplish them all, and needed many times more funds than he was allotted. He spent years simply in organizing and outfitting the expeditions. In one expedition he had discovered the strait that now bears his name, then had had to return and re-outfit his ships for still another voyage which Catherine's successor, the Empress Anna Ivanovna, niece of Peter, ordered him to carry out. Funds, meanwhile, were meager; he was promised much and given little. His orders were countermanded by politicians. Nothing went right. Bering, once full of vigor and interest, became sapped of vitality, enthusiasm, and strength, and could summon little force in urging the ships completed and the voyage begun.

He was to go into the North Pacific and find the fabled Da Gama Land, which was rumored to lie between Asia and America, and then to move on to the North American Continent itself. Since part of this lay close to Siberia, Empress Anna wanted it claimed for Russia.

Meanwhile, in St. Petersburg, Steller was quickly proving himself to be one of the most capable scientists at the Academy. He studied Russian, read the great books in the library, ranged out into the countryside for specimens. And while he was in St. Petersburg he learned to his incredible delight that there was a possibility that he might be appointed to go with Vitus Bering in the exploration of the North Pacific. If this should come true, it would be the fulfillment of a long-held dream, his greatest wish.

Preparing for what he might find in the North, he visited an elderly and ailing botanist named Messerschmidt, whose books he had read. He wanted to know what Messerschmidt had to say about Kamchatka, and where would be the best places to seek for specimens, for if he were to join Bering, he would first spend time collecting on the Kamchatka peninsula. But the old man had been stationed at Bolsheretsk, southward on the peninsula, and he had returned embittered and ruined in health. He tried to dissuade the young man from the same pain and disillusionment, but he could not. He told him of the primitive hardships, the ugliness, the lack of cooperation, the hideous Siberian winters, and the miserable, defeated, hopeless people who were exiles living out their days in this wilderness. One needed superhuman, dedicated zeal, indeed, to overlook these things; one needed an iron constitution to be a scientist and survive in Siberia. Few of them lasted long. And Messerschmidt, old before his time, lay back coughing.

Yet Steller could not be disheartened or his high spirits quenched. Siberia was where he wanted to go. He knew it might take him three years to travel more than seven thousand miles over the wastes and wildernesses of Siberia to reach Kamchatka and then, later, Okhotsk, where Bering's ships would depart. But nothing seemed too severe for Steller. When word came that he had been accepted, he knew he had been offered Paradise across the Siberian snows.

Messerschmidt died. His young wife, Helena, and Georg Steller, attracted to each other from their first meeting, were married. They were happy, until word came at last that Steller was to proceed at once to Siberia, to the laboratory at Bolsheretsk, to collect plants and birds in that area before joining Bering on Avatcha Bay when the time came.

Helena Steller was not pleased with the glorious prospect of traveling by sledge and troika into the hideous wilds of Siberia, or of waiting at the grim base of Okhotsk for her wandering husband to return from Bering's mad expedition. She was with difficulty persuaded to start off with him and, although she relented, there was a tight look about her mouth, and her eyes were wary. Helena liked cities; she hated the wild.

By the time they and their baggage had reached Moscow over a long and desolate stretch of road from St. Petersburg, Helena Steller had made up her mind. With finality she informed her husband that she would not go a step farther. If he insisted on proceeding without her, then he might not find her waiting for him when he returned.

He loved his wife. He also loved duty and science and adventure. He kissed her good-bye, and went on alone.

Reaching Kamchatka after a long, chill journey, he settled himself at the laboratory with a Cossack assigned to him as his assistant and with an artist to make his drawings. The three spent a wonderful season collecting mountain plants on the peninsula. He found many new species, and some birds, too; Kamchatka had been little explored and almost nothing was known of the flora and fauna. Sometimes, dimly, he wondered what Helena was doing, and if she missed him; rather he doubted it. She had never been an affectionate woman. She had seemed self-sufficient and even relieved when he left her in Moscow.

In 1740, Steller left the base in Kamchatka and with his Cossack went over the miserable, muddy, mountainous country to Okhotsk to join Bering at last. In the harbor he found the two ships, the *St.*

Peter and the *St. Paul*, almost ready to weigh anchor. The *St. Peter* was the flagship, and on this, with Bering, Lieutenant Waxell, and other officers, Steller was rather grudgingly given quarters. He was astonished at Bering's noncommittal attitude, his air almost of resentment that a bothersome naturalist should have been assigned to his expedition to make scientific reports and collections. Yet he knew that Steller had come on with the express recommendation of the Empress herself, with orders to be permitted to collect at every opportunity for the benefit of the Russian Academy, and that he also be permitted to act as physician and chaplain when needed. But Bering was a grim, silent, withdrawn individual and would not let Steller do much of anything until, with illness taking over the ship, he had to let him minister to the men and to officiate at their burials.

Steller, trying to disregard the rebuffs and the apathy which he found among the men on the ship, was inwardly glowing with happiness at having reached this point in the long-coveted exploration of the North. He was bound for the fabled Da Gama Land, which he privately did not believe existed. He was sure that only America itself lay out beyond Kamchatka and the Pacific. Natives to whom he had talked said that it was a place with great white mountains and boundless forests, a place called Alayashka, the Great Land.

The ships set off in early June, 1741. Bering retired below and was seldom seen; he seemed sapped of all initiative, will, interest. It was Steller who was out on deck at dawn each day, studying the sea and the sky and the birds; it was Steller who was always peering into the eastern mists for a possible sign of land. But there was no land. Instead of navigating northwest, which the Kamchatka natives had said was the direction to Alayashka, Bering had ordered a course southeast, and there was no land, nothing. Then they came into a violent storm, and the pitching ships were immediately separated in the tumult of wind and waves. The *St. Peter* struggled in the mountainous gray billows. The men were dreadfully ill. When the storm subsided, the *St. Peter* was quite alone on a great and trackless sea which still heaved mightily after the tempest.

Bering came on deck, ordered the northeast course, and returned again to his cabin. Steller, meanwhile, tried to minister to the men, some of whom were showing severe symptoms of scurvy. On the afternoon of July 16, as he stood at the rail, always looking to the northeast, his heart leaped almost with fear. As the mist had parted suddenly he had briefly seen what appeared to be a tremendous white mountain peak ahead. Then the apparition had vanished like a dream.

The men jeered at his excitement. They had done a good deal of this, had made fun of the serious scientist who had promised that as soon as they found land he would feed them weeds and grass to cure their scurvy. They sneered at his aims, at everything he did or said. But a few thought that they, too, had seen the mysterious mountain before it vanished. They talked about it among themselves. Steller knew he had seen the mountain. Land was close.

He was out on deck before dawn, watching, but the fog was thick and impenetrable. Then it parted again and before them lay a great white range of mountains with the huge one even greater now because they were so much closer. It was land! There were islands nearby. The sick men fell out of their bunks and staggered up on deck. The very sight of land refreshed them. The Great Land —Alayashka!

They named the mountain peak after the patron saint of the day —Mount St. Elias. Its height, men later learned, was 18,008 feet. It dominated the coast range with its awe-inspiring altitude and remote snows.

But there was no great elation in Vitus Bering. He had plans for landing just long enough to fill the water casks. He had no plans for exploring. He would not listen to Steller's suggestions of wintering there in a sheltered cove, even of letting him collect wildlife in this unknown, alluring land. Steller himself, hardly able to wait to go ashore, could not understand Bering's indifference.

At first the Captain Commander refused to let Steller go ashore with the water casks. This was too much to endure, and Steller's long-withheld impatience and outrage boiled forth in a stinging tirade which made the men stand back and wonder at his temerity. No one spoke like that to the Captain Commander Bering. But the Commander simply listened, noncommittal and quiet, while Steller accused him of disobeying the Empress's orders, reminding him that "they had not come to North America simply to carry some of its water back to Asia."

Reluctantly Bering gave permission for Steller and his assistant to go with the boats bearing the water casks, but reminded him dully that if he did not come back in time, he would have to stay forever in that terrible wilderness. No, he could not go to the mainland. He would have to be satisfied with the island. That ought to be enough. If he had sense he would stay on the ship and not venture into the unknown. But the unknown was meat and drink to Georg Wilhelm Steller.

With his Cossack he went to the island—Kayak Island, between the present Juneau and Anchorage, near Prince William Bay, Alaska. He knew he had only a brief time to work, that in a small space he must collect everything he could and at the same time his report must not be so haphazard that it would be blurred or incorrect. He must see everything in its relation to every other thing, as if it were imprinted in a picture which he needed only to look at in his mind to recall again what he would see this day. But he had little time, and it was a huge land, pristine and unknown and untouched. He yearned to know it all.

He also knew that if scurvy were to be combated on the return voyage, he must see that antiscorbutic plants—cresses and wild onions and anything else he could find with these properties—were collected. But here and at later stops in the Aleutians, Bering rejected the urgent need, curtly telling him to collect the stuff himself if he wanted it.

For several hours on the island, Steller and the Cossack collected.

Then he sent the man back on one of the boats to carry the load of plants and other specimens to the ship and to ask—to plead—for an extension of time. He needed months, years, not a few hours. It was inhuman; it was cruel; it was impossible!

Waiting for the man to return, Steller wandered up into the deep, mossy trails of a fir forest, pausing now and again to dig a new plant with his Yakut dagger. He examined the rocks, listened to the birds. He went almost four miles up the trail, then realized that no one could possibly find him. He halted and sat down near the rim of a cliff overlooking the sea.

Then he heard a bird. How many an exciting moment in man's life of discovery begins with that short sentence! He heard a bird —a harsh *char-char-char*—with a curious quality in it, quite different from anything he had ever heard before. He saw a flash of magnificent, iridescent, ultramarine blue and black, and a jay-sized bird with a long crest flew across a patch of sunlight and came down to the ground. The bird hopped with a spring-wire gait of tremendous exuberance and energy; it made agreeable, scolding sounds to itself, turning its head from side to side, while its elegant black-blue crest glistened in the sunlight, or rose and fell with the bird's emotions.

Steller's scientifically trained mind went back over what he knew. This bird was a jay, he was positive of that. He had read Catesby's work on the Carolinas, and he knew he had pictured a jay, but not one like this. There was nothing at all about one like this.

He watched the splendid creature whose energy and beauty seemed all a part of the new land. He could not collect it; the Cossack had the gun. Steller hurried back down the path to the shore and found that several of the new jays followed him and gathered not far away as he paused now and again to taste berries that he found. He had just discovered the delicious salmonberry of the Northwest; he rejoiced in its fresh juice and sparkling raspberry flavor, even though the fruit was not quite ripe. He gathered several kinds of plants, made a fire, and brewed a tea of their leaves. Leaves like these, in quantity, could surely save all the men from the ravages of scurvy.

The Cossack came back. He shot a jay for Steller, and before they went back he shot several other birds that were new. Bering, however, would not permit any extension of time. Before dawn next morning, when Steller felt that perhaps there would be another excursion ashore, Bering was up in the dim light, commanding the men to cast off quickly and set sail for home. Steller was sick at heart at the lost opportunity.

But he had his new jay. This was later given his name as its discoverer—Steller's jay, that elegant bird of the mountains, down the Northwest coast and into California. There are many races of the same bird. Its Rocky Mountain kin, the black-headed jay, was to be found by other men at a time of great hardship, hunger, cold, and misery along a place in Montana called the Lolo Trail. But these trials were nothing, perhaps, to the soreness in the heart of the scientist when he saw Alaska disappearing forever into the mists.

The crew of the *St. Peter* lay ill with scurvy, which reached a greater virulence as the days went by. At stops in the Aleutians, once to bury the first victim, named Shumagin—whose name was given to that island where he left his bones—Steller insisted on gathering as many wild cresses as he could in the short time, and with these he began to treat the men who were so ill they could no longer spurn what they termed cattle fodder. Those who were too far gone with the terrible debilitating disease died, one by one, and were buried at sea; but he did save many of them. Then, as if their troubles were not enough, the *St. Peter* came into a violent tempest which hurled it through the waves and battered it, causing leaks that threatened to sink the vessel. The ship was lashed and punished, and on the crest of a huge roller it was thrown over a reef and into a lagoon. The *St. Peter* lay broken on the rocks, but remained above water so that the men who survived struggled to shore. They were more dead than alive, but they were alive, and that was something.

The weary, sick men at first were certain that they had been cast on a shore of Kamchatka. They stared into the mists to see the familiar peak of the volcano, Klyuchevskya, but they could not see it or anything familiar. It was an island, and they were many miles away from even Kamchatka peninsula and the wild base on the mainland called Okhotsk, which to them now spelled civilization and safety and surcease from misery.

They began their long battle to exist. They dug pits in the beach and raised sail-canvas to make a roof and low walls. The pit-houses were chill and damp, but they at least kept off the worst of the weather. The sick men lay in their dank cellars, suffering, dying. And the foxes terrified them. Arctic foxes swarmed on the rocky island. They had never seen men before and were unafraid. Day and night they came on raids. They grew more bold as the men weakened and died, seeming to sense the air of death and defeat. They slipped like shadows about the miserable camp, stole what food they could find, rushed in for a nip at a man's arm or leg or nose; and the men in their weakness wept in fear of these demons and the futility of trying to fight them. Fearful that the animals would come in and eat them alive, the men were often afraid to go to sleep. The foxes seemed to be everywhere, stealing, biting, lurking—waiting.

Georg Steller became Steller the physician. Bering was too desperately ill himself to do anything. His second in command was Waxell, but it was Steller who nursed the sick, found ways to combat starvation, kept up the men's courage during the worst months of the long winter when the foxes seemed sure to triumph. He shot sea otters and other animals, made a vitamin-filled soup of their livers and kidneys, and gathered what vegetation he could find to add to the nourishment. Many of the men at last began to show signs of improvement.

Vitus Bering, however, died, and was buried on this island which later was given his name, Bering Island in the Komandorski group. Waxell took command, but there was little now that he could do. Only Steller, it seemed, had courage and enthusiasm. For once again he was in an unexplored place. He might not have Alayashka, but through fate's intervention he had this island, and it was his to explore at leisure. With paper salvaged from the ship's locker, the remains of the vessel still being above water, he commenced work on his book, *Die Bestiis Marinis*. It was to be his great contribution to natural history, even though he did not live to see it published. While the other men lay dull, complaining, and hopeless, Georg Steller wrote a book.

There was much that was new on this island. He explored all of it, and collected every species of plant and animal he could find. He discovered a great colony of sea lions at one end of the island, enormous animals never before known to science. Daily he went there to watch. He built a crude blind on the rocky beach where the huge creatures consorted, and sat for hours to study them as they mated, or fought, or slept, or bore their young. Their incredible roaring filled the blind, and there were times when he wondered if some monstrous old leathery bull might not shove against the frail structure and knock it down about him.

One day an unbelievably enormous creature washed in over the reef and day on the beach, quite dead, with the gulls already picking at it. It was the biggest animal he had ever seen and it evidently had never been described before, if any man had seen it more than casually as it surfaced and sank near a ship. But this was his specimen, given into his hands for its immortality. It was the sea cow, or northern manatee, which not many years later would become extinct. He measured it, examined it, then persuaded some of the men to take it apart for him so that he could see the skeleton and the organs. The flesh was not unpleasant when roasted for dinner, but the men could not see the use for such careful dissection of the remainder of a carcass which no one intended to eat.

During that winter and spring, Steller found a duck, later called Steller's eider, and studied the colony of large cormorants that roosted and laid eggs on the rocks. This was the spectacled cormorant which, like the sea cow, has since become extinct, devoured by the Aleuts. The cormorants were also a great source of food for the castaways, since one of these big green-and-purple creatures would satisfy three hungry men.

As the weather moderated into a bleak spring, the men under Waxell built a vessel out of the salvaged wood of the wreck. It was a small vessel, and not very seaworthy, but it could take the survivors to the mainland. By spring more than half of the men who had sailed on the *St. Peter* had died. The ship was soon loaded with what they could take with them, but only Steller had anything of any consequence—all his collections and his manuscript. He had an entire sea cow skeleton and its skin, a sea lion, and much more. It was all, suddenly, incredibly bulky.

Waxell looked coldly at the accumulation. He would permit only a small part of it to go aboard the small ship, and Steller would have to choose what he wanted to leave behind. Since he wanted to leave nothing at all behind, the decision was a searing one. He could not, Waxell insisted, take the sea cow or the sea lion. But his bird skins were light in weight; they packed small. The jay, the cormorant, the eider, and a new albatross went back with him.

They got to Okhotsk, finally, and found that no one expected to see any of the *St. Peter's* crew again. The *St. Paul* had long since returned after its own brief experiences on the American coast. Everyone thought the *St. Peter*, with her crew and the eminent Bering, had long since been lost.

The men discovered that changes had taken place during their absence of more than a year. Empress Anna Ivanovna had died and the new Empress, Elizaveta Petrovna, had a strong will and a mind of her own. Steller found that when he reached the scientific base on the Bolshaya River, many of his friends there had been sent home. Elizaveta had brought politics into the Academy, was exiling the foreigners and bringing in her own people. Conditions were growing unbearable at Bolsheretsk, and he was glad to go back to the mountains with his Cossack to finish his study of the Kamchatka peninsula. By special messenger he sent his carefully catalogued collections to St. Petersburg.

Late in the summer of 1744, as he was on his way home, he wondered wistfully, as he had wondered many times, whether his wife had forgiven his absence and would be waiting. He wished now that he could hurry his way over the interminable distances of Siberia. He spent a grim winter in Yakutsk where mail from home was waiting, but not very cheerful mail. A brief letter from Helena told him that she was leaving him.

He still had his work and it took away some of the pain, but now it seemed that everything was going wrong. Suddenly in August, 1745, he was summarily arrested and told to put his affairs in order. He was brought back as a virtual prisoner over miles of desolate country—desolate even in late summer—with no chance to have prepared his recently collected plants so that they would keep. He had, in fact, been compelled to leave most of them behind. He could only hope that his collections from the Bering expedition had reached the Academy safely.

He never knew why he was arrested. It was enough that the High Governing Senate had ordered it. Then in October, again for no reason, he was released and told to go on his own to St. Petersburg. But his collections were now ruined. Perhaps it was this devastating series of blows which brought on a fever. As he traveled home by sledge, he grew worse; he tried to minister to himself, but found himself beyond that. Friends cared for him at Irkutsk, but he died there on a day in November, 1746. He was thirty-seven.

It was the end of a career, the end of a man, but not the end of the discoveries to be made in the land he had just touched, and about which he had felt so much excitement and hope. Alaska, the Great Land, would lie there waiting for other men to come. He had only marked the way. His jays would bounce on spring-wire legs in the forests of the Northwest; his eiders would swim and fly in great flocks in the North Pacific; his records of plants would stand as the first to have been made in that whole wild, pristine, wonderful wilderness.

By the time the next scientist from the Russian Academy, Dr. Peter Simon Pallas, came to the Sea of Okhotsk and the Bering Strait, and to the Aleutian Islands, many changes had taken place. Already some creatures seen by Steller were becoming rare or extinct or even then were lost. His sea cow was gone. So was the spectacled cormorant, or almost gone. Pallas collected several specimens, however, and one of them was sent for ornithological study in London, where the illustration in this book was painted. This bird and Steller's jay, Steller's eider, Steller's sea eagle, with his albatross and sea lion, keep his name alive.

CHAPTER SIX

WILLIAM BARTRAM

THE alligators worried him. Uneasily he built up his campfire and leaned his back firmly against the scaly trunk of a large live oak whose roots formed a sort of armchair for him. He braced himself so that in the dark an alligator might not take him by the foot and drag him into the river. All around him the night was full of sounds. It was spring, and the frogs were loud. Barred owls barked and cajoled; the incessant throaty serenade of a chuck-will's-widow came from the magnolias somewhere in the Florida darkness, and the laughing and cackling of coots and gallinules rose from the marsh. He could place all the sounds—the bullfrogs' thunder, the frog with a voice like a cowbell, the yelping of green frogs, the chirruping of tree frogs, as well as the chorus of clicks which told where dozens of little cricket frogs sat partly submerged in the shallows. His mind drowsily catalogued the sounds until, when he was almost asleep, he jerked upright with a start, the back of his neck tingling. There was a wild and most desperate cry of anguish somewhere out there.

He could see nothing in the blackness of river and swamp, nothing back of him in the woods, but it was so black everywhere that anything could be lurking just beyond the circle of light cast by his fire. He threw on more wood, but even as the fire flared higher, he could see nothing. And the crying burst forth again in a perfect agony of sobs and wails. It was most alarming, and it made him uneasy, made him somehow sad to hear this mourning thing. He wished he knew what it was. The unknown is always so much more terrible than the known.

Each night as he camped in the Florida swamp wilderness he heard it. Now it no longer alarmed him; it simply presented a mystery. Sometimes he crept forward along the banks, or set out quietly in his canoe in search of the maker of the crying, but it was never in the place he thought it was. It was like some disembodied thing, a tantalizing challenge he never seemed able to solve.

Some days later when, in the company of an Indian, he and his canoe pushed through a silent swamp, William Bartram startled a hen-sized bird with brown feathers speckled with white, long legs and short tail, and a down-curved, long, brown bill. The Indian with him explained that this was none other than the Crying Bird, called Ephouskyca by his people, who believed that it was a spirit of some lost swamp creature, mourning through the darkness. The bird did not then utter a sound, but he was sure now, from the Indian's description, that the wailing he had heard had been made by this bird.

He resolved to name it the Crying Bird and give it a scientific name that would commemorate how the bird had teased him for so long—*Tantalus*, for that old Greek king who was punished by never being able to reach a drink of water when he was dying of thirst, or of reaching the fruit hung just out of his starving grasp. *Tantalus*, the Crying Bird; later it was known as the limpkin, but it still keeps the scientific name that Bartram gave it.

He would never forget that night when he had first heard it. Before dusk at this camping place he had watched in fascination the swarming nuptial dance of millions of May flies rising and dipping like frail feathers above the surface; the fish leaped and splashed after them during the insects' brief sojourn above water. Afterward the night had become dark, noisy with frogs and birds and with that spine-tingling crying. There was always, too, the chance that an alligator would lumber out of the swamp and invade his camp.

Then it was morning, the glorious Florida morning, and the wild turkeys were up in the trees to greet the sun in a rare and wonderful salutation to the dawn.

I was awakened in the morning early, by the cheering converse of the wild turkey-cocks . . . saluting each other, from the sun-brightened tops of the lofty Cypresses and Magnolias. . . . They begin at early dawn, and continue till sun-rise, from March to the last of April. The high forests ring with the noise, like the crowing of the domestic cock, of these social sentinels; the watch-word being caught and repeated, from one to another, for hundreds of miles around; insomuch that the whole country is for an hour or more in a universal shout. A little after sun-rise, their crowing gradually ceases, they quit their high lodging places, and alight on the earth, where expanding their silver-bordered train, they strut and dance round about the coy females while the deep forests seem to tremble with their shrill noise.

William Bartram was a rover, a woodsman, an educated man, and a naturalist at a time when there were not many men in America who combined all four qualities. His boyhood had fitted him for it, for his father was the eminent botanist of Philadelphia, John Bartram, who had had correspondence with Mark Catesby, and who possessed an original edition of the *Natural History of Carolina*.

The boy, William, had grown up with this magnificent work in the household, had pored over the pictures and the descriptions, and had seen many birds for himself. When he and his father went on excursions to the woods and mountains, they had both used Catesby's work for identification of the specimens they brought home. This and the more abstruse and poorly illustrated books of Edwards and Latham and Lawson were all he had to help him. He followed Catesby's nomenclature, mostly; but it was still a period in which, if a man preferred a different name for a bird, he could bestow it, and for all he knew it might eventually be accepted as more accurate and lasting then the earlier ones. There was, however, little idea of true classification of birds by family characteristics. Bartram lumped all the birds which ate seeds in the "Granivorous

Tribes"—this included everything from wild turkeys and ruffed grouse to cardinals, goldfinches, and wrens. But he was simply groping, as other scientists were groping in this new and most puzzling land.

In trying to be clear and accurate, he laid out Latin names that were often long and cumbersome. His Whooting Owl, in his bird-Latin, was *Strix acclamator, capite levi, corpore griseo*. The Mallard Duck had a name almost as long as the bird—*Anas fera torquata major, caput et collum viridi splendentia, dorsum griseo fuscum, pectore rufescente, speculum violaceum*. But the name that Bartram and Catesby gave to the robin remains today—*Turdus Migratorius* —and so do some others which have stood the test of time and knowledge.

He knew with humbleness, however, that he had really only made a start. He remarked:

I am convinced there yet are several kinds of land birds, and a great number of aquatic fowl, that have not come under my particular notice; therefore shall leave them to the investigation of future travelling naturalists of greater ability and industry.

To many men in England in the eighteenth century, botany was the thing. Those who could not come to America to collect prevailed upon their friends there to oblige them with as many specimens and plants as possible. So when his friend Dr. Fothergill of London asked him to go down to Carolina and Georgia and into the Floridas to search out and collect rare and useful productions of nature, William Bartram delightedly agreed that it was just what he most wanted to do. It gave him, besides, an excuse for an excursion into new country. Roads being what they were then, he set off, aged thirty-four, in April, 1773, in a brigantine out of Philadelphia.

Heading down the coast, bound for Charleston, South Carolina, the ship promptly ran into a violent spring storm off Hatteras that threatened to wreck the vessel and drown the estimable Mr. Bartram, who wrote later: "The powerful winds, now rushing forth from their secret abodes, suddenly spread terror and devastation; and the wide ocean, which, a few moments past, was gentle and placid, is now thrown into disorder, and heaped into mountains, whose white curling crests seem to sweep the skies!"

After two days of struggling, the ship not getting any nearer safety or shore, the storm at last cleared, and he woke to a brilliant atmosphere full of the cries of sea birds. The smells and sounds of springtime in South Carolina were coming out to meet the ship as it limped into the harbor.

He had a thoroughly delightful time collecting, by canoe and horseback and by carriage and on foot, every plant species he could find. He completed Dr. Fothergill's collection in ample time to get back to the woods for his own pleasure and learning. It was still spring, the birds were calling him, and he certainly couldn't go home now.

Retracing some of his route back to Florida, whose possibilities he had only briefly discovered as he collected plants, he roamed alone through its wilderness. He absorbed everything—insects, birds, reptiles, trees, and always his great love, the flowers. He went by dugout canoe up the St. John's River near St. Augustine and worked south toward its headwaters in Lake George. He quietly explored by himself in a land which perhaps no white man had ever seen so intimately, and none certainly by choice or for pleasure and enlightenment. There were a few scattered plantations, still in imminent danger of Indian attack; there were the distant Seminole towns, and occasionally a trading post sweltering out in the palmetto scrub. But inland along the rivers there was little evidence of white men.

It would have been blissful for William Bartram, quietly paddling his canoe on his private explorations, or putting up a sail and letting the wind take him, if it had not been for the mosquitoes and the alligators. The latter worried him. There were so many of them in Florida. He could never get accustomed to their prehistoric aspect, their relentless determination to attain what their cold-blooded brains wanted; and they were often so big, sometimes ten to twelve feet long, and so heavily armored that he felt helpless in defending himself against them.

Camping one evening, he chose the highest spot along the river—and Florida afforded few of any great elevation—where he built a good fire with a supply of extra wood close at hand for the night. Alligators were down in the river; they had come up around where he had left the canoe. He could see them, could hear them swashing about and grunting, or slashing and splashing in the water. He didn't like the situation.

He was hungry, but unfortunately had left his food in the canoe —and he certainly didn't relish the thought of going down there to get it. As a compromise, he thought he might catch some fish for supper instead. Around the curve of his little promontory he could see a small lagoon that was overgrown with waterlilies, lotuses, rushes, and irises. If he could reach that point quietly without attracting attention from the crocodiles—he called them crocodiles or alligators, one or the other, in his journal—he might be able to catch some fish. He hoped no saurians were there for the same purpose, but he rather doubted that they were; there were so very many of them down in the river. In the marsh he could see coots and gallinules flying about and flapping over the lily leaves. Young broods of wood ducks swam about. There was no alligator in sight.

The wild oranges on the ridge were blossoming. Their fragrance was pleasant in the calm and delicious sunset air as he made his way to the lagoon. He was about to throw in a line when out of the irises there charged a monster which, to his alarm, looked like a behemoth spouting fire and smoke—he was positive he saw fire and smoke, or at least the smoke. The tail lashed, and the animal surged toward the young ducks, but they neatly vanished with their parents somewhere out of reach. The racket which the animal had made aroused a rival, and Bartram stood transfixed, cold to the toes, his fishing line limp in his hand as the rival alligator wallowed across the shallows and attacked the first-comer. They evidently were not even aware that a man was watching.

It was a dreadful battle. He would never forget it. The creatures were wrapped around each other like giant snakes, lashing and thrashing and roaring and wrestling, stirring up mud and water while all the birds flew away. Each alligator tried to clamp snaggle-teeth on the other, but neither quite managed it. Finally the vanquished one lay panting among the mud and sedges, while the victor slopped its way to the edge of the bank, lifted its great muzzle so that Bartram could see half-way down its awful, gray-pink throat, and bellowed a tremendous roar of triumph.

William Bartram was a persistent man, especially when he was hungry, and he certainly was not a coward. Although he really didn't admire the way the sun was setting so rapidly, or how the alligators seemed to be gathering by dozens in the river, he decided to give up his idea of fishing at the marsh and to make a run for the canoe. If he could get into it fast, shoving off before the animals gathered their slow wits to attack him, he could try to fish at a place not far away. The boldness of his pushing the heavy canoe into their faces threw them off for a bit, and he thought he had escaped. He hadn't brought his gun for fear that he might lose it overboard, but he had provided a stout club in case they attacked—though how he could beat off so many he did not really know and did not like to think about.

Bartram must have been very hungry, because he continued with his plan, while the alligators surged toward him and crowded against the canoe. They clapped their jaws together with menace; they snorted and grunted. He neither liked the way they smelled nor the way they looked. He hastily shoved the canoe toward the shore again, thinking that if he paralleled it closely enough he would have them only one one side. Then he finally gave up and leaped ashore.

This worked. They drew off and looked up at him. They watched. They swam along in the river as he walked the bank toward the lagoon once more. And there, in spite of his tormentors, he finally caught some fish.

Returning to his shore camp, he settled down on his haunches to clean and scale the fish. He was so intent on his work that he almost forgot the alligators. The smell of fish, however, had brought them back, and he looked up suddenly to see a very large alligator slowly moving toward him. William stepped back hastily just as the animal lashed its horny tail across the place where he had been squatting and swept off most of the fish.

He was clearly frightened. He hauled the canoe high up on the bank, kicking the alligators out of the way. Then he built up a big fire. He reconnoitered his camp spot and to his dismay found that he was on a narrow isthmus, with a cypress swamp at the back and the river at the front. He had barricaded himself on a ridge from which there was no escape except by the river.

But fear would have to wait upon hunger. He cooked and ate what remained of his fish, and was listening to the mockingbird in the orange trees, when he heard a strange noise in the dusk, something disturbing and somehow awesome. He went cautiously to the bank and found the river crowded with masses of fish moving upstream. Alligators were leaping and snapping and sloshing and beating into the fish, which were flapping and splashing, too.

The fish-run was no doubt what had brought the alligators, and in a way this was consoling; they were there to eat fish, not him. He did not anticipate the fact that bears came here to catch fish, too, when they were running, or that he would have to frighten away two of them from his camp that evening.

In spite of everything—the wailing of the Crying Birds, the owls barking, the racketing of the frogs and rails and gallinules, the splashing of the fish and alligators, and an occasional roar from one monster who objected to something—he actually slept a little, though he woke now and again when the wood rats rustled over the fallen dried leaves of the oaks and once in a while took a short cut over his face with their little cold white feet.

The next morning was calm, sweet, peaceful, flavored with orange blossoms and scented with dawn. He could almost think the alligators had been a nightmare, until a large one charged his canoe as he was departing. He indignantly beat it over the snout with his paddle and it retreated in a surge of bubbles.

But he was not the sort of man to go home after a night of this sort. Will Bartram was an explorer, and he really loved a degree of danger, if it didn't get too spicy. He continued placidly on his trip, enumerating the kinds of trees and flowers on the banks, writing, at each evening's camp, an account of the birds he saw. There were curious ones in these swamps.

One day he came upon a strange gaunt creature standing motionless on a dead cypress snag, with broad black and white wings outstretched like two flags. The bird held its long, sinuous neck at a strange angle, quite frozen in an oriental-like posture until he startled it. Then the creature dropped like a plummet into the dark swamp water and slowly sank out of sight, the head with its sharp beak and keen eye the last to submerge as it watched him and he watched it. This was the snake bird or anhinga. There was nothing else in all America just like it, not even its closest kin, the cormorants.

Another day he watched white ibises rising on perfectly coordinated wings in flight that took them up and up and up from the sunny Florida savannahs, to hang on upward air currents, circling, drifting, without moving their white wings with the black tips, then slowly sinking again, still in perfect accord, to lose themselves in the tall grass.

William Bartram came back as browned as a Seminole from his adventures in Florida and Georgia. But he did not stay home very long at a time. He didn't have to earn a living; his father evidently was wealthy. So when the wilderness called, William went. He followed the trails up into the mountains to the west, and over the ridge to the headwaters of the Tennessee River, in the land of the great rhododendron mountains and the Overhill Cherokees. They, too, were his friends. It seems that everyone but the alligators were the friends of this gentle, thoughtful man with his notebooks and his collecting case and his insatiable curiosity about what lay over the next hill or around the next bend of the river. The lure and love of birds led him into innumerable adventures, none more exciting, perhaps, than that time when he battled the alligators and listened to the Crying Bird on a warm spring Florida night.

CHAPTER SEVEN

CAPTAIN COOK, JOHN LEDYARD, AND THE THRUSH OF NOOTKA SOUND

J OHN LEDYARD felt a curious sensation somewhere in his chest as he stood at the rail of the *Resolution* and watched the new land come into focus through the mists.

To Captain James Cook this was a land he had never seen before. As an explorer he was obliged to find out what he could about the place, and he was, besides, going to hunt for a possible northwest passage connecting the Pacific with the Atlantic. This unknown shoreline of the northwest coast of North America might conceal such a route. Men had been searching for it for centuries. To David Nelson, botanist of the expedition, it was a new land of unknown flowers and trees. To Dr. William Anderson, coughing in the chill wind, it was a land of birds and mammals.

But to John Ledyard, breathing spring in the air, that was *home* out there. As he stood by the rail, he felt a sudden surge of an almost physical pain. This was his own land, and he had not been home for a long time. He had been serving with the Royal Navy of King George III when the American Revolution began. He had refused to fight with British forces against the colonists, his kins-

men, had been imprisoned for a time, and then had been released to
go off to the South Seas with Captain Cook. He may have wondered, suddenly and with belated concern, how matters stood with
his countrymen, wondered if the English had now, by 1778, beaten
the revolutionists as they had boasted they would. Anything could
have happened, but all he could tell now was that America was still
there. He was smelling the good spring smells of his own land, and
he was homesick.

More than three thousand miles of unexplored wilderness lay between this point and his old home in Connecticut, but that mattered
very little just then. For a long time he had almost forgotten that
he was an American. There had been that interlude in Tahiti, the
girl there whom he had loved and who had put her tattoo on his
wrist to show that he belonged to her. There had been the Sandwich Islands, too. But now the land itself reminded John Ledyard
that, in spite of all he had done, he was still an American.

Even from the ship he could recognize the American pines and
maples and birches, the great dark hemlocks with long, sweeping
boughs as he remembered them in the forests of the Northeast when
he had gone off to live with the Iroquois. These were not like the
lush tropical trees he had been seeing for so long wherever the ships
had touched land in the South Seas. He decided he was tired of
palm trees and the cloying perfumes of frangipani and ginger. The
vigorous scent of American trees and the songs of American birds
came out to meet him.

. . . it soothed a homesick heart, and rendered me very tolerably happy.
. . . It was the first time too that I had been so near the shores of that
continent that gave me birth; and though more than 2000 miles distant
from the nearest part of New England I felt myself painfully affected.
All the affectionate passions incident to natural attachments and early
prejudices played round my heart, and I indulged them because they
were prejudices. I was harmonized by it.

He wondered suddenly how far it was to Boston, and how it
would be to walk home. It would be a high honor for him to be

the first man to walk from coast to coast, home to Connecticut!

Very likely no white men had come to the northwest coast of America since Georg Wilhelm Steller had seen it fading into the mists, except for the fur trappers and fishermen from Russia, who were not noted for observation. The eminent Dr. Peter Simon Pallas, a German naturalist in the Russian Academy of Science who was amassing a tremendous museum for Catherine the Great, had collected variously in the Aleutians and the Arctic and had received bird specimens brought to him by the fur men ten years before Cook reached North America. The coastline was largely unmapped. It lay smooth and unknown except where the map-makers had employed a little imagination and embellished it nicely with whales and sea serpents and islands that did not exist. But no one really knew what it was like or what was up there. They did not know whether there might actually be unknown routes leading to the North Atlantic, or land connections with Asia itself. Captain James Cook and his two ships, the *Resolution* and the *Discovery*, had come to find out.

This was Cook's third voyage to the Pacific, and it was to be his last. He was an intelligent man, an excellent navigator, and a ship's master who was far ahead of his time in the care of his men, his knowledge of antiscorbutics, and the ability to prevent outbreaks of disease. He insisted on cleanliness, on the proper food, on discipline. His ships were well run and noted for the lowest loss of life on voyages three and four years long—unheard of before at any time in history. He was, moreover, interested in natural history and made it his business to collect what he could at places where they landed. With the help of Nelson, Anderson, and Ledyard, much had been collected already.

On this third voyage, Captain Cook had first explored in the South Pacific, had found New Caledonia and Polynesia, had stayed for blissful months in Tahiti, or Otaheite, where his men found amours to suit each man, and a lovely, lazy life that was hard to exchange for the rigors of the ship. Cook knew he would have to get underway while he could still pull his men back into harness. It was with great regret that they left Tahiti, never to return; but at the Sandwich Islands they found a situation almost as pleasant. The ships made a lengthy stay here, to pass the winter until time to head northeast to the coast of America.

Captain Cook had been ordered to hunt for the elusive Northwest Passage. As soon as winter had left the upper reaches of the world, he knew he must be on his way. He announced a handsome bonus for every man of the crew if he should at last succeed in a search which men had been attempting since the first navigators had come to the northern regions. It was, however, a poor substitute for the pleasures of Hawaii, the Sandwich Islands.

Day after day the empty Pacific lay all about the ships—empty of life, empty of birds—until they came into a part of the sea which was filled with phosphorescent light made by minute creatures that Cook had never seen before. They were tiny and colorful, glowing and shimmering like cool fire. He thought they were a phosphorescent shrimp, but they were probably *Noctiluca*, a protozoan living by billions in those waters. In their incessant movement, the whole sea took on a changing pattern of scarlet or blue or green or purple. Cook and his ship's doctor, Anderson, who was also a naturalist, scooped up some in a glass and watched the colors change, then die. At night the vessels drifted through a sea of eerie light and color, ethereal and wonderful in their mysterious glow, with the ships' wakes trailing fire.

One day they saw a shearwater, a sea bird which roams far from shore. On the sixth of March several whales were sighted, blowing spray and vapor; some seals came and disappeared and rose again around the ships. And on March 7, 1778, the long looked-for shores of what he felt must be North America lay ahead in the breaking mists. Cook could see mountains and endless banks of old snow and coniferous forests; then the mists blew in again, and there came wind and rain and hail and deluges of stinging sleet. The ships did not dare come any closer, so they simply coasted along, northward, hoping to find some sort of harbor or haven from the terrible weather. Captain Cook, catching more glimpses of the land, disliked its desolate look with its patches of snow, yet thought it might be pleasant enough to visit in summer. He had too recently come from the tropical isles of Hawaii and Tahiti to favor the chill northern aspect of March in northern California and Oregon. They passed a great range of mountains that may have been the Olympic peninsula, passed a point which he called Cape Flattery, where they missed the straits that would have led him past this cape into Puget Sound and calmer waters.

Instead, the two weather-tossed vessels continued northward until, on March 29, more than three weeks after they had first seen land, they found a harbor, sailed in, and dropped anchor. They thought they were on the mainland, but instead it was Vancouver Island. They had come into Nootka Sound on the west shore of this island.

Even before the first boats could put to shore, three large wooden canoes with high prows well carved and ornamented, crowded with natives, came out to welcome the newcomers. In greeting, the natives scattered handfuls of feathers on the water, while the head man, in full regalia, carried on a long harangue with much gesturing of hands and shoulders. Captain Cook felt that the man could have saved himself the trouble—no one could understand a word he said. John Ledyard, however, simply stood at the rail and absorbed the welcome sight of American Indians again, and an American landscape.

Cook evidently took an immediate dislike to the natives of Nootka Sound and his further acquaintance did not brighten his regard. They were inexpressibly dirty people, encrusted with grease and paint, and they had the nauseating habit of eating with relish the lice from each other's heads. These people evidently abhorred water for washing purposes. Their houses, though well built and large, were mere garbage dumps of the most foul-smelling sort. Cook was disgusted with them; nevertheless, in his thorough way, he made a careful study of Nootka Sound natives, the first European to have done so. His artist, John Webber, drew pictures of them, braved the interior of one of the houses to make a record of it, and drew action scenes of native life. David Nelson, the botanist, went ashore at every opportunity to collect plants, and William Anderson and John Ledyard went along to collect birds and mammals, and to study the natives.

Captain Cook decided that there was not enough time for any extensive exploration on land at this point, not if he were to search for the possible route inland before winter. Three weeks, however, were spent at Nootka Sound, refitting the ships, gathering plants for food to combat scurvy, studying the natives, and collecting natural history specimens.

Birds were rare and shy, and Cook decided that this must be because the Nootkas killed so many of them for their feathers, which were a preferred ornament and were also scattered on the water as a gesture of welcome to strangers. Except for the sea birds, which ranged from here to Siberia and frequently around the entire circumpolar seas, little was known of the wildlife of the area except for the few species that Steller had found. Pallas had identified a good many others which had been brought to him, among them the snow goose. But the land birds were still strangers.

Very few were even vaguely familiar to the Englishmen. But one morning there was a song which John Ledyard must have found instantly familiar. It was not quite as he thought he remembered it, but there was a nostalgic similarity about it, a lovely, homey sound. It brought back to him bright spring mornings in Connecticut when the arbutus was in bloom in the pine woods and the first migrant birds had come back. It reminded him of April on the campus at Dartmouth, of the wonderful surge and excitement of a rainy morning in spring—a robin song! He was sure that he was hearing a robin, an ordinary, delightful, back-yard kind of robin, the American kind, not the English species which was very different. It had been so long since he had heard an American robin.

The men could not at first find the bird, though it sang beautifully in the firs. They tramped silently over the soft, resilient mosses and heard the song again. The singer was in the tip of a fir and was brought down. John Ledyard knew then that he had been mistaken and that it was not, after all, a robin that he held in his hand. It was robin-like in form, and had the same cinnamon color on its breast which he remembered as characteristic, but it had a cinnamon eye-brow, wing-bars on dark brown, and a striking black crescent across the throat. It was a creature that naturalists had never seen before, and at the moment it did not have a name.

Neither did the small singing birds which, for want of a better name, Captain Cook called wrens, but none of these, evidently, was brought back. One day a hummingbird plummeted like a bullet around the ships and dashed off toward land. They saw others, and the tiny skin of one was added by William Anderson to the precious collection. Before the ships departed, they also added a new flicker and a new sapsucker.

The collection eventually came to Sir Joseph Banks, a noted English naturalist who, with the help of the zoologists, Latham and Pennant, identified the mute, dead skins brought from the final tragedy of the Cook expedition. In the striking brick-brown of the bird Ledyard had thought was a robin, the English ornithologists saw nothing of the cool fir forests of Nootka Sound. They simply realized that here was a new thrush which had a confusion of markings unlike those of any other of the genus, so they named it the Pacific varied thrush. The hummingbird was new—the rufous hummingbird; and so were the red-shafted flicker, the Pacific Canada jay, and the red-breasted sapsucker.

After the ships left Nootka Sound they ranged up along the coast, searching without any luck for the possible passage to the east. Cook may have inwardly doubted that he would find such a thing; he already knew that Mackenzie, Hearne, and the Frobishers had been exploring inland, had found and traced the Mackenzie River and the Coppermine which emptied into the Arctic Ocean, so that if, in that latitude, there had been any east-west passage, they would certainly have found it. But Cook's orders had been to explore for a passage; he explored dutifully, and he found no passage.

The coastline carried him up along Alaska, then trending westward with the line of the Aleutians. With winter upon them, they hastened to Hawaii where it was sure to be warm and pleasant, the food abundant, and the people agreeable. But the natives of Hawaii, soured from the experiences they had had with Cook's men on the earlier visit, and from the diseases they had left behind as souvenirs, set upon and repulsed the landing parties eager for Hawaiian hospitality. Captain Cook was stabbed in the back, burned, and dismembered, before the fragments of his body were returned to the ships.

Shocked, horrified, and disillusioned, the expedition fled Hawaii. John Gore was now in charge and he, with the men and the specimens and all the records of Cook's last voyage, eventually got back to England. John Ledyard sought and obtained his discharge. He had another idea in mind. The thought of walking from Indian tribe to Indian tribe, from Nootka Sound to Boston, had taken hold of his imagination. To him would belong that incomparable treasure of wilderness, of seeing for the first time the pristine country between the Pacific Ocean and the Mississippi River, and from that river to the Atlantic.

John Ledyard was in Paris in 1782 when Thomas Jefferson was the newly appointed American minister. Jefferson was a scientist, a scholar, a naturalist, an adventurer at heart who for a long time had wished for a way to explore the land west of the Mississippi, to find out about the Indians, the birds, the flowers, the mountains. John Ledyard with his ideas of walking from coast to coast was just the man for him. It seemed ordained that the two should meet. For Ledyard had a plan.

The plan was to interest some Yankee businessman in a venture by which Ledyard at the same time could get himself back to Nootka Sound. If a merchant should outfit a good ship, or ships, and go up to Nootka Sound, there to barter with the Indians for a load of fine furs, the ship, after letting off John Ledyard at the Sound, could then proceed to China and sell the furs at an immense profit. The wealthy Chinese adored the furs of the sea otter, and the Nootka Sound natives had no idea of the value of what they obtained and owned so easily. From this point, John would commence his big hike home.

Jefferson thought it was a capital idea, and workable. But the pair had a hard time finding anyone willing to go on with the plan. He and Jefferson had almost persuaded the cautious John Paul Jones to do it, but Jones, overcome by obscure qualms that he might offend the French King, backed out. Still Jefferson and Ledyard would not give up. If they could not find a way to convey Ledyard by sea to Nootka Sound, then he might go overland through Russia and Siberia, reach Kamchatka, and take passage on a fishing or trading vessel across to America. The distance was very little by water.

The proper passports were obtained to permit him to pass through the countries lying between France and Russia, and Catherine the Great granted him permission to travel in the name of science across her lands. In a comparatively easy manner he reached St. Petersburg, where he was entertained and dined by Dr. Pallas. Then he went on, mostly on foot now because his money was going fast. He liked to walk. Distances were nothing—ten miles, ten thousand miles, all you had to do was put one foot before the other, and you'd eventually get there. The peasants along the way gave him their meager hospitality. He pushed on to Irkutsk in Siberia, and to bleak Yakutsk, which was still only half-way across the terrible wastes of Siberia.

The Russian officials, meanwhile, were letting their suspicions grow. Some more astute than Catherine were brooding over what this man was really aiming at in his incredible journey to reach Okhotsk and the narrow crossing to America. The great fur lands of Russia were out there, not yet fully claimed, and if Russia did not hasten and take over Alaska, the British or the Americans might move in and usurp all that wealth of otter and seal and fish. It had been a matter for suspicion when Cook had come there in 1778, but now one of his own confederates, and an American besides, with some strange tale of wanting to walk across America, was traveling alone in Siberia to some secret rendezvous with a mysterious expedition waiting for him at Okhotsk. After they had let their imaginations dwell on these disturbing conjectures, the Russian officials began to get busy.

Politely, at first, they detained John Ledyard. They threw obstacles in his path—and there were enough obstacles in the natural landscape without any made by man. There were ruts of frozen Siberian mud that turned boggy and bottomless in a thaw, and a wind that was relentless and cold, even in summer, and always the poorest of shelter and food. In desperation at further hindrance, he was compelled to retreat 1,500 miles back to Irkutsk for the long winter of 1787. While he was there, and with no explanation, he was suddenly arrested, put into a horse-drawn sledge and, later, into a closed coach that was little better, and hurried back across the route over which he had walked for half a year. A thousand miles in a week they raced and jounced him over ruts and rocks, with the captive given little time either to eat or to sleep. He was suffering from a severe cold, was ill and feverish and coughing. They dumped him out at the border of Poland to fend for himself. The Empress, his captors would only explain, had changed her mind. He could no longer trespass with his own secret schemes upon Russia.

John Ledyard was broken in health. He never came back to his America. Trying to regain his strength in the mild climate of Egypt, he became involved in an expedition to explore the upper Nile, but died in Cairo before he could begin this new venture.

Thomas Jefferson was grieved. He had liked young, enthusiastic, intelligent John Ledyard with his affection for natural history and for America. But Jefferson did not give up his idea of exploring beyond the Mississippi. Back in the United States again, he tried to form an expedition to be led by George Rogers Clark, but that fell through. So did the expedition on which he sent André Michaux, the eminent French botanist who had been sent by his country to collect American plants for propagation in France.

Jefferson had proposed this latest plan to Congress and had suggested that his friend, Meriwether Lewis, a young man who was an expert naturalist and an excellent woodsman, would be the one to send. Congress would do nothing, but the Philosophical Society at Philadelphia offered to put up a subscription to finance M. Michaux, not Lewis. The cautious Society warned, however, that M. Michaux would be paid the full amount only if he reached the Pacific Ocean by way of the Missouri River and the Columbia; he would receive part of it if he went beyond the Mississippi, but nothing at all if he did not get even so far. Michaux was already on his way when France stepped in and ordered him elsewhere. The French had other plans; he was to assist in the recapture of New Orleans from the Spanish. And so the expedition again fell through —so also did the proposed taking of New Orleans—and still unknown birds and mammals and men lived beyond the Mississippi. An additional uncertainty and growing worriment to the United States Government was the fact that the fur lands of the northwest coast and the interior of North America were yielding more and more wealth to British and Russian owners.

CHAPTER EIGHT

LEWIS AND CLARK

MARKING the edge of the unknown, there was always the river. It was like the great wall of China, with civilization on one side and wilderness and barbarians on the other. To people venturing away from the settlements, the Mississippi formed the boundaries of America's West, defined the nation's reaches. At the edge of the Mississippi lay the western rim of the United States, and the river left no doubt as to definition. There were Spanish, French, and British lands on the farther side. It might be all North America, but it was no more ours than Canada was, or Mexico, or Brazil. It was foreign territory, yet our birds might fly across the river into Spain's holdings, or Spanish-based geese might pause a while in an Illinois slough before going to Canadian nesting places. Russian-American thrushes might pass through Indiana and linger in Florida before going to South America. It was a confusion to men, but not to the birds, to whom there were no boundaries.

When Thomas Jefferson became President in 1801, along with the new century came a new era of exploration and the urgent desire for development of knowledge of America. He now had the power to persuade Congress that a small expedition to explore the West was a necessity. Practically speaking, it was important to find out the extent of the fur lands up the Missouri, to carry out treaties with the Indians in the fur countries, to find if possible an overland route to the Columbia River and the Pacific, even though it must cross foreign territory.

The young man who had been so eager to go earlier, when Michaux had been chosen instead—Meriwether Lewis—had meanwhile become Thomas Jefferson's secretary. This was primarily so that Jefferson could study his possibilities and implant in him at the same time some of his own drive and enthusiasm for the wild things of the west. He trained him in writing accounts with full details, though Jefferson could never teach Meriwether Lewis how to spell properly.

Lewis was a self-taught naturalist of keen perception and judgment, who since boyhood had roamed the woods of Virginia and studied its wildlife. He had grown up with a love and knowledge of science. He was, besides, honest and completely trustworthy and he knew how to get on with men. He was exactly the kind of person Jefferson needed.

To include in the party a man of almost equal proficiency and ability in case something happened to Lewis, President Jefferson appointed their mutual friend, William Clark of Louisville, Kentucky, as captain immediately under Lewis but with equal powers. This could have been a touchy situation between two men of different temperaments; there could have been bitter rivalry, enmity, and a breakup of the whole fabric of discovery and discipline. Yet as the expedition proceeded it was considered a beautiful thing to see how the two leaders deferred to each other, how one would let the other have credit for some new find. Neither was self-seeking or petty or envious of the other. Jefferson had chosen wisely.

Permission and passports from the ministers of Great Britain, France, and Spain had been obtained so that the party might pass freely beyond the Mississippi. Then politics changed rapidly and spectacularly. To avoid trouble with the British, Spain transferred its holdings of Louisiana back to France, and Napoleon, to finance his current war, sold the whole area to the United States for fifteen million dollars. Consequently, when Lewis and Clark in 1803 set off they were not, after all, entering foreign territory, or traveling dangerously among suspicious or hostile Europeans. The Indians might prove difficult, but at least there would be no international incidents to be wary of, and the men would be on American soil all the way.

The instructions which Thomas Jefferson formulated for Lewis and Clark were tremendous in scope, exhibiting great thought on the part of the President as well as a reflection of his deep interest in natural history and ethnology.

The party was to find out all it could about the Indians, was to note the soil and the "face of the country," the vegetation, the animals, and the remains of anything rare or extinct (the President fondly hoped they would find remains of mammoths). Minerals were to be noted and collected, as well as limestone, pit-coal, salt-peter, salines, and mineral waters. They must look for volcanic evidences; note the climate—the proportion of rainy, cloudy, and clear days, as well as lightning, hail, snow, ice, the coming and going of frost, winds, the dates when particular plants put forth their flowers or leaves, and the time of arrival and departure of birds, reptiles, insects, mammals. Jefferson's specific directions could have kept ten expeditions busy for ten years.

With exuberant spirits and growing excitement, Meriwether Lewis went to Pittsburgh, the headwaters of the Ohio and the first link with the Pacific. With him went his big, devoted servant, York, and his large Newfoundland dog. At Pittsburgh he outfitted a heavy keelboat fifty-five feet long, drawing three feet of water, and carrying one large square sail and twenty-two oars. The deck extended ten feet across the bow, and the stern formed a forecastle and cabin. The middle of the boat was covered with lockers which might be raised to form a breastwork in case of attack by Indians. There were also two large pirogues for shallow water duty. The keelboat was finally loaded with nearly seven tons of equipment. There were guns and containers of gunpowder made of lead; the gunpowder was thus safe from dampness and, when needed, the lead could be melted down to make rifle balls. There was food, including portable soup; medicines in considerable variety to cover every known affliction which might beset the party. There were even an anvil and a forge.

With Lewis went a number of Virginians, including young George Shannon, who was barely sixteen years old and tremendously excited about the whole coming adventure. At Louisville the keelboat lay to while William Clark and his Kentucky recruits brought on more supplies and equipment; then they were all on their way. They left Louisville in August, 1803, and, after stops and lay-overs at Cairo, Ste. Genevieve, Kaskaskia, and Cape Girardeau, finally reached St. Louis in December.

To provide accommodations there for thirty-odd men and the equipment and a large-sized dog would have been prohibitive, so they moved up the Mississippi a few miles and set up camp on the shore of the little Rivière du Bois, or Wood River, opposite the mouth of the Missouri. All winter, on the steep banks of the Wood River where it met the Mississippi, the men could watch the changing situation on the yellow-brown Missouri River just opposite. That was their river, their unknown quantity. None knew what he would find up its mysterious and unexplored lengths; none knew how far it went or what connection might be found with the Columbia River which would take them, they hoped, to the Pacific. They knew only that the water they saw had come from where they were going.

It was a long winter, but at last, with a great grinding and rumbling, the ice went out of the rivers. It surged downstream in the swirling yellow-brown water as the freshets of the Missouri poured its mud into the Mississippi. Now and again a dead buffalo came rolling and tumbling on the rushing water and lodged soddenly on a sand bar. The geese went north. Robins sang in the willows; the red-winged blackbirds and grackles streamed in at sundown and settled in creaking, caroling flocks in the willows and marshes.

Carolina wrens were singing among the exposed willow roots along the river.

Spring! May 14, 1804. It was high spring when the keelboat was loaded and it was time to go. With some effort, they navigated the vessel slantwise across the surging waters of the Mississippi to the Missouri River's mouth, on the west. After a winter of inactivity, the men were soon weary from the unaccustomed effort of rowing and before they had gone half a dozen miles up the Missouri they were almost exhausted. It would take a while to toughen their muscles.

The trip upriver was slow. It was stimulating because it was new, but the landscape for some time was not unduly different, the wildlife not especially exciting. On July 4 they camped at a spot in Missouri which they named Independence in honor of the day. From July 21 to August 4 they stayed at a place they called Council Bluffs, where they held conferences with the Otoes and Iowas. Every day they took careful notes of weather and landscape and Indians, went ashore to collect natural history specimens, noted the birds and mammals. Things were going well, except for the death of Sergeant Floyd, who had been ill when they started and died as they proceeded up the Missouri. He was buried on a high bank and a wooden marker placed to record the fact.

As they neared the mouth of the Little Sioux River, passing between the yellow-brown, wind-carved bluffs of the Missouri, they began to notice a strange sight. The surface of the river was covered with white, downy feathers. For three miles or more the boat pushed up through the feathery flood. Ahead of them, at last, they discovered the source—a great flock of white pelicans which, moulting now in August, was sending this white covering down the Missouri. The birds, Lewis wrote, where so many that their numbers were incredible. They occupied several acres of the sand bars, and when the boat came close the birds rose with a great swirl of wings, with a wingspread of nine feet. The men fired among them and brought one down. Lewis examined it in detail and wrote a careful account in his journal. The white pelican was not a new species, but it was the first interesting bird they had found on the expedition, and Lewis had never examined a creature like this before.

Ahead, the way grew harder. Sometimes they met such low water between the tremendous sand bars that the men had to pull the boat upstream by ropes and pole it over shoals. Shannon, the boy, went ashore to hunt and was lost overnight, which scared him a great deal and alarmed the men. On September 17, 1804, the party camped at the mouth of Crow Creek, a few miles above the White River in South Dakota. Meriwether Lewis went out with his gun and a couple of men, as Clark wrote: "with a View to See the Countrey and its productions, he killed a Buffalow and a remarkable bird. . . ." The buffalo was much-needed food, and the bird was something new for science. It was the first new bird on the trip.

They had heard something crying *twait, twait, twait,* but had not discovered it at first. Then they forgot it momentarily when the men, creeping over a rise, saw a dozen buffalo beyond a clump of cottonwoods and a dry wash. The men dropped back in excitement to tell Lewis, who was still hunting for the maker of the unexplained noise. Food was needed; a fat buffalo would take care of the situation. The bird could wait. They shot a fine young animal, and while the rest of the herd snorted and thundered in dust across the plain, the sound of the rifle stirred up the birds. Several strange, large, crow-sized birds with extraordinarily long black and white tails flashed up from a thicket and flew slowly away. One man had the presence of mind to shoot a specimen before they had all disappeared.

It was a magpie. Lewis had never seen anything like this bird before. It was a splendid creature with large black eyes, the glossy black feathers covered with a wonderful sheen of purple and blue and green. There were white wing patches that had showed strikingly in flight, and white on the belly—and that elegant tail! He wished he could send one, alive, to the President.

About a week after they found the magpies, they got into some trouble with the Indians which could have ended the expedition there in Dakota. They had camped on a sand bar in order to confer with the Indians. To further friendly relations, Lewis invited the chiefs to come on the boat and inspect it, but made the mistake of offering refreshments. He gave each one a fourth of a glass of whiskey. They liked this. They sucked the bottle after it was quite empty, and then began to grow troublesome when he refused to open another. Lewis and Clark knew that the chiefs could not have become drunk on the small ration of whiskey and could see that the disorderliness which ensued was largely pretended. The chiefs grew noisy and demanding; they insisted that the two leaders come ashore with them, but Clark prudently stayed aboard with most of the men while Lewis went. He was shoved about. The Indians staggered up against him and his men and almost knocked them down. Several braves hugged the mast of the keelboat and declared they would not let the party proceed any farther.

Lewis and Clark certainly didn't want any trouble, but it seemed that they were having it anyway. They were greatly outnumbered. Then Lewis, who had had all he could take, drew his sword and gave a quick signal to Clark on the boat, who ordered all the men under arms at once. The young warriers, meanwhile, had fitted their arrows in their bows. Then one of the chiefs, seeing how matters were going and observing the soldiers to be armed, ordered the hotheads to desist and to let go of the mast and rope. The situation cooled down, but, in an understatement, Clark later said: "I felt myself very warm and spoke in very positive terms." Jefferson had told them not to start any trouble with the Indians, but there was a limit to what a man could stand.

The journey had been slow and winter was already beginning to make itself felt with the forewarnings of yellowing leaves on the cottonwoods and cold winds out of the north. In the Mandan Indian country, near the present Bismarck, North Dakota, the party stopped, and on the left bank of the river they set about building a fort which they named Fort Mandan. They laid in supplies of meat for the long winter and brought in wood for the fires.

The Mandans came often to visit and stare. One day there arrived a pompous French-Canadian named Toussaint Charbonneau who had an entourage of no less than three Indian wives. He had heard of the expedition and now offered himself in the position of interpreter. Charbonneau was a talkative, conceited nuisance; Lewis and Clark did not want him along. They knew his sort. But when he casually mentioned that his youngest wife was a Shoshone whom he had bought from her captors, Lewis and Clark revised their first decision. The girl, whose name was Sacajawea, or Sa-ga-ja-wea, knew enough English to be useful as an interpreter and go-between with the Shoshones, in whose land they would be traveling, and her knowledge of the country could be very useful. This might offset the bothersome Charbonneau.

Lewis and Clark, however, were not much impressed with the girl when they saw her crouching in a corner where Charbonneau had ordered her to wait. She did not look up when they spoke to her. They could see with some disillusion that she was pregnant. This would mean that in the spring they would have a baby to look out for on the rigors of the trip. Charbonneau promised effusively that the child would not be any bother. Neither would his wives.

Lewis, outraged at the man's effrontery in thinking he could bring along all three of his squaws, coldly informed him that only one wife would accompany the interpreter, since he was now going to have to behave like a white man if he expected to travel with them. More than one wife was illegal, indecent, and not per-mitted on this expedition. Charbonneau meekly agreed. He sent the other two unprotesting squaws back to their people. Sacajawea stayed.

On the bleak, wind-swept, snow-drifted Mandan country they lived through the winter. They had a Christmas celebration—

Cruzatte, one of the French-Canadians Clark had brought along, had his fiddle. He tuned up on Christmas night for a dance. There was whiskey to go around and roast elk meat, but not a great deal else. Still, it was Christmas, even if it was far below zero outside, with a knife-edged wind blowing snow as high as the fort.

Spring again seemed to be a long time in coming. When in March the thaw came at last and the river was open again, it was time to break the expedition's link with home and the East. The keelboat could not continue farther because of shallow water and a narrowing of the river; it would be impossible, besides, to portage so large a craft over the mountains. They made plans to send it back with some of the men whose time of enlistment was up and who wished to return, together with a pair who had been court-martialed during the winter. With the boat would go letters to families, and a report to the President. They would also send back specimens which had been thus far collected.

On April 3, 1805, the boat was loaded with the pressed plants, skins of mammals and birds, Indian artifacts, weapons, pottery, costumes, and detailed reports of the expedition. With the gifts for Jefferson also went four live magpies in a large wooden cage. The shipment eventually reached St. Louis and proceeded to New Orleans, from which point it was loaded on to a sailing vessel that carried it to Washington. Two of the magpies lived. They were put in Peale's Museum in Philadelphia where naturalists came to see and wonder at these rarities from the Far West.

As the expedition of thirty men, an Indian woman, and a baby set off into the unknown country, they had six small canoes and two large pirogues. Lewis wrote fondly:

This little fleet, altho' not quite so rispectable as those of Columbus or Capt. Cook, were still viewed by us with as much pleasure as those deservedly famed adventurers ever beheld theirs; and I dare say with quite as much anxiety for their safety and preservation. We were now about to penetrate a country at least two thousand miles in width, on which the foot of civilized man had never trod; the good or evil it had in store for us was for experiment yet to determine, and these little vessells contained every article by which we were to expect to subsist or defend ourselves. . . . I could but esteem this moment of my departure as among the most happy of my life.

The expedition slowly moved up the Missouri. It was April and ice formed at night or collected on the oars by day. At the mouth of a river which they named Maria's River, in honor of Lewis's cousin, Miss Maria Wood, they left a cache of powder and the pirogues.

Sacajawea by this time was very ill. She had not been feeling well when they set out from the fort, but she had not complained. Her baby, which had been born that winter at Fort Mandan, had ridden on her back, a placid, agreeable, French-Indian baby who was no bother and who seldom cried. The men were growing fond of little Baptiste—Clark called him his little Pomp—and took turns caring for him when Sacajawea became too ill to do so. Finally, she lay in one of the canoes all day as they traveled, and suffered silently day and night. They delayed the expedition because she could not go on. They despaired of her life, yet they could not let her die. They not only needed her, but Lewis and Clark were both growing fond of Sacajawea as a person. She had blossomed into an individual; she was no longer merely a silent, subjective squaw. She had opinions, a voice in the party.

Clark worked over her. He ransacked the store of medicines for something that would help; he wished they had included several potions used for female maladies, but when they had left the East no one had expected to have a woman on the expedition. And she must not die. Then, miraculously after Clark's ministering, she was better and could eat some of the soup he had made for her. She walked again one day, weakly at first; suddenly craving raw camas roots, she wandered out from the camp to find them. When she did not return, Clark went hastily in search of her and discovered her face down in the grass, desperately ill again. He carried her back and made her rest for several days, eating only what he gave her. William Clark took Charbonneau aside and thundered reproof at him for letting his wife eat what she wanted, ordering him to keep better watch over her so that she could not indulge her reckless Indian tastes until she was well.

Slowly, slowly, they moved up the Missouri—listening to the far-off tootling and drumming and stamping of the prairie chickens at their courting, listening to the strange, far, high voices of the whooping cranes flying north. They found a new bird that would be called the white-rumped shrike. They continued up through the mountains where the narrowing forks of the Missouri offered a confusion of routes and much time was lost in exploring them. Passing the Great Falls with its torrents, they reached the head-waters of the Missouri River at last.

One of the men made a big thing of straddling this little rivulet before they went on toward the country over the divide where Sacajawea said they would surely find her people. She grew more excited as they traveled, knowing she was coming home. And one morning they came to where the Shoshones, her people, were camped.

Sacajawea's sister looked up to see the lost one approaching and ran to clasp her in her arms; they embraced, weeping, then laughed over the fat baby. Cameahwait, the chief, who was Sacajawea's brother, solemnly offered a welcome to the white men, glad his sister had come back from her captivity. She had brought him a very special present, a lump of white sugar which she had cherished and had refrained from eating herself. She knew he had never tasted such a delicious confection before. Lewis and Clark gave him some dried squash from the Mandans, and this too the chief relished with delight. The Shoshones were fascinated by the party, by the accounts given by Sacajawea of the journey; they were awed by the strange black man, York, who exerted himself to dance and sing for them. York's horseplay kept the Indians happy and at ease, helped the negotiations, and eased any possible tensions among them. More than once on that expedition York saved the day—discouraged though he might be, his ankles sore from cactus spines, hungry as the others, tired as they, he could entertain the Indians if it kept things from exploding into trouble. So also did merry old Cruzatte and the violin.

Near the Shoshone camp on August 22, 1805, Lewis found another new bird. In spite of the serious business of getting horses and enough food, and dickering endlessly with the Indians, the leaders still had time to record their notes and look for new things. When he heard the bird at first he thought it might be a sort of crow. Then he saw a shower of pine-cone fragments and seed hulls come tumbling out of a yellow pine, and he moved closer. He now could see the bird. Its tail and wing-patches were white, a striking contrast against the black wings and light gray body. It was, he thought, about the size of a robin. That was the bird, of all those found on the expedition, which now bears the name of Clark—Clark's nutcracker, then called Clark's crow. Lewis had a bird of his own, too —Lewis's woodpecker, with its curious rose-colored breast and glossy black-green head and back, which they had found a few weeks earlier on the trail.

They saw more of the unique black-and-white birds as they departed with the horses, which had been obtained after much dickering with the Shoshones. Sacajawea led the way. They came in early September to the difficult Lolo Trail leading them painfully through the Bitterroot Mountains. For a time they followed a rocky Indian trail, but finally were surrounded by such dense tangles and thickets that they had to cut their way before the horses could proceed at all. The mountain slope below the path was so steep, so covered with loose rock, that the horses often lost their footing and were, as Lewis said, "in perpetual danger of slipping to their certain destruction."

Some of them did fall, some turned over and over, rolling downhill. Packs were damaged; one horse was badly crippled, and another simply gave out. With the risk and incredible difficulty, the men only made five miles on September 2. When they needed a camping place, they had only a mountainside, with a creek rushing below and stones everywhere.

There was now very little to eat; for days they had been on short rations, for there was almost no game. The Lolo Trail was a place evidently shunned by most game because of the steepness. The men did manage one day to shoot nine grouse. These and a little corn had to feed the whole party. Then, in the chill mountain dusk, it began to snow. The flakes swept down with a hissing sibilance through the pines, quickly capping the needle tufts and piling up heavily on the slant boughs of the firs until they were borne to earth. By morning the snow had changed to rain and then to sleet. Ice glazed every twig and rock; the world was a glitter of ice and snow when the sun broke through the clouds. It was beautiful and strange, but it was more dangerous to travel than before, for the trail was now doubly hazardous.

Yet as they came cautiously down to the lower altitudes, the sleet vanished and there was no sign of snow. They came into a pleasant valley where a village of Tushepaw Indians lived, who had enough horses to trade some to the white men. It was wonderful to find fresh mounts in this wilderness, but there was no replenishment of food or energy for the men. They were sore and sick and weary. Yet they did not complain—the complainers had gone back on the keelboat from Fort Mandan. The others continued doggedly, as if they knew they were making history and could thus endure anything.

Again the trail led them through the valley of the Bitterroot and up into the Kookooske River country, over steeps and incredible tangles. Up and down the trail wound in every direction to get up the ascents and around the numbers of fallen trees that lay on the south side of the mountain.

Things grew no better. More snow began to fall and by night it was six to eight inches deep. It was difficult to find the trail in the veiling of snow and among the heaped pines which, when brushed against, cascaded snow on to the travelers. Lewis said, "I have been wet and as cold in every part as I ever was in my life; indeed I was at one time fearful my feet would freeze in the thin Mockirsons which I wore."

Following a supper provided by a luckless colt that could be spared from the caravan, the men slept cold. After the snowstorm, the sun came out and pine needles dripped live sparks. Birds were all about—birds largely unknown to the explorers. There must have been many kinds singing in the bright morning, but Lewis specifically mentioned one which was later named the black-headed jay, as well as the Rocky Mountain Canada jay, and the interior varied thrush.

He had heard the thrush singing and had tracked it through the snowy trees to a tangle of sumac bushes where a beautiful creature of brick-red, brown, and black was feeding. Captain Cook had found the Pacific varied thrush at Nootka Sound in 1778. Twenty-seven years later, Meriwether Lewis found this inland variety. The black-headed jay was a subspecies of the Steller's jay. The other was a sleek, quiet individual with a long, swooping flight, a voice like a cat's mewing, white head, blue-gray back and wings, and a black cap well back on the white head. The pink-and-black woodpeckers which he had discovered earlier were busy in the trees.

Birds as splendid as these were infinitely refreshing to the scientific spirit, but food was still the constant concern. Anything edible was now used. Some crayfish, which Cruzatte had caught in the creek and cooked French-Canadian style, were added to a meal that consisted of a few grouse and a roasted coyote. That was all to sustain thirty men and a woman with a baby. All but the baby were losing much weight and energy on their meager diet. Many of them broke out in sores and infections; some had dysentery and stomach pains. But they kept on, with stops at times of several days when Lewis himself was sick and could not travel. Clark with difficulty continued in spite of the boils which had appeared on his ankles where the cactus spines had stabbed them.

Then at last, on a glorious day, the hungry band stood on the banks of the Columbia, whence the Kookooske had taken them. They made canoes and eventually started down the powerful river, portaging around the falls of Celilo. Indians catching salmon at this point shared some with the travelers. They saw in the distance the white heights of Mount Hood and Mount St. Helens, and came down at last into the broad mouth of the Columbia.

There were waves and a taste of salt; the men were sure they had reached the sea at last. The river was so wide, the day so foggy, but Clark was premature in his delight when he wrote: "Ocian in view! O! the joy." It was not until November 19, 1805, that some of the party did finally stand on the shores of the Pacific Ocean, where the waves thundered and the sea birds cried. The gaunt men were jubilant. This was the reward of the whole trip, the aim which had made their sufferings endurable. The waves were wonderful! Clark and his party—Lewis and the others had not yet come this far—dined that night on Columbia black-tail deer, on the foggy shores of the Pacific Ocean.

Some days later, when the party was together inland, the Clatsop Indians came to camp with news of a whale on the shore. The men were about to start out eagerly to see this wonder, when Sacajawea, who on occasion could express herself very well and succinctly and without the submission of a squaw, spoke up. She said that it was very hard on her to be left behind after she had come all this way to behold the great waters and had, besides, never, never laid eyes on a whale. To be left behind like this all the time was very unkind and heartless of the white men.

Few Indian women would have dared speak like this, but Sacajawea was a special person now. So Captain Lewis, who might have suggested it if he had only thought, invited her, her child, and her husband to come along. Sacajawea, in complete wonderment and huge delight, at last saw the ocean and heard the waves roar, and saw the incredible form of the whale lying on the beach.

Seven miles inland, away from the sea storms, they built Fort Clatsop as winter quarters. It was not a pleasant winter, or a comfortable one, for it rained three-fourths of the time. Blankets and clothing were always damp. In spite of the wet weather and scanty food, the party existed, and Lewis and Clark continued earnestly to observe the flora and fauna and study the ways of the Indians and their languages. It was here that they had time to write careful descriptions and draw pictures of some of the new birds and plants they had found. One of them was the cock-of-the-plains, or sage grouse. It was the size of a small turkey, had a black belly and a tail composed of long, spike-shaped feathers. It had been brought in primarily as food, but the meat was disagreeably dark and rank-flavored because of the sagebrush the bird had eaten. It was, however, another new species to add to their list.

Early in February, Clark sent Shannon, Labiesh, and Frazier on a hunting excursion up the Kil-haw-a-nak-kle River which flowed into Meriwether Bay. This was necessary to keep the fort fed and was also a good way to combat boredom. That evening the trio came back lugging a half-dead creature of truly enormous size that fought and bit and flapped, while the men tried to tell at once how they shot it and what a hard time it had given them. It was an amazing bird, and Clark was certain it must be the largest in all of North America. He found that it weighed twenty-five pounds, but because it was in poor condition he felt that thirty-five pounds might be an average weight. He had seen turkey buzzards, but no vulture was like this, yet he was sure it was of that species—the glistening black wings with a white stripe, the naked head and neck, covered with bright orange-yellow skin, the strange pale eye with red iris and sea-green pupil, the vicious, hooked beak.

It was the California condor. It had been found by Spanish explorers farther south, but had never been described before or its picture drawn. The Lewis and Clark expedition did both.

In the spring they set off for home. Sacajawea's baby was now able to walk and was the pet of the party. Clark was already thinking of asking permission of the child's parents to educate him in the East. He could not bear to see a bright child like this brought up among the Shoshones or in Charbonneau's doubtful care.

Still exploring, and still finding new birds, the party reached the headwaters of the Missouri where they had left the canoes. Thankfully they paddled downstream. They had added the strikingly beautiful yellow, red, and black Louisiana tanager to the list of new birds, as well as the mountain quail. Their skins, with many of the other specimens, eventually reached Peale's Museum.

Finally, after nearly three years of travel since leaving the Ohio River, the great journey was over. In triumph the canoes reached St. Louis on September 23, 1806, and were greeted with acclaim and celebration. They had traversed the continent from the Mississippi to the sea and back again, had traveled the endless pine forests and mountains, through country hitherto unknown, and had brought to light the first of the western birds which would be the lure of many another ornithologist yearning for that country.

CHAPTER NINE

THE YELLOWSTONE EXPEDITION

THE Yellowstone Expedition had high aims but a low budget. It went up the Missouri in a steamboat disguised as a dragon, and returned on foot with as undernourished and as enduringly enthusiastic a set of scientists as any expedition ever had. This was in 1819, when few ornithologists and botanists dared to venture alone or even in small groups into the West; their hope was to be included on one of the military parties exploring the unknown lands beyond the Mississippi. Lewis and Clark had blazed the way—one way. Zebulon Pike in 1806 had dragged his weary troops over the plains to the Rocky Mountains south of where Lewis and Clark had explored, had gone too far into Spanish territory, had been arrested by Spanish authorities, and his expedition ended.

In 1819 there was a new President—James Monroe, who had done much to bring about the Louisiana Purchase in whose territory he still had deep interest. Lewis and Clark had covered the northern part of the area. Monroe wanted to send other expeditions in various directions so that all that land would be known. As part of this plan, he sent Major Stephen Harriman Long in 1819 to the central and southern Rocky Mountains to explore all the land between there and the Mississippi.

This was the first western expedition to use a steamboat in part of its operations. The *Western Engineer* was a small, side-wheel vessel with weak engines and a propensity for running aground on any sand bar or mud bank that presented itself.

Steamboats were still in their infancy. Only eight years earlier the first one had navigated the Ohio and lower Mississippi in what proved to be a one-way trip. Aside from Henry Shreve's important improvements which permitted a steamboat to go upstream as well as down, they had not advanced a great deal since. The often faltering *Western Engineer* was to carry a whole party of scientists and soldiers down the Ohio and up the Mississippi, then up the Missouri to places where it was intended to set army posts. The original plans called for going up to the Yellowstone River and exploring its length.

In cheerful excitement, the party embarked on May 5, 1819, from the landing at Pittsburgh. Several of the best scientists of the day were aboard. Major John Biddle was journalist of the party, though every man kept a private journal; Dr. William Baldwin was physician and botanist; Dr. Thomas Say, eminent zoologist of New Harmony, Indiana, was a specialist in birds and insects; Augustus E. Jessup was geologist; Titian Ramsey Peale was assistant naturalist and artist; Samuel Seymour was painter; Lieutenant James D. Graham and Lieutenant William H. Swift were assistant topographers.

All were keyed to a high pitch of excitement as the *Western Engineer* left Pittsburgh and paddled nobly around the bends of the Ohio, blew black smoke, and coughed rhythmically in her chimneys. The naturalists, except Dr. Baldwin who was ill, stayed on deck all hours in order not to miss anything. At wooding stops they were first ashore, collecting until time to proceed again.

On June 5 the *Western Engineer* rounded Cairo point and was in the Mississippi. There the vessel promptly struck a snag which knocked a hole in the wooden hull. This necessitated a long delay for repairs, but the scientific party didn't mind that. They welcomed any excuse to go ashore.

At St. Louis some changes were made on the outside of the steamboat. Since the boat was heading into Indian country, it might be a good idea, someone thought, considering that the Indians had never seen or heard of a steamboat before, to ornament this pioneering vessel in such a way as to startle and amaze the savages. Utilizing the general shape of the boat, they added some boarding and paint and created the general shape of a writhing serpent along the side of the boat, the housing for the paddle wheels taking care of the humping of the body. Steam would be exhausted in the region of the creature's nostrils, and the disturbance of the paddle wheels, the coughing of the exhausts, and the noise of the engines might be calculated to present an astonishing and awe-inspiring picture to any Indian bold enough to look at it. There had never been a steamboat like this before—or since, for that matter.

Proceeding at last into the Missouri River, the dragon-boat got into difficulty at once, not with Indians but with mud. In the first four miles the steamer grounded twice. The boilers were in trouble with the thick yellow-brown Missouri's sediment, which clogged the valves, cut down on power and steam, and required a halt every fifteen hours or less while the boilers were cooled down, unbolted, and a man sent inside to scrape out the thick muck. One of the engineers, not relishing this endless and distasteful job, invented a valve to blow out the mud. The innovation—a valuable improvement used on later steamboats—still did not prevent the *Western Engineer's* groundings and other difficulties.

At Franklin, Missouri, Dr. Baldwin was taken ashore, where he died next day. His death cast a damper over the expedition; they had all liked him. He had looked forward eagerly to collecting new plants in the Rocky Mountains.

The scientific crew, irked with having had to stay on the boat while all the wildlife was on shore, now left the steamer at Franklin for an excursion on foot across the prairie, and met the boat at Fort Osage. On August 6, Thomas Say with his group left Fort Osage bound for the principal village of Kansa Indians near what is now

Manhattan, Kansas. It was a two-weeks' ride over the hot Kansas plains, but Dr. Say was too busy collecting insects to be unduly annoyed by the heat. At the Indian village they were cordially entertained for four days; then, making camp on the way back, they saw trouble in the form of a cloud of dust approaching over the baked-dry plains.

One hundred and forty Pawnee Indians on horseback raced toward the small, undefended camp of the naturalists. The Pawnees were in an irritable mood, but they would not attack; they simply tried to be so annoying that they would provoke the white men into shooting first. The Pawnees dismounted, gave oily evidence of false affection, and then milled about the camp and stole everything in sight, including the four horses and other items. Several Pawnees cut the ropes of Dr. Say's tent and down it collapsed on his specimens, records, drawings, and personal effects. The Pawnees, whooping and grinning in evil delight, dived underneath and went off with everything.

Thomas Say's hands fairly itched to kill them all, but he held his fury. He motioned to the others not to retaliate. There were too few of them to risk an attack, and 140 Pawnees could kill them all very easily if they wished. The miracle was that they had not done so already. So the outraged and angry white men did not shoot, and the disappointed Indians, with much yelling and brandishing of spears and the loot they had taken, galloped off across the broiling Kansas plains, now and again scattering the specimens and papers behind them.

Wearily, the scientists gathered up what was left and set off on foot to meet the boat. Dr. Say, later on, tried to recall what he had written in his stolen notebook and could do so fairly well, but he regretted the loss of the specimens and drawings. At least he and his companions were alive. And, as if in recompense for their misfortunes, they found a bird never before described. It was trim, brown and white, with chestnut markings on crown and face, a bird to be known as the lark sparrow.

The shore expeditions several times encountered the strange illusions of prairie mirage. The journals relate:

Nothing is more difficult to estimate by the eye than the distance of objects seen on these plains. A small animal, as a wolf or a turkey, sometimes appears of the magnitude of a horse, on account of an erroneous impression of distance. Three elk, which were the first we had seen, crossed our path at some distance before us. The effect of the mirage, together with our indefinite idea of the distance, magnified these animals to a most prodigious size. For a moment we thought we saw the mastodon of America, moving in these vast plains, which seem to have been created for his dwelling place. We discovered near the Grand River several large animals feeding on the prairie, at a distance of half a mile. These, we believed, could be no other than bisons; and after a consultation, respecting the best method of surprising them, two of our party dismounted, and creeping with great care and caution, about one-fourth of a mile through the high grass, arrived at the spot, and discovered an old turkey with her brood of half-grown young, the only animals now to be seen.

The *Western Engineer* finally churned and chugged its way to Council Bluffs and the fort they named Engineer Cantonment, where the whole expedition would spend the winter. They would study the Indians and the natural history of the area until spring made it possible for the steamboat to proceed to the mouth of the Yellowstone. Major Long went back east to spend the winter, and Mr. Jessup went with him. He had been ill and could not remain with the group for the next season's work. Say was ill, too, from fever and dysentery incurred on the trip, but he refused to leave. He was too close to the Rocky Mountains to retreat now, and perhaps during the winter he would recover.

When spring came to the upper Missouri and the bluffs and marshes around the fort, Thomas Say had indeed fully recovered. He was outdoors every day, hunting for birds. Great flights of geese and swans and cranes were going over, and the night was filled with the sounds of remote voices of birds going north. One of his discoveries that spring was the long-billed dowitcher, a snipe-like bird with a beak almost as long as its legs, and another was a very special little bird which would eventually bear his name. It reminded him of a small-sized robin as it sat on a willow twig, but it darted out into the air after insects as a flycatcher would. It had a red-brown breast and dark brown upper parts. This was Say's phoebe.

The first boat to arrive at Engineer Cantonment after the ice went out in March brought Major Long and two new members of the party, Captain J. R. Bell to replace Major Biddle, who had been summoned back, and Dr. Edwin James to replace both Baldwin and Jessup in the fields of botany and geology. But Major Long also brought bad news to the eager party. Congress had become annoyed at how little, outwardly, had been accomplished during one season's operations. The expenditures, the Congressmen agreed, had been too great for the results; besides, it was a time of recession. The expedition was not important enough to warrant spending much more on it, and further appropriations and had been denied. They would have to use the small amount that was left—enough, however, so that Major Long might continue overland to the Platte River, find its source, and return to the Mississippi by way of the Rocky Mountains and the Arkansas and Red Rivers. The steamboat, with Lieutenant Graham, was to return for duty on the Mississippi.

On a spring day the *Western Engineer's* wheels splashed the mud-water of the Missouri. She sounded a whistle that slowed the engines because so much steam was required to blow it, and passed around the bend below Council Bluffs. The expedition was on its own.

There were now twenty in the party, including the scientific staff, four interpreters and baggage handlers, and seven soldiers from the fort. There were twenty-eight horses that had been secured from the Indians, and an inadequate supply of coffee, sugar, salt, pork, biscuit, parched corn, corn meal, and whiskey. For the Indians they had a supply of vermilion paint, looking glasses, beads, knives, combs, firesteels, hawks' bells, moccasin awls, and tobacco. There also were the collecting equipment, two thermometers, blank books, portfolios, compasses, a sextant, and mercury.

On a fine June day in 1820 the expedition left Council Bluffs, crossed to where Omaha now stands, and headed into the largely unknown lands to the west.

Some days later, surmounting a rise, the party drew rein in awe. This was not the optical illusion of wild turkeys; these were the buffalo at last! An immense herd grazed placidly over the broad plains. There were at least ten thousand magnificent dark brown animals that raised small columns of dust as they moved about. As the party camped quietly on the ridge, night hid the herd. The great arch of sky held thousands of stars as the dark plains held thousands of animals.

In the early morning, when Dr. Say raised his head from his blanket to look eagerly to the west to see the buffalo again, he saw only mists lying across the prairie grass, only mists and nothing more. The great herd had vanished somewhere in the night.

The men slept on blankets on the ground, yet rested well after a long day in the saddle. Major Long, however, would not let them feel too much at ease, or get too comfortable or too confident. He knew they were in Pawnee country and that their whereabouts was no secret to the Indians. So every now and again without warning he held what he termed a "fire-drill," a sudden alarm of Indians to see how fast the men leaped into action. On a chilly morning before sunrise where they had camped on the buffalo plains, he sounded the alarm, fired off a gun and yelled, and the men rolled out with commendable speed, grasping their weapons and leaping up to meet the grinning Major with his watch in hand. Dr. James was agreeable enough to this preparedness program, but he did rather dislike those early morning routs. He wrote plaintively in his journal:

Since leaving the Missouri, we had never indulged a disposition to sluggishness, accustoming ourselves to rise every morning long before the sun, but we still found that we left that small spot of earth, on which we had rested our limbs, and which had become warm and dry by the heat of our bodies, with as much reluctance as we have felt at quitting softer beds.

On the morning of June 30, as they traveled west over the Colorado plains, seeing prairie dog towns and burrowing owls, Indian paintbrush and purple pentstemon, the men noticed something low on the western horizon. It might be only low cumulus clouds, but it also might be the snow-capped peaks of the Rocky Mountains. There was a sudden, wonderful feeling of excitement, a lift of the heart. The men could hardly take their eyes from the strangely portentous rim of white to look at the magpies in the dry washes, or the odd little owls standing on prairie dog burrow-mounds and bobbing their heads like little Chinese figurines.

By noon they were sure—the Rocky Mountains, as Pike had described them, lay ahead. A high mountain, they were certain, must be Pike's Peak, but there was something not quite right about it. This had two peaks, not one. French trappers had mentioned a mountain, very high, called *Les Deux Oreilles*. This it proved to be, and it was renamed Long's Peak for the leader of the expedition.

It seemed to take an interminable length of time to reach those everlastingly distant mountains. They had hoped to spend the Fourth of July there, but by then they had reached only the place where Denver would one day stand. They could never realize just how far away something was, especially mountains.

. Following southward along the Great Front Range, the expedition passed Castle Rock, where Dr. Say discovered the rock wren skipping about among the boulders. In the strange sandstone formations of the Garden of the Gods, pink house finches or linnets were singing—new, also—and he found a lovely pale blue, brown, and white bird flitting among the mesquite bushes and white prickly poppies—the lazuli bunting. The cliff swallow was still another new one for Dr. Say. Many men evidently had seen cliff swallows before, but none had bothered to describe them or to give them a name.

They were now in the vicinity of Pike's Peak and could see its formidable snow-capped bulk looming beyond the red sandstone cliffs. As they turned into Cheyenne Canyon, one of the hunters brought in a strange new pigeon with purple head and a long, squared-off tail marked with a light band across the end. Another hunter contributed a partridge which was about the same size as the familiar ruffed grouse of the eastern forests. But this bird was almost black below, dark gray above, and it had a curious yellow-orange eyebrow. It proved to be poor food at dinner, because its dark flesh was flavored with the bitter sage the bird had been eating. But to Dr. Say this bird, the dusky grouse, like the band-tailed pigeon, was still another treasure discovered in the very shadow of the peak which Zebulon Pike had found but never climbed.

Meanwhile, Dr. James, scrambling about on the mountainside and canyon trails, was finding new flowers. He came back to camp that evening with a transcendent glow on his face and a splendid blue and cream-colored flower, an exquisite thing of elegance and grace. He had found the Rocky Mountain columbine, which was to become the state flower of Colorado and which would add its strain of color and beauty to the cultivated columbines of America and England.

Pike's Peak looked down at them and beckoned. Pike himself had declared that no one would ever be able to climb it. The sides were too steep; the sliding rock was a hazard. But Edwin James looked up toward its purple-gray bulk and knew that there were alpine flowers up there. He would have to try to climb Pike's Peak. Dr. Say was too busy with the birds and reptiles he was discovering in the lower levels; he had just found the Arkansas goldfinch and a new warbler, the orange-crowned. Besides, he had plans to study the burrowing owls in the colony nearby.

So Dr. James took two men with him, and on July 13 at sunrise they started off into the canyon. They carried a picnic lunch, or what passed for one on expeditions of this sort—a saddle of venison and some already-cooked bison ribs. Two other men went along to care for the horses after the trio continued on foot when the trail grew too steep. At the boiling spring (Manitou Springs) they ate their lunch, hung the spare provisions in a large cedar, and leaving the horses and their handlers, began to climb. They had a blanket each, some meat and corn, and a small kettle in which to boil water for tea.

Climbing was hard. Much of the surface of the mountain, as Pike had said, was covered with loose, crumbled granite. They slid back, scrambled and fell. Their breathing was more difficult. They had not gone more than two miles before they knew that they had to rest for the night, but there was no level place to camp. The mountain side was too steep; they had to secure themselves with a pole placed against two trees to keep from rolling into the mountain stream that tumbled noisily past their camping place. The night was cold and uncomfortable. They started again as soon as it was light. They left their blankets and provisions hung up in the trees and expected to be back by nightfall. They still had not realized the measure of this mountain.

Through the thin, brilliant, chill air, they passed timberline and the stunted spruces which lay low in the punishment of the high mountaintop's winds, then out into the tundra where the ptarmigans were nesting and the white-crowned sparrows were singing from the six-inch willows that hugged the rocks. The men walked over low alpine flowers of utmost beauty—brilliant, half-inch-high, azure forget-me-nots, the pink alpine phlox, the blue sky-pilot shaking in the wind, the fairy primroses, androsace and elephantella, alpine clovers, snow buttercups, king's crown, alp-lilies, and many more.

Edwin James was frustrated at the futility of trying to collect them all. And he was tired—exhausted—but he would not rest until he had gathered what he could.

By two o'clock they had to stop, whether they wanted to or not. They lay down in the chill, bright sunshine and caught their breath.

When they had rested a while they ate the little food they had, and wished they had brought more. They went on into patches of old snow where Dr. James, with renewed energy, found more and more exquisite treasures for his collecting case. It was almost stuffed now; he could find little room for more.

By four in the afternoon, men for the first time stood on the summit of Pike's Peak. They had done the impossible. From the windswept crest they could see the Arkansas River far in the distance, and the plains shining in pinkish gold, like a map, far and small, and the mountains rising, blue and purple in unending ridges to the west and north. Clouds of grasshoppers were coming up over the snow banks. The sunshine glittered on their wings as they rattled past on the wind. Of all the things he had thought to find up here, more than 14,000 feet above sea level, James had not expected grasshoppers. More logically, there were the tracks and horns of bighorn sheep on the rocky summit. A cony yipped from a rock cairn and scooted out of sight as a golden eagle coasted over.

They stayed no more than half an hour on the summit. It was bitingly cold up there. They descended to the shelter of the trees, and knew that they could not get back to the midway camp that night. They had no food, no blankets, but they kindled a fire and made themselves as comfortable as they could for the night. Next morning, as they continued down the mountain, they were horrified to see smoke below them in the vicinity of the earlier camping place. They hurried, feeling that something must be wrong; smoke would attract Indians and Major Long had told them specifically not to make any more than they could help.

Apparently a large part of the mountainside was on fire, and as they came to the old camp they found the smoldering remains of their blankets and food. They realized then, sheepishly and with no little embarrassment, what had happened. They had simply forgotten to put out their campfire and it had raced over several acres of Pike's Peak. They salvaged a small amount of scorched food for breakfast, put out the fire as well as they could, and went down to the main camp. That evening Dr. James, in a pleasant daze, carefully sorted and pressed the innumerable new plants from the mountain. It had been one of the great experiences of his life.

During his absence, Thomas Say had also been having a memorable experience. He had gone out to a prairie dog village and had spent the day sitting on a burrow-mound, trying to understand the lives of small owls and marmots living amicably in the same community and apparently not too much discommoded by the occasional presence of a rattlesnake. He had never seen an owl like this one, with such long legs, an owl very much at home in the brilliance of sunlight all day long, and which sat upright almost exactly like a prairie dog on the burrow-mound. From where he watched he could count two dozen on as many mounds, but at a little distance it was difficult to tell owl from marmot. They were both sandy-brown, round-headed, cylindrical in shape. Both had the same low clucking sound and whistle of warning. Say wondered in scientific humor if the prairie dogs had not tutored the young owls so that they had picked up prairie dog lingo instead of owl talk. But then he recalled more soberly that where the burrowing owl had been known in the West Indies, there were no prairie dogs, and the birds uttered the same notes. It was a strange coincidence, however (if there ever were real coincidences in nature), to find bird and mammal appearing so much alike at a distance and both nesting in deep burrows which had been excavated on the hot, windswept high plains by the prairie dogs.

On his way back to camp, his fair skin more sunburned than it had been before, he found another bird that pleased him very much —a bird of considerable character and force, a yellow-breasted, brown flycatcher with a bit of red for a crest, the Arkansas kingbird. Meanwhile, back at the camp, Titian Peale had shot an elegant scissor-tailed flycatcher and was engaged in painting its portrait when Say returned with his own specimens. This and several others of Peale's paintings made on the expedition in Colorado subsequently were added to Bonaparte's *Ornithology*.

When the expedition left the Pike's Peak area and moved south through arid country, conditions grew worse. Food was now exceedingly scarce. Hunters who went out for a day and a half came back with one deer or an old turkey and her scrawny young. The men were reduced to living on cornmeal mush and parched corn. The coffee, tea, and sugar were now being reserved for hospital stores. It was almost worth while getting sick if you could have a cup of coffee again. Much of the salt was gone, and after they had been without this condiment for many days, it was found that even the perspiration on their faces had lost its saltiness. A thousand miles of heat and hardship and danger lay between the men and what they fondly recalled as the "enjoyments and indulgences of civilized countries."

They were fairly cheerful about it, all but three soldiers who had been the complainers and shirkers all the way from Engineer Cantonment. There were a number of times when Major Long wished he had never seen Bernard, Nolan, and Myers. Some weeks later, Lieutenant Swift and Thomas Say were to wish it even more fervently.

The party now divided so that more ground could be covered. Dr. Say and his group, including Swift, set out to explore the course of the Red River and the Arkansas. Long's group pushed on through dry country to within 150 miles of Spanish-held Santa Fe, toward which they dared approach no closer for fear of being arrested. The two parties were to meet at Fort Smith, on the Arkansas River, whenever they should get there. Fort Smith was located on the boundary of what is now Oklahoma and Arkansas.

Long's party fared rather well at first in finding a mule deer, the only meat they had seen in days. They knew that it was a hitherto unknown species, knew also that they were extremely hungry— were, in fact, close to starvation. But the dimensions of the animal were dutifully and hastily taken, a hurried sketch made by the light of the campfire by the hungry Mr. Peale—and then the soldiers skinned the animal, cut up the meat, and cooked it quickly. It was pleasant to serve both science and one's stomach without undue neglect of either.

This was the last good food they were to have for some time. They were in the barren country of southern Colorado and upper New Mexico where there was neither wood nor even buffalo chips with which to kindle a fire. A fourth of a biscuit remained for each man. When someone shot a badger, and another hopefully brought in a young burrowing owl which, when the feathers and head were off, was little bigger or fatter than a sparrow, the game could not be cooked because there was no fuel. The men were not as yet so hungry that they could stomach raw badger and raw owl. There was no water. The sun was pitiless in the broiling bowl of sky.

Finally they came upon a stagnant pool which deer and javelinas had muddied with their feet. They found a little wood and managed to cook the badger and the owl before they entirely spoiled. Then they thankfully shot a wild horse, cooked the flesh, and ate it with relish. In spite of hunger, however, the imperturbable scientists continued to collect, and Mr. Peale continued to draw pictures before using the specimens for dinner.

There was on August 9 a laconic entry in James's journal:

We breakfasted on the last of the horse, which, having been killed on the 5th, and the weather since unusually warm, had suffered from long keeping. We ate it cheerfully, only regretting that we could not promise ourselves as good for dinner.

Slowly the desperate days dragged across the barren country, which Major Long later described as the Great American Desert, until the men at last reached the Arkansas River and its trees and greenery and life. With renewed courage they pushed on to the fort. Thomas Say and Lieutenant Swift and their men had not yet arrived. No one had heard any news of them. The famished expedition promptly ate so much of the delicious food given them at Fort Smith that they were ill until their systems could get used to nourishment again, especially such niceties as salt and sugar, starches, and vegetables.

Meanwhile, Thomas Say and his group also rode through hungry country. They were growing weak and debilitated from lack of food; the heat was oppressive, and there were frequent August thunderstorms that sent deluges of heavy rain against the camp. There was no indication that Fort Smith or the river were near.

On August 31 they camped in a rocky valley and went to sleep hungry. The man who was delegated to cook, when there was anything to prepare, woke first from force of habit and discovered that his knapsack had been rifled. He leaped to his feet to give the alarm, and found that three of the best horses were missing. He roused the others in a hurry. There was no sign of Indians, and there also was no sign of those complainers and do-nothings, Myers, Bernard, and Nolan. They had decamped with the horses and had stolen everything else they could lay hands on.

Lieutenant Swift and Thomas Say were aghast. They could not believe what they saw—their own knapsacks empty, all their spare clothing gone, also their personal property, including money and watches. Worst of all was the loss of the manuscripts and note-books. The three deserters could not have wanted them; they were of no value to them—the meteorological records and journal of Swift, and Say's five priceless books in which he had written his observations of the manners and habits of mountain Indians and their history, two books of vocabularies, the topographical journal, and his notes on the mammals, reptiles, insects, and birds he had found on the expedition.

The three thieves apparently had been increasingly irked by the futility and discomfort of the endless journey, by the stops to examine some insignificant lizard or plant or bird; they could not understand what it was all about. They were fed up, finished, ready to clear out. They simply vented their fury on the scientific materials that had been so painfully collected.

It was enough to destroy a man's whole scientific courage. To Lieutenant Swift and to Dr. Say, the bottom had dropped out of the world. Weakened from hunger and discouragement, they went on. The wild grapes and green persimmons which were all they found to eat that day were somehow fitting to the occasion.

When they came at last to Fort Smith, the commanding officer at once sent out a posse to find the thieves, but nothing was ever heard of them again, or of the manuscripts and materials. Say was thankful that the majority of his collected specimens, had been in the pack-saddles of horses with the other group and were now safe at the fort.

After a few days of rest and food, the group continued together back to civilization. Thomas Say went home to the sweet Middle Western landscape of New Harmony, Indiana, to recuperate from the rigors of the trip and to enjoy his wife's cooking again. Lucy Say, also a skilled zoologist, assisted him in cataloguing his new specimens, among which were twelve birds not found by Lewis and Clark and several thousand insects, of which many hundreds were new. Edwin James had collected nearly five hundred undescribed plants and many mineral specimens, shells, and fossils. Peale and Seymour had made 122 animal sketches and 150 landscape views. Much territory had been mapped; Pike's Peak had been climbed; and a great deal of knowledge had been gained about the Indians.

The expedition may have been considered something of a failure from the standpoint of the government's financial expenditure, but the understanding of the natural history of the West had been materially advanced—in the singing of the lazuli buntings and pink linnets, in the strutting of the dusky grouse, in the pigeon with purple head and a band on its tail, in that new little black-and-russet flycatcher which would be known forever as Say's phoebe.

CHAPTER TEN

ALEXANDER WILSON

AN object of mockery, he stood in the public square and, while his neighbors laughed at him, he set fire to the satiric poem he had written which had brought about his disgrace. He watched the fragments flare up quickly; they were consumed much faster than it had taken him to compose the objectionable words. Stung by the indifference of the mill-owners toward their workers, he had written this fitting lampoon of the man responsible for much of the labor trouble in Paisley. The man had objected, had sought out the author, had had him disgraced in the public square and then put in prison. Alexander Wilson, thin, pale, bony, felt himself die inside. He wanted no more of Scotland, no more of the kind of justice his countrymen meted out.

Alexander Wilson was born in 1766 in the Scottish town where the Paisley designs in women's shawls were developed. His mother died when he was ten. He was never a well child, a condition that worried young Alec's father. Then there was a stepmother in the household, with whom the boy could never get along. She was firm in having him learn a trade, so he was apprenticed to a relative to be a weaver. By the time he was eighteen he had had enough of weaving. He hated sitting indoors all day and part of the night, while the outdoors called. Therefore, in order to get himself outside, do a little traveling, and earn a little money at the same time, he became a peddler.

Later, back in Paisley, he saw the labor difficulties that stemmed from the recession caused by the French Revolution; saw the employers getting unaccountably rich, while the weavers grew poorer and want and hunger were everywhere. So Alexander Wilson, who was a better-than-average poet, turned his hand to satire. The outcome was disgrace. He was hurt and bitter. He had never been a cheerful man; he frequently felt that everyone, including fate, was against him. The treatment by his fellow men only confirmed this, and it galled him. When he was out of prison, poor and with no prospect of bettering himself in Scotland, and hating Paisley for its treatment of him, he heard the call to America. There was freedom in America. He would go.

The sailing vessel *American Swift* set him down at Newcastle, Delaware, though he had wanted to go to Philadelphia, that center of culture and brotherly love and equality among men. With hardly any money at all, with only meager hand luggage and his gun, he set off to walk. It was thirty-three miles to Philadelphia, but to a one-time peddler in an exciting new land, this was nothing. The very air smelled exciting. There was something different about it. It brought the whiff of adventure and a cleanness of wilderness with every breath he drew. To lungs that were none too good even then, it was the best medicine he could have had.

He walked. The road took him through an oak woods whose shade on a July day was pleasant. He heard birds, but did not see them. Then he heard a yammering—and he caught his breath as an incredible thing on wings swooped across the road and clapped itself against the side of a tree. It was so beautiful, so completely magnificent—so American. He lifted his fowling piece and shot his first American bird. He held it in his hand, the neck wobbling now, a spot of blood no redder than the bird's crimson head and neck, sharp in contrast against a snowy breast and blue-black back and wings. He pulled open the vanes of the wing to see where the white had gone that he had seen so sharply as the bird flashed in front of him, and found it. He had downed a red-headed wood-pecker. It was not rare; most people in the eastern United States were very likely familiar with it. Catesby had illustrated and described it. But to Alexander Wilson, this was the most splendid thing in the world, and it was his. He kept it with him during his long walk, until the July heat made him aware of the fact that this was flesh and he could not prevent it from decay. He wished he knew how to keep it forever as beautiful as it was on that first day of his in America.

In and around Philadelphia he obtained work. He went to Virginia and disliked it. He peddled a bit, but didn't do well. He taught school in Pennsylvania and New Jersey, but did not find it inspiring. He had, however, become increasingly aware of the natural history of America. His travels had shown him more and more of it, had impressed upon him how little he knew—nothing, nothing at all, and most of the people with whom he was associated knew as little. But then, moving to a place about four miles from Philadelphia to teach in a small school, he paid a visit to Mr. Bartram's Botanical Garden not far away and met the venerable Mr. William Bartram—he who had had the adventure with the alligators long ago in Florida.

Bartram had written *Travels Through North and South Carolina, Georgia, East and West Florida,* and had been instrumental in collecting many birds which George Ord and he had sent to European naturalists for classification. Buffon, Cuvier, and Viellot, however, could not do much with American wildlife, although Viellot, to find out, came to do a little field work for himself in the United States and Mexico. Most American birds did not tally easily with European species. Linnaeus had worked hard at naming them, and so had the others, but knowledgeable men like Bartram knew that they were often wrong. American wildlife simply was different, and it had to be seen to be understood.

When young Alexander Wilson met the elderly William Bartram, the spark was kindled. Bartram had a library of books, all the ornithology books and botany books of the day. Wilson saw the magnificent plates of Catesby and pored over his pictures, coming across names for some of the birds he had been seeing. It was possible, he decided, that Catesby had not gone far enough. At first awed and delighted, he then became critical. He could find points to criticize in Catesby's pictures, arguments with Edwards's, Latham's, and Buffon's often absurd classifications and descriptions. Few of the ornithologists had ranged through the woods and along shores and in swamps to study birds, as Mr. Bartram had done, or to paint them from life; all but Catesby, and he had been limited in his scope. Although Wilson respected Catesby, he felt that perhaps he, Wilson, could do better.

When his day's classes were over, he bent over paper with pencil and brush, a dead bird before him under the candlelight, trying to copy its lines and make the dead thing come alive on the paper. His first attempts were not very satisfying. He started over, and when he had some drawings which he thought were at least passable, he took them with trepidation and inner nervousness for Mr. Bartram to examine and make suggestions. Bartram himself had painted birds; he had been a careful observer besides. He worked with Wilson to bring out the best in the paintings which were taking form. Wilson always had a hard time drawing a decent-looking flower that both resembled its original and satisfied William Bartram, but with the birds it seemed that, without any artistic training or any ability he had known existed, he was empowered and inspired to draw. His pictures usually did not have the feeling of life and animation that he sought, and they were almost always drawn in profile because he did that best, but they captured the likenesses of birds far better than Catesby had done. The technique of feathers was masterful under Alexander Wilson's brush; some, like the almost full-sized ruffed grouse, could scarcely be improved on today. Wilson was certain that his paintings excelled even Catesby's and those of every other bird painter. That was before he knew about a certain young man in Kentucky who was also painting birds.

In the flush of a dedicated enthusiasm and inspiration, Alexander Wilson wanted to amass portraits of all the birds of America and to have them published in books that would be more available to the public than Catesby's rare and costly tomes. Bartram, who knew some of the difficulties attending publication of any book, even when one had plenty of money, could not encourage him much; but Wilson had gone beyond that now. He had his own inner fire. He continued to teach school, but his heart was not in it; he did it only to provide himself with food and lodging and enough clothing, with money to buy paper and paints so that he could work on his book. He traveled when he could and collected more birds wherever he went.

Though not realizing it, he was, at the same time, finding birds that had not hitherto been discovered and described. Wilson, perhaps, added more species to the list of American birds than any other ornithologist before or after him. He became known, long after his death, as the Father of American Ornithology, but he had no idea of this during those exalted, frustrating years when he was finding birds, painting their pictures, writing his text, and trying to sell his books.

He always sent his finished plates to Bartram for criticism. Then, so flushed was he with his own feeling of success and dedication, he painted two birds which he had collected along the Mohawk River, one of them a Canada jay, and sent them to Thomas Jefferson who, in 1805, had just been re-elected President of the United States. Wilson admired Jefferson, and he was deeply thrilled when the President, acknowledging the gift of the painting, wrote him, in his own hand:

Sir,

I received here yesterday your favor of March 18th, with the elegant drawings of the new birds you found on your tour to Niagara, for which I pray you to accept my thanks. The jay is quite unknown to me. From my observations while in Europe, on the birds and quadrupeds of that quarter, I am of opinion there is not in our continent a single bird or quadruped which is not sufficiently unlike all the members of its family there to be considered as specifically different; on this general observation I conclude with confidence that your jay is not a European bird. . . .

As you are curious in birds, there is one well worthy your attention, to be found, or rather heard, in every part of America, and yet scarcely ever to be seen; it is in all the forests, from spring to fall, and never but on the tops of the tallest trees, from which it perpetually serenades us with some of the sweetest notes, and as clear as those of the nightingale. I have followed it for miles without ever, but once, getting a good view of it. It is of the size and make of the mocking-bird, lightly thrush-colored on the back, and a grayish-white on the breast and belly. Mr. Randolph, my son-in-law, was in possession of one which had been shot by a neighbor; he pronounces this also a Muscicapa, and I think it much resembling the *Mouche-rolle de la Martinique*, 8 Buffon, 374, Pl. enlum. 568. As it abounds in all the neighborhood of Philadelphia, you may perhaps by patience and perseverance (of which much will be requisite) get a sight, if not a possession of it. I have for twenty years interested the young sportsmen of my neighborhood to shoot me one; but as yet without success. Accept my salutations and assurances of respect.

Th. Jefferson

This was thrilling! The President himself had never seen the new jay before, and he had asked Wilson to find out what another bird was, evidently the towhee. He was at once on fire to track it down and paint its picture.

Slowly his paintings were being finished, and he was working with his nephew, William Duncan, in making the plates, some of which he engraved himself. On a polished copper plate a coat of varnish of a particular composition was thinly spread and allowed to harden. The picture was then traced on this, and cut down to the copper with a pointed stylus. Then a bank of wax was raised as a dam around the entire plate, and an acid called *aquafortis* was poured into this enclosure. The acid ate into the copper only where the design with all its fine lines had been cut. When the plate was inked, paper was pressed upon it to receive the print. This, then, had to be colored by hand by the artist, or by his hired colorists who worked from the master copy.

Wilson could not find a publisher to finance his great work, but he managed to have a sample copy printed and bound. Then he had to go out with it to get subscriptions for the rest. He would charge $120 for the complete set. This was considered a lot of money for bird books; a good many gentlemen of means declared they would not pay twenty cents to look at a bird.

He was at the same time still traveling about whenever he could. He and old Mr. Bartram for a time were making wild plans to explore the Mississippi and the West. Wilson knew they would need protection and conveyance; he knew also that Thomas Jefferson was sending out expeditions to explore beyond the Mississippi to the Rocky Mountains, exactly the places Wilson yearned to visit. Lewis and Clark had been sent up the Missouri. Wilson had seen and admired the bird specimens they had sent back, even before the expedition itself returned. He knew that Pike was to be sent west; if only Wilson and Mr. Bartram could go with this group!

Bartram knew that he was too old to tackle such an adventure, but he wanted his young friend to go. He wrote to Jefferson to recommend that Wilson go along as naturalist to collect wildlife of the new lands to be explored. Then Wilson, not being able to contain himself in his eagerness, perhaps saying too much and upsetting Bartram's good offices in his behalf, wrote personally to the President, pleading:

Accustomed to the hardships of travelling, without a family, and an enthusiast in the pursuit of Natural History, I will devote my whole powers to merit your excellency's approbation; and ardently wish for an opportunity of testifying the sincerity of my professions, and the deep veneration with which I have the honor to be. . . .

But Pike and his expedition had departed in July, 1806, and a naturalist had not been assigned. Pike himself, who was no naturalist and not interested in being one, involved as he was in managing the expedition and dickering with Indians, could have made good use of someone like Alexander Wilson. The President never answered either Bartram's or Wilson's letters. There was no explanation, just silence.

Hurt and disappointed, Alexander Wilson continued to work on his paintings. He set out with his sample volume to obtain subscriptions. After weeks of hard work, traveling and soliciting in New York State and Massachusetts, he had only forty-one subscriptions. He could not see why everyone was not overwhelmed with the glory of his work, or why everyone he approached did not immediately put down his name for a set. He was bitter about it. Then he went south and visited every city and town as far as Savannah, Georgia. He obtained only a few subscriptions, not enough to pay for the journey. In Baltimore he got sixteen; in Washington, seventeen; Jefferson himself was one of these subscribers.

However, the journey brought him, if not many supporters, more unfamiliar birds and some unforgettable experiences. Here in the South he saw his first ivory-billed woodpecker and was impressed. On his way to Wilmington he had shot one, winging it only enough to bring it down. The bird yelled piteously, like a young child, he thought. The horse shied and threw Wilson head-over-end as soon as he had mounted with his noisy and protesting captive. He wrapped it in his coat to quiet its racket and to avoid being stabbed by the white beak. As he rode through the streets of Wilmington the bird let loose with even louder screams and would not be muffled. Women, hearing it, ran to their doors and windows to see who was mistreating a child.

He went to an inn and, with the bird still shrilly protesting inside his coat, he dismounted and sought lodging. The loungers with one accord suspended their slow chewing, got up, and gathered around; the inn keeper came forward. Wilson solemnly asked if he had lodging for himself and his baby. The man looked blank. The others looked at each other and touched their heads. The "baby" shrieked and gave him a jab, and Wilson hastily drew it forth, to the general astonishment and mirth of the gathering.

He took it upstairs with him to the room assigned and locked the bird in while he went to see to his horse and have something to eat. When he returned in an hour the room was a ruin. The bird had climbed up the side of the window nearly as high as the ceiling, and had proceeded to hack off large pieces of plaster. The bed was covered with chunks of debris; the lath was exposed for at least fifteen inches square, and a hole had been made in the weather-boarding on the outside. If he had come back fifteen minutes later, the bird would have made its escape through the hole.

The woodpecker screeched and cackled and complained as he climbed up on a chair and brought it down, then tied it with a cord around its leg and fastened this to a table leg. He hurried out to see if he could find something for his obstreperous pet to eat besides the plaster. When he came back with a piece of pork, he found to his mortification that the bird had chopped through the leg of the mahogany table and quite ruined it. With food in front of it, the bird would not eat.

It attacked him several times while he was drawing its picture. He kept it for three days. Then the ivory-billed woodpecker, big-gest of its race, perhaps the only one any man ever kept in captivity, died, whether of starvation or of yearning for the wilderness, or of both, we cannot know. And Wilson had an enormous charge of repairs to pay before he left that inn at Wilmington.

His first book was published in 1808, his second in 1810. He was going to have to find more subscribers and at the same time to find more birds. He had been told that towns along the Ohio had cul-ture and refinement among people of means who would no doubt all subscribe, so he set off, after having begged old Mr. Bartram to come along. Bartram yearned to do so, as in his youth, but he was too infirm now.

Wilson traveled by stagecoach, by rowboat and raft, and then on foot, when his money ran low. He did not do well in Cincinnati. He commented wryly that people there told him they would think of it (subscribing), and he added, "they are very thoughtful people." He went to Louisville and lodged at the Indian Queen tavern.

On March 19, 1810, he went rambling about the town with his book and his gun and stopped in at a merchant's establishment, one of many at which he called. "Examined Mr. . . . 's drawings in crayons—very good. Saw two new birds he had, both Motacillidae." But he added next day, "No naturalist to keep me company." And on March 23 he packed up, gave his pet Carolina parakeet to the tavern keeper, and left Louisville where he had received not one subscription.

He said: "I had four letters of recommendation, and was taught to expect much of everything there; but neither received one act of civility from those to whom I was recommended, one subscriber, nor *one new bird;* though I delivered my letters, ransacked the woods repeatedly, and visited all the characters likely to subscribe. *Science* or *literature* has not one friend in this place. . . ."

One of the "characters" he had met had been John James Audubon. The meeting of these two has been one of the enigmas of ornithological history, a minor tragedy, and one of the strange coincidences and puzzles of history. Far different from what Wilson wrote, Audubon said of the same encounter:

One fair morning I was surprised by the sudden entrance into our counting room of Mr. Alexander Wilson, the celebrated author of the "American Ornithology," of whose existence I had never until that moment been appraised. This happened in March, 1810. How well do I remember him, as he walked up to me! His long, rather hooked nose, the keenness of his eyes, and his prominent cheek bones, stamped his countenance with a peculiar character. . . . His stature was not above the middle size. He had two volumes under his arm, and as he approached the table at which I was working, I thought I discovered something like astonishment in his countenance. He, however, immediately proceeded to disclose the object of his visit, which was to procure subscriptions for his work. He opened his books, explained the nature of his occupations, and requested my patronage.

Audubon apparently felt no jealousy. He examined the books

and impulsively was about to sign his name as a subscriber when his partner, Rozier, spluttered to him in French, "My dear Audubon, what induces you to subscribe to this work? Your drawings are certainly far better, and again, you must know as much of the habits of American birds as this gentleman."

Wilson may or may not have understood French, but he did understand with mounting anger and bitterness that he had just lost a sale. He could not have known that John James Audubon at that time certainly was not able to afford to pay $120 for books; it was all he could do just then to feed his family and keep his store from bankruptcy. He did understand, however, that he had a rival in this backwoods community where there was no culture or appreciation of the arts. He asked, thin-lipped, if he might see Audubon's pictures. So Audubon, a friendly individual, with the same respect that Wilson had shown him his own books, laid open his own splendid plates for the inspection of the visiting ornithologist.

Wilson was more and more hurt and confounded and filled with cold anger. He had had no idea that anyone was doing the same thing which had so engrosed him these long years. It was unjust. Wilson cautiously asked Audubon if he intended publishing his paintings, and seemed surprised and somewhat relieved to hear that he did not. It was not until much later, after Wilson's death, that Audubon decided on his own venture.

Wilson asked to borrow a few of Audubon's plates during his stay and was willingly loaned a stack, which he took to his room at the Indian Queen. The Audubons also lodged there, so they were handily situated. Audubon promised Wilson that they should go out together and hunt birds; it was wonderful to be with someone who knew them. They would have a famous time of it together, and he promised to show Wilson where to find some birds which he did not now have.

The two went on several expeditions into the forests along the Ohio. They dined together with Audubon's friends. Audubon offered to let Wilson take some of his plates to publish in his book, if he would give him credit for them, but Wilson disdained to reply to this insult. He already could feel that this man had something he would never have. At night in the Indian Queen, Wilson sat alone in his room and played melancholy airs on his flute. It made John Audubon sad to hear him.

Wilson left Louisville without saying good-bye to the Audubons or to friends who had entertained him. When Audubon was in Philadelphia later on, he visited Wilson but was not cordially greeted. And when Wilson's ninth volume of *American Ornithology* came out, Audubon with dismay read in the text that Wilson had "neither received one act of civility [in Louisville] . . . *Science* or *literature* had not one friend in this place."

Three years after Wilson and Audubon met so unsatisfactorily in Louisville, Alexander Wilson died of dysentery in Philadelphia. He had not been well for a long time, and the disease carried him off.

Charles Lucian Bonaparte, Prince of Musignano, nephew of Napoleon Bonaparte and a noted ornithologist, completed Wilson's final volumes. Other artists contributed their work in illustrating birds that Wilson never found. Titian Peale's plates of birds painted on the Yellowstone Expedition are among them. And a Steller's jay in the possession of Mr. Leadbeater of London, which may have been the original jay shot by Steller himself, was lent to Bonaparte so that A. Rider could paint its picture for the completed works of Wilson.

The pages of this and all the ornithology books and popular bird guides from Wilson's time onward credit him with the discovery of many American birds, while his name was given by his admirers and friends in his memory to Wilson's plover, Wilson's phalarope, Wilson's warbler, Wilson's thrush, Wilson's petrel, and Wilson's snipe.

CHAPTER ELEVEN

JOHN JAMES AUDUBON

HE lay on his elbows in the buffalo grass and looked over the low ridge at the animals grazing in the distance. He waited for the hunters to proceed and rather wished they would get it over with. On the hard-baked earth of midsummer he let his mind wander, waiting. The root-clumps of the buffalo grass hurt his elbows. There was a locoweed almost under his nose, and he moved a bit so he could focus on it. Now that he was fifty-eight, he could not see things sharply close to his face; but the distant view was still bright and clear-cut, especially if there was a bird in sight.

Looking back as if this Montana prairie were a precipice in time from which John James Audubon could see down the years that were past, he could remember birds and the adventures in finding them. There had always been birds. He quickly calculated: that new one which he had named for his friend Harris, and the one for Bell, brought the grand total to 499. Four hundred and ninety-nine plates of birds identified and painted. A pity that he had found them all; a pity, too, that he could not have made it a round five hundred.

He never dreamed that they would snowball so tremendously, all those birds, and the experiences he had had in finding them. They had been his life. His Lucy and the two boys had been wonderful, such an endless help as they still were, always understanding of his need for birds. He tried to remember his first bird, but he could not; it was too long ago. Perhaps the very first had been that unfortunate parrot named *Mignonne* which had belonged to his stepmother in France, and which he had seen killed by her pet monkey. It had certainly made an indelible impression upon his young mind; he had felt so desperately sorry for the poor parrot. No—he remembered now. The kingfisher had been the first bird he ever painted from life, long ago in Pennsylvania.

He remembered how it had been along the Ohio, when he was a struggling storekeeper in Kentucky, and how he and his surly partner, Rozier, had examined those bird portraits that Wilson had painted, and how angry Wilson was to find that Audubon would not subscribe to his work. Wilson could not have known how poor the Audubons were then. It had been only a short time afterward, in December of that same year, 1810, that he and Rozier determined to make an attempt at repairing their losses by taking their goods and whiskey to Ste. Genevieve on the Mississippi, which offered a better chance to make some money. It was also an opportunity to find more birds. Birds were free; he needed no money to enjoy them.

John James Audubon never lost his interest in or his total fascination for birds, their beauty, their habits, their songs. Even when he was most afflicted by poverty, grief, hardship, and discouragement; when he had no work, no money, no hope of succeeding in his life's dedicated work; when fire destroyed his journals; when rats chewed up his paintings; when his baby daughter died; when there was no food in the house—he still had his birds. He remembered how he had said:

One of the most extraordinary things among all these adverse circumstances was that I never for a day gave up listening to the songs of our birds, or watching their peculiar habits, or delineating them in the best way that I could; nay, during my deepest troubles I frequently would wrench myself from the persons around me, and retire to some secluded part of our noble forests; and many a time, at the sound of the wood-thrush's melodies have I fallen on my knees, and there prayed earnestly to our God.

The journey to Ste. Genevieve with Rozier by river was one of the adventures he would never forget. Poor Rozier was not always the most agreeable of companions. He failed to get into the spirit of adventure which always filled the bright-eyed Audubon. Discomfort was discomfort to Rozier; mud was mud; cold was cold; it was all execrable. Rozier complained openly and sulked. Discomfort to Audubon was just part of the exhilaration of adventure. He had an unquenchable cheerfulness and optimism which must have been infuriating to his partner, who by now had come to the conclusion that he had been soft-headed to combine forces with this irredeemable dreamer and ne'er-do-well. When they parted company, with mutual satisfaction, by the following spring, April 11, 1811, each wrote:

"Rozier cared only for money, and liked Ste. Genevieve." "Audubon had no taste for commerce, and was continually in the forest." This was a pretty good evaluation of both.

In December, 1810, however, when Audubon was twenty-five, the pair set off in a heavy, wet snowstorm in a keelboat loaded with three hundred barrels of whiskey, various dry goods, and gunpowder. The craft moved quietly through the smother of snow at five miles an hour downstream from Henderson, Kentucky. At stopping points they learned that even so early in the season the Mississippi was already choked with a vast ice gorge, though the Ohio was still open. The pair decided to wait it out a short distance above the mouth of the Ohio until they had word of the Mississippi's opening. Rozier fumed.

Near Cache Creek, above the dismal village of Cairo, Illinois, the two pulled into shore and found another keelboat, also loaded with up-river produce, waiting at the same place. Audubon—never one to consider delay a hardship—was making plans to explore the shores and forests; who knew what birds might not lurk there, or what interesting adventures? The sycamores were gigantic trees, their smooth upper boughs shining chalk-white in the winter light. The forest floor was almost covered with a tall stand of dark green cane, where now and then he saw wild turkeys picking and scratching in the leaves. He watched how the little green parakeets at dusk poured by hundreds into hollows of old sycamores, some of which were big enough to have housed a horse and carriage in their lower parts. The parakeets evidently clung with their claws to the rough inner wood of the hollows.

Rozier and Audubon woke the next morning after their arrival to find their bivouac part of a busy community. A large encampment of Shawnees had arrived. This was the place where they came each year to harvest the big crop of pecans, as well as hunt the bears, deer, and raccoons which also were attracted to the nuts. Rozier was alarmed; he distrusted savages. Audubon perversely liked Indians and refused to call them savages, but natives. He spoke a little Shawnee and he was, besides, so friendly that the Indians, like most people, became fond of him at once and made him welcome.

They were eager to help him get specimens. The squaws set small traps for little animals, and when, in return for what they caught, he presented them with a knife, a pair of scissors, or some other trinket, they expressed their gratitude as gracefully as the most educated lady he had ever known.

Rozier was petulant. He brooded in gloomy silence on the boat, pining with ennui, irritated at being detained. He sometimes complained bitterly to the men of the other keelboat, but he never had any sympathy from Audubon. *He* liked it here.

Audubon woke one morning to find a stir of activity in the camp. A canoe with half a dozen squaws and the same number of hunters was about to leave the Illinois shore for the Kentucky side of the river to hunt wild swans. He could not miss this opportunity. They made room for him, and the canoe paddled quickly into the dawn-lit width of the Ohio from which mist rose over the whole surface, like a kettle simmering. The winter sun struck the steam with glints of gold and apricot that licked upward like pale flames across the entire river. The winter dawn had that early-morning turquoise and apple green, silent and cold and crystalline.

As the canoe started across the river, Audubon was privately amused and not at all astonished that the women manned the paddles while the hunters simply went to sleep until the canoe pushed into the congealing mud of the Kentucky bank. The squaws scrambled out and secured the boat, then went hunting for nuts. The hunters woke up. They and Audubon pushed their way through the tangle of cottonwood and willow saplings and half-frozen slough ponds to their goal, the lake where the swans gathered.

There were hundreds of the large white or rich cream-colored birds. They had paddled about on the lake all night to keep it from freezing, and there were so many of them that they almost whitened the surface. They were beautiful to see as they arched their necks and dipped their black beaks into the water, or leaned backward and gently rested with one leg extended. When the swans saw the Indians, they were immediately on the alert and swam toward the far shore. But the Indians had divided forces, half on each side, so that no matter where the swans turned, there were hunters behind the trees. Fifty whistling swans were killed that morning, birds whose skins would later be sold to the traders— delicate, snowy, swan-skins bound eventually for evening wraps for the fine ladies of Europe.

The shooting done, the men retired to rest from their exertions while the women came, dragging the canoe through the willows and weeds, to retrieve the birds. Back at camp after a supper of pecans and bear's fat, the women worked late while the men reclined by the fire and slept. Then, and perhaps only then, John James Audubon, writing the date in his journal, realized with a start what day it was: Christmas Day. He had spent it in the company of a party of Shawnees hunting swans, and had had nuts and grease for his Christmas dinner!

It was something to remember with pleasure. Coming back to the present, he shifted his position a trifle on the ridge above the grazing buffalo. The hunters were swinging in nearer for a shot. The larks sang in the distance, and he thought he heard a sparrow-like trill that was different, but in all that expanse of grass and sky and grasshopper-buzzing, he could not be sure or know exactly what he had heard.

His life had carried him far in search of birds. There had been the day when he was livelier and younger, when no strange bird-voice went unchallenged or unfound. He remembered how wonderful the birds had been in the live oak forests around Bayou Sara in Louisiana, when he took time from his teaching and went out to sketch birds; so many had come from there to fill his book. He remembered the flatboat trip down the Mississippi when he had found the white-headed eagle. Aboard the craft, he had managed to paint its portrait, downbound on the big river, and had caught its untamed and fierce eye almost exactly. He had felt at the time that his colors were not so clear and bright because he had had to dip up river water for his paints.

He remembered how anxious he had been, once he had exhausted the possibilities of lower Louisiana for birds, to get out into the semi-tropical world along the Florida coast and to the Keys and the Tortugas. It was not easy to find passage on a boat that would go where he wanted to go, and which he could afford. But miraculously he obtained passage on the Coast Guard cutter *Marion*. This had been perfect, for the *Marion* of necessity had to put in at odd points, probing the coastline and edging into the mangrove swamps to seek out the haunts of pirates and wreckers.

Audubon had spent all his waking hours on deck watching the ibises and spoonbills and herons and cormorants of this fascinating region. One of the birds he saw became a discovery of his own—the great white heron, bigger than an egret, a glorious snowy thing poised in the mangroves as the tide left the sticky flats. Through the kind offices of a wrecker, he had obtained a specimen.

His life had been studded and highlighted by these excursions, as well as by the people who had helped him attain his goals. His beloved Lucy and the boys had done much for him, had taken over the down-to-earth business and hard work of securing subscriptions for his book, and getting the plates engraved and published. As he grew older, he was more and more aware of and grateful for their concerted help, and for the aid of his good friend John Bachman, whose two daughters had married Audubon's sons; grateful for John Townsend and Thomas Nuttall who had brought back more than seventy wonderful western birds for him to paint when he could not get out there himself.

It had been his pleasure to name many of his discoveries after his friends. During his lifetime, however, he did not know that some birds he found and named so lovingly were not accepted as new species; some were even suspected as never having been seen at all. Yet he had not knowingly been dishonest. Birds were puzzles. There were the variations in individuals, the different plumages of females and immatures, the chance hybrids. How could a man know, especially when he was pioneering and had so little to guide him except his own instinct and luck?

He had much trouble with the immature yellow warbler. Thinking he had a new species, he named it Rathbone's warbler after a merchant in Liverpool whom he knew well. He named a bird for his friend Townsend—the Townsend bunting—which has never since been seen outside his plate. He painted the small-headed flycatcher, and so in fact did Wilson, but this bird has never been seen again. He painted a pretty little thing that looked something like a ruby-crowned kinglet on a handsome branch of mountain laurel, and he called it Cuvier's Regulus, in honor of the eminent naturalist, Baron Georges Cuvier. But no bird like this has ever been seen, nor has the carbonated warbler, which is known only from Audubon's plate Number 60, made from two specimens which he said he found in May, 1811, in Kentucky. No one has ever seen his bemaculated duck—it was probably a hybrid between the mallard and the gadwall. He could not know. He was not trying to be a nature faker; he painted what he found. The happiest days of his life were those on which he discovered a bird. But the splendid days of his youth, when almost every bird he found was a new one, had long gone. It now took work and travel to find a new species, if he was lucky.

In June, 1833, while his elder son Victor was in London carrying out the business of getting the *Birds of America* published, John James Audubon had sailed from Eastport, Maine, for new adventure in the north. With him he took his son, John, and four other young men—Dr. George Shattuck, Thomas Lincoln, William Ingalls, and Joseph Coolidge, all eager to collect birds, both for their own interest and for his uses in painting more bird portraits. He had chartered a schooner called the *Ripley*, for which he paid $1,500. He could afford it now.

There was rough weather for several days and Audubon was seasick, yet he could not stay below. Well bundled against the cold wind and spits of snow and gusts of rain, he dragged himself out on deck. He saw great black-backed gulls coasting by, saw Wilson's petrels and the islands that were pocked with their nesting holes, rocks and islands literally covered with white gannets, and the black guillemots and curious parrot-beaked puffins. As the ship came into the Gulf of St. Lawrence he saw the great Bird Rock where sea birds nested as thickly as snow on all the red sandstone ledges. He thought at first it really was snow that he was seeing.

I rubbed my eyes, took my spy-glass, and in an instant the strangest picture stood before me. They were birds we saw,—a mass of birds of such size as I never before cast my eyes on. The whole of my party stood astounded and amazed, and all came to the conclusion that such a sight was of itself sufficient to invite anyone to visit this place.

He had seen wonderful sights before—the egret rookeries in Florida, terns standing thick on the beaches of the Tortugas, pelicans white as snowbanks on Mississippi River sand bars—but nothing like this. Here was an island of birds. Every available ledge or space was occupied by the big white gannets sitting on their eggs

or guarding their newly hatched, fuzzy young. The heads of all
the adults were turned toward the ship as it surged through the
rough water, the yellow beaks, the suspicious pale eyes—a marvelous sight. The schooner bobbed and rolled so heavily that it was
difficult to keep the telescope on the birds. And as it came as close
as it dared, thousands of large white birds soared suddenly into the
air, turning so that their black wing-tips were sharp accents in
all that white, before the gannets swerved back to their ledges.

The black-green waves thundered in huge curling white comb-
ers over the rocks around the base of the island, and the pilot knew
it was too rough for him to attempt a landing. Although Audubon
was having a hard time with his stomach on the rough sea, he
almost forgot this physical distress when he learned that he would
not be able to land on this incredible island. The young men, seeing
disappointment on a face upon which all emotions were fluidly
revealed, and rather wanting to try to go ashore themselves, asked
the pilot about the possibility of putting out the whale boat for a
landing on the calmer side of the island. The pilot thought it could
be done. It would be risky, and he would not recommend that old
Mr. Audubon go, but the young men could if they wanted to
chance it.

The boat was put overboard in the heaving sea. Tom Lincoln
and John Audubon got in with their guns and clubs and sacks. They
would bring back some birds for the artist to paint. Audubon admonished them to be careful. If he were only younger! The ship
stood by. As the stench from the island blew through the damp air
—an odor comprised of the remains of putrid fish, rotten eggs,
dead birds, and excreta from thousands of large birds—it was in-
tensified in the moist and foggy day and was almost unbearable to
those waiting on the ship.

He grew worried about the boys; they were staying too long.
But eventually the whale boat came back on the swells, and everyone was safely aboard. The young men had their sacks filled with

gannets and puffins and kittiwakes and murres. It was treasure enough to keep him busy for several days at his drawing table under the big lamp in his cabin.

Rounding Anticosti Island, they came to the coast of Labrador, where he had a chance at last to go ashore. He had never seen a tundra before. The very walking here was different; it was a curious kind of terrain. In the spongy moss that covered almost every foot of earth, his feet sank so deeply that the soft cushion quite closed over them, and he had to drag them out again—wet— over and over, step by step. It became a wonderful relief to find a rock to rest upon. Over the tundra, with its dwarfed, wind-tattered spruces and its acres of hummocky sphagnum of the muskeg, its white tassels of cottony sedge waving in the wind, the very look of the land was almost terrifying. The clouds boiled low; they blackened and shadowed the great masses of bare, rugged rock, the bird-laden sea cliffs, and the dim, endless acres of the tundra itself.

Out here he found a brown sparrow with a gentle, tinkling song that echoed back and forth from spruce to spruce. He named it for his friend Tom, calling it Lincoln's sparrow, and wherever he saw it after that he would remember the grim, cold, exciting days along the coast of Labrador where he had found it first.

The trip was strenuous for Audubon. He went to bed exhausted every night. "I am growing old too fast," he mourned. "Alas! I feel it—and yet work I will, and may God grant me life to see the last plate of my mammoth work finished."

Now another ten years had gone by. His books were finished but he himself was far from ended. Needing another project, he decided on *Quadrupeds of North America* as a companion work to the birds. It would not be as extensive, not as large, but with the help of his family he might be spared long enough to complete it. His sons would help a great deal. John, who was excellent on the backgrounds, eventually painted a number of the mammals. John Bachman helped him obtain specimens, as did all his family and friends. And so here he was now, fifty-eight years old, lying on his elbows on the Montana plains! His long curling hair was white, and he was heavier, but how could he have thought that his strength was nearly gone ten years ago in Labrador! His eyes were still keen, his frame erect, his body strong. Strong enough to have come by steamer down the Ohio, up the Mississippi, up the Missouri, and now to lie here where the hard roots dug into his muscles, while his companions were about to kill buffaloes before his eyes.

The journey had begun with a good deal of excitement. He wrote back home from St. Louis, the jumping-off place:

Such a steamer as we have come in from Louisville—the very filthiest of all filthy old rat-traps I ever travelled in; and the fare worse, certainly much worse, and so scanty withal that our worthy commander could not have given us another meal had we been detained a night longer. . . . the "Gallant"—a pretty name, too, for as she struck a sawyer one night we all ran like mad to make ready to leap overboard; but as God would have it, our lives and the "Gallant" were spared—she from sinking, and we from swimming amid rolling and crashing hard ice. The LADIES screamed, the babies squalled, the dogs yelled, the steam roared, the captain (who, by the way, is a very gallant man) swore—not like an angel, but like the very devil—and all was confusion and uproar, just as if Miller's prophecy had actually been nigh.

Our *compagnons de voyage*, about one hundred and fifty, were composed of Buckeyes, Wolverines, Suckers, Hoosiers, and gamblers, with drunkards of each and every denomination, their ladies and babies of the same nature, and specifically the dirtiest of the dirty. We had to dip the water for washing from the river in tin basins, soap ourselves all from the same cake, and wipe the one hundred and fifty with the same solitary towel rolling over a pin, until it would have been difficult to say . . . whether it was manufactured of hemp, tow, flax or cotton. . . .

With him again were young men who were all ornithologists under his aegis; the wealthy Edward Harris, Isaac Sprague, Lewis Squires, and the celebrated taxidermist, John G. Bell. Reaching St.

Louis at last, thankful to have escaped the doubtful pleasures of the *Gallant*, Audubon saw to getting supplies for the expedition on which he hoped to secure mammals for his new work, while the younger men went on hunting expeditions into Illinois and Missouri. It was necessary for them all to wait until the ice went out of the Missouri before they could proceed up to Fort Union at the mouth of the Yellowstone in Dakota territory.

While he was in St. Louis, Mr. Audubon was entertained extensively; he was a celebrity and was treated as such. But even finer than the parties and friends and adulation was the first specimen for his mammal collection. He had been taken in a wagon to see old Mr. Pierre Chouteau who lived outside the city—and Mr. Chouteau had *pocket gophers* undermining his front lawn! They were downright pests, he declared, and Mr. Audubon was welcome to take them all. But Audubon wanted only a pair of these unique little beasts; he cherished them, carrying them back to St. Louis where he painted their portraits. They were, he felt, a good omen for his journey.

The steamer *Omega* took the party up the Missouri. Pushing against the brown flood, running aground on sand bars several times a day, stopping daily for wood and letting Audubon and his young men get off for brief excursions at the same time, the vessel moved up the river. Audubon wished that the times ashore were not so brief. For the shore and its marshes, its willows and patches of cottonwoods, were full of birds on their great northward migration. Singing, flying, calling, flashing colors, he thought he knew them all. But there was just the chance that somewhere ashore there was a bird he had not yet found, one new to science. Although the expedition was planned principally for him to obtain his quadrupeds, he was still instantly alert to birds. As the boat passed slowly upstream, almost brushing the willows in the bends, he stood at the rail and scanned the trees.

The Missouri was in a cantankerous mood. The boat grounded, floated off, grounded again, was stuck broadside; then as it shoved

1. Red-headed Woodpecker 2. Yellow bellied W. 3. Hairy W. 4. Downy W.

The red-headed woodpecker was the first American bird to be seen by
Alexander Wilson and was always one of his favorites, probably because
of this early association. Four woodpeckers are arranged on this page,
with the red-head in the center, the yellow-bellied sapsucker to the left,
hairy woodpecker to the right, and the downy woodpecker below, showing their comparative sizes.

Swallow-tailed Flycatcher.   Arkansaw Flycatcher.   Says Flycatcher.   Female Golden crested Wan.
Muscicapa forficata.   Muscicapa verticalis.   Muscicapa Saya.   Regulus Cristatus.

Titian Ramsey Peale, artist on the Yellowstone Expedition, painted portraits of the scissor-tailed flycatcher and golden-crowned kinglet, above, the Arkansas or western kingbird, bottom left, and Say's phoebe, right, August 24, 1820, Canadian Fork of the Arkansas River. (*American Ornithology*, Prince Charles Lucien Bonaparte, 1825.)

1. *Aulocus or Cliff Swallow.*
Hirundo fulva
2. *Burrowing Owl*
Strix Cunicularia

In Colorado, Thomas Say studied the burrowing owl and Peale painted its portrait, with the cliff swallow and its strange, flask-shaped mud nests plastered on a wall of rock. (*American Ornithology*, Bonaparte, 1825.)

These were Alexander Wilson's favorite woodpeckers: red-headed wood-pecker, lower right; pileated woodpecker, left; and the impressive ivory-billed woodpecker, top right. The latter was drawn from the captive bird which hacked a hole in the wall and ruined a mahogany table before Wilson had finished its portrait. (*American Ornithology*, Wilson, 1811.)

The first bird which John James Audubon ever painted, he recalled in his journals, was the belted kingfisher, when he was a youth in Pennsylvania. The plate above was no doubt painted years afterward when he had set about in earnest to depict the birds of America.

Carolina paroquets eating clot-bur seeds compose one of Audubon's more effective and beautiful paintings. The little bright green birds with their red and yellow heads—"the parrot with the sunrise on its head," as Du Pratz called it—were irresistible to the artist and a fascination to the naturalist. (*Birds of America*, Audubon, 1827–30.)

In honor of Prince Maximilian of Wied-Neuwied, Prussian naturalist who discovered it in Montana, this slate-blue bird was named Maximilian's jay. The specimen was painted by John Cassin for his *Illustrations of the Birds of California, Texas, Oregon, British and Russian America*, 1856.

PLATE VII

E.Lear del

Dr. William Collie, physician and naturalist on the voyage of the *Blossom* in 1828, collected birds from Mexico to the Arctic. The unique long-tailed, bright blue, Collie's magpie-jay honors an all but forgotten man. The portrait, painted by E. Lear in London, appeared in an account of birds of the voyage, by N. A. Vigors, 1839.

into deeper water, a wild storm blew across the bluffs and plains and struck the boat. There was wind and there was lightning, while rolling crashes of thunder reverberated from the clay hills. The boat, guided by the wind, went on to another sand bar, and there it stuck fast.

After the storm was over and the rain had ended, the boat was still stuck. There was plenty of time to go ashore. Edward Harris went into the dripping woods. He shot a small brown bird in the undergrowth and brought it back—and Audubon felt a delighted twinge of nostalgia. Here was his Lincoln's sparrow, named for young Tom who had been with him in Labrador ten years ago. The Lincoln sparrow in Kansas—"strange place for it, when it breeds so vary far north as Labrador."

Harris returned to his hunt. Bell, Squires, and Sprague were also ashore. Audubon, not wanting to get wet, stayed aboard. He could see almost as much by remaining on deck. The woods close by were alive with song as the sun came out after the rain. Then Harris returned again, and he held out something in his hand. He was in a poorly concealed state of excitement. He was ornithologist enough to know that no Audubon painting had ever shown the bird he brought. Audubon took it and examined it carefully. He had never seen one like this—this large finch with the black velvet head and throat, the white breast, the brown back and wings with their prominent streaking. The old thrill surged back. In his hand he held, incredibly, another new bird.

He painted its portrait that evening. Later they found these birds again and again as they migrated north. He was certain that he had a new species now. It had taken a grounded steamboat, a violent storm, the strange wild terrain of the river, and the help of his good friend to find it for him. So he named it for "the best friend I ever had"—Edward Harris, who had brought it to him on the steamer *Omega*, stuck on a sand bar in the Missouri River above Leavenworth, Kansas. And as Harris's sparrow it is still known today.

Later, on May 6, a chill and windy day, the men again went ashore. J. R. Bell followed a small, gabbling song which led him along a thicket in an attempt to see the singer. It was a tantalizing creature, singing and flitting along, and not showing itself. He finally cornered it and brought it back. He laid the tiny gray-green body on Audubon's drawing table.

The vireo was very small, without any prominent markings. He named it for the man who had found it—J. G. Bell. At Fort Union he found a bird which he named for Isaac Sprague—Sprague's pipit —but he evidently found none he wanted to name for the fourth member of the party, young Lewis Squires, who had been some-what temperamental and was hard to get along with at times.

Daily, as they proceeded up the Missouri, Audubon had been hearing a different sort of meadowlark song; it was not the familiar eastern meadowlark. From the boat he caught glimpses of the birds; they looked like the familiar sort. But the song was a beautiful con-tralto warble. Lewis and Clark had noticed it, but had done nothing more about it. No doubt Townsend and Nuttall heard it, too. But it waited for Audubon to distinguish between the eastern and the western meadowlarks and thus add still another species to his list.

At Fort Union, at the mouth of the Yellowstone River, the steamer let off all its passengers and departed downstream. With the fort as a base, the younger men ranged out on hunting trips, some as far as the mountains. But Audubon, feeling the rigors of the trip, feared to tackle so much adventure and did not go far from the fort at first.

Mr. Culbertson, manager of the fort, was sorry for him. There-fore, on a warm July day he arranged a buffalo hunt and invited Audubon to go along. He would make it as easy for him as possible, because he must not go back to civilization without taking part in a hunt. Audubon was as excited as a child; he was going to have his buffalo hunt after all!

The expedition set out with two wagons carrying baggage, as well as Mr. Culbertson and Mr. Audubon, while the younger men rode on horses. They traveled about fifty miles across the plains toward the mountains, where the three strange peaks called the *Trois Mamelles* stood up as landmarks.

He had seen buffaloes many times around the fort, but it was a different matter to go out now on their own level to shoot them. When he spied four bulls at a little distance, grazing, he felt his heart pound like that of a young man on his first hunt. It hurt him, it pounded so. They got down on the ground and lay there, resting on their elbows. They used the telescope to see the animals better; then they moved slowly forward with the wagons but were concealed by a ridge from the animals. The four hunters, including Harris, Bell and Squires, were ready; Audubon and the others inched their way through the locoweed and short-grass prairie vegetation to the crest of the ridge. The locusts buzzed. The rough ground hurt his elbows. He lay there, panting a little and watching.

There was a shot, and the first bull wheeled. Blood flowing from nose and mouth, it lunged toward the spot where Audubon and Culbertson lay, then fell dead at about sixty yards. They shot three; one escaped. Squires' horse, perhaps stepping into a prairie dog hole or frightened by a snake, bucked, and pitched its rider over its head fully ten feet. He landed on his powder horn. It knocked his wind for a moment, but he was up again yelling for Harris to catch his horse, then dropped down on the grass to recover his breath and strength.

Squires was out of the hunt. The others galloped after the fleeing bulls. It was over, suddenly, with three bloody animals lying inert and dark on the prairie. Culbertson and Audubon walked toward the one which had been about to charge them as they lay on the ridge. This, said Culbertson, must be Mr. Audubon's buffalo, and he should therefore have the honor of cutting off the tail-brush. He was proud as he cut off the tail and put it in his hat band. He felt it gave him quite an air, made him feel like a proper buffalo hunter.

They took the tongue and some choice cuts off the hump, and that was all right. But Audubon's stomach quite turned over when he saw Culbertson break open the skull of the first buffalo, dip into the brains with his hands, and eat them raw. Even Squires, recovered from his fall, bravely followed suit and so did most of the others, but this was a little too uncivilized for John James Audubon.

He had had enough of buffalo hunting. The appalling waste of life sickened him as much as the barbaric habits of the hunters. He could not reconcile the slaughter to the gains.

What a terrible destruction of life, as it were for nothing, or next to it, as the tongues only were brought in, and the flesh of these fine animals was left to beasts and birds of prey, or to rot on the spots where they fell. The prairies are literally *covered* with the skulls of the victims. . . . This cannot last; even now there is a perceptible difference in the size of the herds, and before many years the Buffalo, like the Great Auk, will have disappeared; surely this should not be permitted.

The excitement and disgust of the buffalo hunt had all but put out of his mind the discovery of still another bird. It was a pale, streaked sparrow found near the fort. He named it for his young friend back east, Spencer Fullerton Baird of Carlisle, Pennsylvania. This bird, found on July 26, 1843, was the last new species that John James Audubon ever discovered. It was, at the same time, exactly Plate Number 500 in his *Birds of America*, the last picture in the book.

There was a peculiar importance in this little bird that was named for Baird—the first, but not the last, to be named for this man. For Baird became one of the leading ornithologists of the mid-century, picking up the torch of ornithology as Audubon was putting it down, and bridging the period between the wilderness and the pioneer bird men and the scientific endeavors of the late nineteenth century. Baird knew and helped almost every one of the coming bird men in that period.

One day in November, 1843, a big man in a hunting coat with a large fur collar, a man with white curls hanging to his shoulders, long white whiskers on a sun-tanned face, and a gun in his hand, appeared at the gate of a large comfortable house outside New York City. The door opened, the family poured forth, he was enveloped with love and welcome. Audubon was home, and his adventures were finished. Eight years later he died.

CHAPTER TWELVE

PRINCE MAXIMILIAN
OF WIED

THREE men rode through the forest along the Wabash on a
fine day in early spring when anemones were blooming and
maple sap was dripping from broken twigs, along the muddy trail
between New Harmony and Mount Vernon, Indiana. They were
a curious trio, very far from home, heading now to board the
steamboat *Paragon* on the Ohio. One was a small, slight figure in a
large white felt hat, a rusty black velvet jacket that had seen a good
deal of use but was beloved for its roomy pockets and its imper-
viousness to burs, briars, and mosquitoes; and, as one observer said,
"probably the greasiest pair of trousers that ever encased princely
legs." He had no teeth; a large meerschaum pipe was almost always
in evidence.

This was Alexander Philip Maximilian, Prince of Wied-Neuwied,
naturalist and explorer, major-general in the Prussian Army, and
author of outstanding books on the natural history of Brazil. With
him was young Charles Bodmer, a German artist who had been
hired by the Prince to paint portraits of American Indians, wildlife, and landscapes. The third member of the party was Dreidoppel,
the Prince's devoted valet.

It was Dreidoppel's often despairing task to keep his master's white felt hat fairly clean, his clothes presentable, and his health good. Dreidoppel went wherever the Prince went, with a faithfulness and devotion that frequently took him into situations which terrified him and from which he fervently wished himself elsewhere. Dreidoppel had had some harrowing experiences in Brazil. Now he was in America, and although he was pleased to see a new country, he did not relish what lay ahead. He had heard altogether too many unsavory tales about the Indians of the West.

It was true that the winter had been pleasant and civilized enough. The three had been guests at the home of Thomas Say, where the wonderful libraries and cultural facilities of Robert Owen's vanished communal experiment still remained. The Prince had been enriched by the latest European books of science, as well as the original illustrations and copperplates of Viellot's American birds, and of Audebert's hummingbirds, flycatchers, and jacamars. The trio, sometimes accompanied by Say, who was not as spry as he had been on the Yellowstone Expedition, had gone hunting in the bottomlands along the Wabash; in studying the vegetation and birds, the Prince had had an enjoyable winter.

They boarded the waiting *Paragon* at Mount Vernon, which steamed to the confluence with the Mississippi, started up that river, and promptly stuck on a sand bar. Delays of this sort pleased the Prince. But the steamboat itself terrified Dreidoppel; he always had visions of fires, explosions, and sinkings in the great Mississippi.

Reaching St. Louis on a cold March day, they were met and entertained by General William Clark, who was now Indian agent of the area. Maximilian was delighted to meet this man to whom adventure had called. He had read and pored over the accounts of the Lewis and Clark expedition, had longed to come out to do the same thing. Now he was here, and Clark himself could help him attain the rest of the goal. The Prince was grieved to learn, when he inquired about him, that poor Captain Meriwether Lewis had, only a few years after the journey, chosen to shoot himself in the head—in a fit of despondency, some said. Clark, who knew his friend so well, privately told the Prince that he suspected Lewis had been waylaid and murdered at the inn near Nashville where he had been staying. But it was too long ago now to prove anything. Lewis was dead, whether killed by a bandit or by his own hand.

Maximilian had expected to join a "caravan," as he called it, probably a company of soldiers or fur men, or both, heading overland to the Rocky Mountains. He knew that St. Louis was the place where these expeditions were outfitted, and whence they set off into the land of the Indian and the buffalo. They would be just the ones with whom to throw in their lot so that he could study Indians and collect birds. In order to do so, the Prince tried to secure passports for his party from General Clark. Clark was shocked at the naive request.

This was not, he explained carefully, exactly the way to go about the touchy business of studying the American aborigines, who were not usually of a placid nature when white men invaded their territory. The Plains Indians, in particular, were far more likely to attack a caravan and kill everyone in it, than to submit to being studied and measured by the scholarly Prince, or to sit for their portraits by the talented Bodmer. He could not, in fact, permit their going. He would suggest, however, that the Prince and his party go instead on the steamer *Yellowstone*, which was departing for the American Fur Company's post on the upper Missouri. There he could have a base of operation at one of the forts. He would have protection, yet a degree of freedom to range out on expeditions, especially if the Indians were in a peaceable mood; and from the boat he could see a good deal of the country. It was a route which in retrospect was particularly pleasant to Clark.

Prince Maximilian set off up the Missouri on April 10, 1833, ten years before Audubon was to embark from the same place, for the same goal. Audubon, in fact, slept in the same bed at Fort Union which Maximilian occupied. It was twenty-nine years since Lewis and Clark had led the way. The adventure was all unutterably exciting, and the Prince had a great treasure to accompany and inspire him. General Clark had given him a manuscript map copied from one made by Lewis and Clark on their journey. It was a cherished item and used constantly, for there were as yet no other maps for the Missouri. By this means, Maximilian could identify where he was, name the streams and the forts, locate the Indian tribes and the mountains.

Twelve days later the steamboat reached Fort Leavenworth, and ten days after that came to the place now called Omaha, Nebraska, where at the time the Omaha Indians had their village. All this while Maximilian had been eager to see buffalo, but they had been strangely absent until May 18, when to his extreme delight at their size and numbers darkening the prairies, he saw the herds at last. It was a great moment in his life.

At Fort Pierre, up in the land of the Sioux, the *Yellowstone* let off its passengers to board the *Assiniboine*, a newer and larger boat which could travel on the shallows of the upper Missouri with greater ease and safety than the deeper-draught *Yellowstone*. The latter returned to St. Louis, and Dreidoppel may have rather wistfully watched it go.

For two weeks the oddly assorted trio stayed at Fort Union near the mouth of the Yellowstone, then proceeded by keelboat to Fort McKenzie on Maria's River in the Blackfoot country and the mountains. The Prince's two-months' stay here was filled with excursions into Montana and the Rockies. He studied the Blackfeet, the Gros Ventres, and the Assiniboines. Bodmer painted portraits of any Indian he could induce to sit for him; he painted the landscape, the animals, the birds. The Prince went out every day, especially during the cooler hours of morning, to look for birds. There were none familiar to him, none like those in Germany or Brazil, or those he had found in Indiana. He was finding the birds which Lewis and Clark had seen—the magpies, the black-headed jays, the Louisiana tanager, as brilliant as anything in Brazil. The Prince at times wished he might be privileged to find a bird that was new to science. It would be a way in which he could leave a mark of immortality in America—a bird never before seen or described by all those earlier hawk-eyed American ornithologists.

But autumn was approaching, and it was time to leave Fort Mc-Kenzie before he was trapped there for the winter. Maximilian had been busy for days collecting specimens to take back with him. He had hundreds of plants and with Dreidoppel's expert help had pressed them carefully between papers. He had bird skins and mammal skins, and in cages there were two large, live bears which he hoped he could transport back to Germany. He also had a prairie dog in a small cage.

A barge had been built for him by the fort's carpenter, which he had thought would be ample for all his collections. But as they were being loaded, the Prince began to wonder if he would get them all aboard. He needed to take a supply of food, too, to feed the twenty-one men from the fort who were going to guide the barge down to the Missouri for him. When a party of Gros Ventres contributed eighteen horse-loads of fresh buffalo meat, he found that this also took a good deal of space; so did the men themselves, not to mention the cages with the bears, the bedding and kitchen equipment, the collections, the boxes. He wished he had asked for a barge twice the size.

By noon on September 14 everything was loaded. The bear cages —he never identified the species—were put on top of the cargo in the middle of the boat, but this arrangement prevented the men from passing from one end of the craft to the other. There was just not enough room for all to sleep on board, a most unfavorable circumstance, the Prince thought, because this meant they would always have to sleep on shore, at the mercy of Indians and wild animals.

Everyone at Fort McKenzie came down to the landing for the impressive departure. They brought a cannon for a farewell salute, which Maximilian, his white felt hat pressed firmly down on his brow, thought was a touching gesture. He was sorry for all the people at the fort who would have to spend the long winter there.

The manager's wife was a handsome Indian princess who had quite taken the German Prince's fancy with her expert riding and way of life. He rather wished he could show her off in Germany. What a sensation!

The barge proceeded easily downstream, moved ponderously around the bends of the high cliffs and past the mouth of Maria's River. Near this point they watched a herd of antelope flashing their white signals in rapid departure, saw deer, many birds, especially Lewis and Clark's jays, and sparrow hawks. And there was another bird. . . .

The party had paused for a belated lunch at two o'clock. Maximilian saw the bird swoop down to the ground, but unfortunately did not have his gun handy; besides he was rather involved in cutting off pieces of tough buffalo meat so he could masticate them with his toothless jaws. But one of the men saw the bird and brought it to him. The prince at once put aside his knife and examined this dark gray-blue bird which had a certain silvery cast to the feathers. It was of the jay family, he thought, one of the Corvus kind. He could not recall having seen it on any of Viellot's plates, or in Catesby's, or Audubon's, neither could he remember anything like it in Lewis and Clark's discoveries. He began to grow more excited and a light shone in his face as he realized that this must, indeed, be a new bird, *his* new bird. Without really seeking, he had found it.

It was the pinyon jay (as it was called much later) and it had been seen before, almost in this very same place, by Lewis and Clark. They had mentioned having found a dark blue bird of the Corvus family, but they had not collected it or commented further. Prince Maximilian of Wied-Neuwied, therefore, had had to come halfway across a world to find it and to give it a name:

. . . this bird, which is nearly allied to the jay, or the roller, has not yet been mentioned by either Townsend or Audubon. In the form of bill, its figure, and mode of living, it much resembles the nutcracker; only the nostrils are not covered with bristles, like those of the jay and crow, but lie quite free on the fore part of the skin of the nose. . . .

As this bird seems to form a new genus, from the above-mentioned peculiarity, I call it Gymnorhinus cyano cephalus.

For many years it was appropriately known as Maximilian's jay, but because it eats the seeds of pinyon pine, this name has now been dropped in favor of pinyon jay. Maximilian's name, however, is still appended to the Latin name as the bird's discoverer.

The journey back was filled with mishap and with comedy that was not funny at the time. At the place where they had found the new jay, they camped for the night. A storm was brewing dark over the mountains, and the weather looked increasingly ugly. About four o'clock in the afternoon the tempest broke furiously out of dark, boiling clouds. The wind and rain and thunder and lightning were awe-inspiring. In addition to the worriment caused by the storm and a possible rise in the river, the men were fearful of Indians who lately had been unpleasantly hostile. The party did not want to stay here; they had to make the best of it, however, by being as quiet as possible and posting a continuous guard.

But the storm had disturbed the bears who, "unusually dissatisfied with their confinement . . . manifested their feelings by moaning and growling, which might very easily have attracted some hostile visitors." There was no way in which to muffle the unhappy animals, especially after the noise of the storm passed and the rain continued in an echoing calm, punctuated by the bears' loud complaints. Dreidoppel was most uneasy, and Prince himself didn't care for the situation.

The party passed an uncomfortable night. They had stayed crowded on the boat for fear of attack. The wet and cramped conditions and the intermittent racket of the bears made it impossible to get much sleep. The next morning things were in a dreadful plight. The men were wet and numb with the cold, and on the unprotected deck all the baggage was soaked through. Water had gathered in the hold. The bears were soggy and miserable; the unfortunate prairie dog had drowned in its cage. The buffalo robes he was taking back to Germany were wet, and so were the botanical specimens and the bird skins.

The party pushed on, however, before doing anything about the situation, until they could land at the mouth of the Yellowstone on the Missouri where the shores were safer. Here they built a large camp fire and spread out the wet items in an attempt to dry them. The bears groaned; their soaked fur stank. They licked themselves, and groaned again. One of the Frenchmen, in an attempt to be helpful to science, shot a skunk on shore, thinking the Prince might want it; its stench did not add to the merriment of the day. Dreidoppel muttered Prussian imprecations that he had not needed since the war against Napoleon. Even the usually imperturbable Prince was upset.

Laboriously, they unpacked everything—the baggage, the chests, the boxes. The large chests which had been made for him at the fort had swelled in the water and burst their joints. They were useless. But what afflicted the Prince most was the loss of the fine botanical specimens which, with much care and no little personal danger, in view of the Indian situation, he had obtained and pressed. All the papers on which they were mounted were soggy, and there was no more to remount them. The Indian costumes he was bringing back were already turning moldly. They smelled rank and horrible.

The only thing to do, to save as much as he could, was to camp where they were and spread things carefully out to dry. A wind rose and sent the drying items flying. Soon the prairie was covered with scattered effects; Dreidoppel and Bodmer chased after them while Maximilian skipped distractedly hither and to in pursuit of some cherished bit which the prairie wind was tossing about. He rescued most of his herbarium, and because the wind was so impossibly strong as an aftermath of yesterday's storm, he had to lay out the specimens in the shelter of a ravine. This took him all day, yet even so all the plants became black and moldy. It was a great grief to him—so much work and planning, and all lost.

With what he could salvage, he finally reached Fort Clark, about three-quarters of a mile below Fort Mandan, where Lewis and Clark had spent the winter of 1804–05. Here he was pleased to meet an elderly French-Canadian named Toussaint Charbonneau— none other than old Charbonneau himself, who had traveled with Lewis and Clark to the coast.

Charbonneau was very proud of what he considered his part in the expedition, though in reality he had not been of very much use. He had malingered and complained, had given wrong directions, and had been of little help as an interpreter or as anything else. His wife, Sacajawea, had been the indispensable one. Yet now, years later, he made himself out to be a celebrated character without whom the expedition would have failed. It had sustained and given him stature.

Sacajawea, Charbonneau told Maximilian, had left him. She had been married twice after that. Clark himself had educated her son, of whom he had grown fond on the expedition, as well as the little girl who had been born later. Charbonneau complained of the desertion, and the Prince, a naive sort who believed everything he heard, sympathized. He drew him out and listened with eagerness to the far-fetched tales Charbonneau related of the trip. He took the talkative old man into his party for some time as an interpreter, and wrote down everything he said, including a great deal of misinformation which Charbonneau passed off as solemn truth.

Prince Max, Dreidoppel, and the energetic Bodmer spent the long winter on the upper Missouri. They filled their time with a careful and detailed study of the Indians, chiefly the Mandans and Arikarees and Minitarees. It was with considerable relief to Dreidoppel when the whole party finally set off in the spring, bound for civilization and home.

Their collections, now much increased, and still including the two bears, were to follow on the steamer *Assiniboine* and go on directly from St. Louis down the Mississippi to New Orleans, thence by ship to Germany. But after their departure the *Assiniboine* ran aground and caught fire. All those carefully amassed collections of the German Prince were lost, and the bears were, too. Few of the specimens from Maximilian's journey ever reached Wied-Neuwied in Rhenish Prussia, but his notebooks did, and so did Charles Bodmer's beautiful drawings, which became the illustrations for the published journals. The skins of some of the birds evidently were safe, too, including that silvery-blue bird called Maximilian's jay.

CHAPTER THIRTEEN

TOWNSEND, NUTTALL, AND THE WESTWARD TRAIL

THE West called. Many men, following the trail of Lewis and Clark, of Long and Pike and Maximilian, answered that call to explore the dangerous country beyond the Mississippi. There was so much promise, often so little reward. There were usually only hardship and punishment and hunger, and sometimes death in its more hideous forms. After the stories came back relating the calamities that befell some of them, the wonder was that other men went at all. But there was a bravado, the eternal feeling, perhaps, of "it can't happen to me." So they packed up their inadequate supplies and set off with their inadequate knowledge, into an unknown land where Indians were fierce and full of hatred, where food supplies were unreliable or entirely lacking, and where the very terrain was an endless menace. Men with enthusiasm and undying excitement for adventure went west, and they found birds.

One of those who heard the call of the western wilderness was John Kirk Townsend, a member of the Academy of Natural Sciences in Philadelphia. He was an ornithologist of great enthusiasm and a good deal of physical energy. With him went the man few understood or knew well, the shy and withdrawn Thomas Nuttall.

Nuttall seemed to dislike people, or to be afraid of them—one could not be sure. He preferred being by himself, studying, or taking long excursions. He had gone alone to explore the Arkansas River country and, as ornithologist and botanist, had brought back many new finds. He had published two volumes on birds, in 1834; and in that same year he was persuaded by John Townsend to come long on a birding expedition to the Northwest.

Although Nuttall might have felt that he had completed his work on birds, he was even more vitally interested in botany. Thinking of the unknown lands and unknown plants in the Columbia River country, he could not resist. Townsend would collect birds; he had promised his friend Audubon to bring back new species for him to paint; and Nuttall would attend to the botanizing. Those who knew him best—they were not many—were astounded that the retiring Mr. Nuttall should actually go with a caravan of people to the West Coast.

The pair made arrangements to join Captain Nathaniel Wyeth's group going out of St. Louis in the spring of '34, bound for the Columbia River with settlers and a party of missionaries with their cattle.

On the evening of March 24, Townsend and Nuttall disembarked at St. Louis from the steamboat that had carried them from Pittsburgh and prepared for their big adventure. They made contact with Captain Wyeth, who took them next day to an outfitting store so that they might buy some of the needed equipment together. This included, among other items, several pairs of leather pants, enormous overcoats made of green blanketing material, and white wool hats with round crowns—hats that would fit tightly to the head and had brims five inches wide. Townsend declared that this sort of headgear was hard enough to resist a rifle ball, if need be, and sturdy enough to withstand a hurricane. With one of these secured to his skull, he had no fear of being scalped by an Indian—the Indian could never dislodge it from his head.

After the equipment had been purchased and put in Captain

Wyeth's charge, the eager pair set off. They disliked St. Louis; they had had all they wished of cities for some time and could not wait to get started on their westward jaunt. They therefore decided to go ahead of the party, who would be coming by steamer up to Independence, Missouri, to finish outfitting for the overland trail. The two would walk to Independence and collect specimens at leisure along the way. The steamer would bring their gear so that they could travel light. Captain Wyeth may have given a significant look at his companions as the two naturalists declared their intentions, but he was helpful and assured them that he would bring their things and would meet them at Independence. He watched them trudge out of St. Louis. It was three hundred miles to Independence.

It was delightful early-spring weather when they set out, though Thomas Nuttall was unhappy because the flowers were not yet out. But he and Townsend, heads in the air, breathing deeply, watched the flights of sandhill cranes passing northward, found pileated woodpeckers in the oak woods near St. Charles, saw hundreds of plovers on the prairie. They traveled slowly, stopping where they wished, pausing at farm houses to ask a drink of water and often being invited to stay to supper or for the night. Then hard spring rains and resultant prairie mud slowed them down. Travel in the next few days was distinctly difficult and unpleasant. Independence suddenly seemed inordinately far away, and each may have privately regretted being so rash as to have foregone a ride.

They were in the river woods watching flocks of parakeets, and resting out of the mud, when they heard a steamboat whistle signaling for the landing at Boonville. With complete delight they discovered that it was the steamer on which Captain Wyeth was a passenger, with their wilderness equipment. It was the answer to prayer! They had had enough of walking in Missouri mud, and thankfully they embarked to ride the rest of the way to Independence. There they completed their outfitting, bought horses, and joined the rest of the party, fifty of them, as well as the five missionaries and their horned cattle, all eager to get started to the west.

"As we rode out from the encampment, our horses prancing, and neighing, and pawing the ground, it was altogether so exciting that I could scarcely contain myself," said Mr. Townsend.

In the broad prairies and extensive marshes, the naturalists saw with delight the yellow-headed blackbirds glistening in the spring sunlight as they teetered on old reed stalks, spreading their glossy jet tails and wings and bending forward their glorious orange-gold heads to utter their unmusical screeks and calls that passed for songs. Larks caroled; hawks drifted over. It was the best of all days for starting adventure.

That night a storm brewed, and by next day the wind was racing in gusts over the prairies; rain was beating at a slant with violent lightning and loud thunder. While the party tried to find some sort of shelter—willows and cottonwoods as yet had no leaves and provided poor cover—a tremendous hailstorm fell from the low clouds. On the unprotected prairie with nowhere to run, this was serious. Townsend had not quite realized how it would be out here in the great open West—so *very* open. Torrents of hail the size of musket balls peppered and hammered and banged. The horses were terrified. They panicked, plunged, kicked, threw their loads, and dashed high-tailed and wildly neighing over the prairie. There was no place for them to go. The hail was everywhere.

When it was over, and the skittery animals were at last rounded up, the exuberant spirits of the caravan had been somewhat subdued. The wet blankets in which everyone had to sleep also served as a sobering influence. But wet blankets became a common occurrence, and Townsend wryly reminded Nuttall of what Townsend's worried grandmother had admonished them before they had set off for western adventure. "Now, boys," she had said, "take care *never, never* to sleep in damp beds!"

After the storm, spring really blossomed over the plains. Nuttall was wild with the beauty of prairie flowers. By the time the party had reached the Platte River, flowers were everywhere, in great swaths and beds and lakes of color. Even the other men of the caravan exclaimed at the sight of acres of wild pink phlox and shooting star, white star-grass and yellow puccoon and violets, and the pale lavender-blue of the camas lily or wild hyacinth.

Nuttall was in a transport of delight. He was in some rarefied atmosphere of communion with nature, with ecstasy quite apart from reality. He rode on ahead of the company and anxiously got down to clear a trail for the oncoming horses, putting aside the flowers with a trembling and eager hand and looking worriedly at the approaching party as if he feared the horses would come before he had finished collecting and trample his blossoms. It was three beautiful, flowery miles through this ravine near what is now Scott's Bluff, Nebraska, before they came out to grass and sand near the Platte again. Nuttall had lingered far behind, still frantically collecting, and finally, breathless but happy, caught up.

Along the Platte that day one of the men caught a baby antelope, a charming little creature whose mother was nowhere about. An expedition was certainly no place to carry a pet, especially a wild one like this, all legs and life, but the men adored the little thing, and it soon was so tame that it would drink milk from a tin cup—milk contributed from one of the missionaries' cows. The men named the pet "Zip Coon," and it came running when called. Someone made a willow basket for it and tied it on the back of one of the mules. When the camp moved from its nightly rest in the morning, the little antelope danced about on rubber-toed bounces to its station beside the mule, then bleated and squeaked with impatience to be lifted in.

When they had been traveling for days over barren plains, they came at last to magnificent cottonwoods and willows growing at the edge of the Platte. This was heaven for the naturalists. They knew they did not dare ask for extra time to collect in terrain like this, with Indians near. Yet they could not bear to leave without getting everything they possibly could find and take. Nuttall and

Townsend were up before dawn next day, just as the first birds were wakening and calling in the cool, pre-dawn light. The wet cottonwoods were full of birds. The two left the sleeping camp and strolled through the woods, breathing the glorious, bracing air. Their guns rang out again and again. They had to shoot—there was no other way to prove what they had seen, or to bring back specimens for museums and for Audubon.

Townsend couldn't remember where he had ever seen so many different kinds of birds in so small a space—vireos and warblers and tanagers and finches and orioles. All were beautiful, he said, and many were new to him. His game bag was full, but the woods extended tantalizingly farther and farther. He hated to go back, yet he knew they must. They had been gone more than an hour, the camp would be stirring, and they must be back for breakfast and in time to make ready to leave. Nevertheless, he knew that he had at least one brand-new bird, a long, sleek gray bird with streaked breast and pale eye, later known as the sage thrasher. Its songs had been part of that morning of many songs, in which the music of birds unknown to Townsend and Nuttall had stood out distinctly.

Several times in his ardor Townsend was left behind. On June 19 they arrived at the Green River and camped on the bank. It was still broad daylight. He ate a hasty meal—in his journal he does not tell where Nuttall was just then—and hurried out with his gun to roam the neighborhood for several hours before dark. It was delightful and quiet, the sky still suffused with light.

When he returned to the camp toward evening, it was not there. He had the right spot. He was sure of this. The horse dung showed where fifty beasts had been hobbled. As he approached, several coyotes loped off, and ravens and magpies got up clacking from where they had been scavenging remains of the camp's meal. But no one was about. He could not understand it. They could not have gone off and left him stranded, and there was no sign of any attack. He was on foot and was growing worried when he heard a neigh in the bushes. His own horse was carefully tied there, the saddle on the ground nearby. He was thankful for that; evidently no mishap had come to the camp; they must simply have gone off to another place, and had thoughtfully left him his horse. Probably Nuttall had seen to that.

But if he was to locate them that night, he would have to work fast while he still had some daylight. He knew that the alluvial banks of the river would show hoofmarks, and he could follow them easily. His horse seemed to know where to go; it took off at a gallop along the river bank for fully half an hour. Townsend had to watch the low-hanging limbs of the cottonwoods to keep from being decapitated in his horse's rush. The animal came to a halt, snuffling the trail. Horses had entered the river at this point. There were tracks farther down, too, but Townsend decided that the crossing must be here and urged his steed to enter the water. The animal waded in cautiously, then with a great surge and splash went over its depth—the bank went straight down and this was no fording place at all. He turned the horse's head against the swift current and the animal swam, snorting and blowing and paddling hard for the opposite shore. Townsend was soaked. But in a few minutes he was on the opposite bank, and not far down the river he found the new camp.

Captain Wyeth blandly explained that he had decided to move to this more favorable location because there was better pasture for the horses, and added that there was a good fording place some fifty yards below where Townsend had gone in too deep. Townsend didn't mind this, however; it was a warm evening. Then he discovered that his coat was missing. He had been warm when he mounted and had attached his coat to the saddle. When the horse submerged, the coat must have floated off. He didn't mind that loss so much; it was an old coat and well used. But in the pockets had been the second volume of his journal, a compass, and other items of great value to him. The book, especially, was a hard loss; he would have given everything else if he could have retrieved that book. It contained his notes, ornithological data and all, from the Black Hills to the present place. Fortunately Nuttall had his own journal and could supply some of the items, but he felt unhappy about the loss. A traveler's journal, he said, is his most priceless possession.

By the time they came into the pine forests of the Montana mountains, he was finding many new specimens for Audubon, as well as for the excitement and delight of the two naturalists themselves. Days were not long enough for everything they wanted to see. They found with pleasure the birds which had been discovered by Lewis and Clark and took some back for Audubon.

Travel grew difficult. One day they had an encounter with a grizzly bear, in which the animal came off the loser. Then, up on the precipitous trail, the mule carrying the baby antelope in its basket slipped and fell, and the antelope broke its leg. The little thing had to be put to death and everyone was sorry. They might readily and without any qualms have devoured as food any antelope shot by the party for this purpose, but little Zip Coon was different; he had been one of them. They somehow craved pets in this violent, wild land. For a time they had a young grizzly bear named Ephraim, but he was much too snappish and cross for a satisfactory pet.

Townsend thought that he would like a pet buffalo. He actually managed to capture a large bull calf one day and with considerable difficulty contrived to drag it back, the calf objecting and holding back and digging the dirt at every step. He had attached a rope from the calf's neck to the high pommel of his saddle. Finally, panting, the horse in a lather, he reached the camp with his pet. There he pounded a heavy stake into the ground and fastened the rope around it. But the young buffalo kicked and tugged and bucked, and broke his fastenings. He stormed out of the camp, blatting in disgust as he high-tailed it for the herd and his mother. Townsend tore after his pet and promptly stumbled and fell flat in a muddy ditch. He got up and continued after the buffalo, finding him where the rope had become entangled quite hopelessly in some oak scrub. He ran up, grabbed the rope—and was knocked down by the irritated animal, who had had all he was going to take. With his hard, tight-curled forehead he butted his captor firmly in the chest and left him breathless on the ground. Then the calf stood back snuffling heavily and rolling his eyes till the bloodshot whites showed. Saliva drooled in a long stream from his lips. He was braced to butt again as soon as Townsend got to his feet.

Townsend lay there, watching the animal warily, waiting for the next move; then, still holding the rope, he eased himself slowly to his knees, to his feet, watching the rebellious calf. He tugged gently on the rope. The animal did not budge. Then he got behind and shoved on the buffalo's rump. The calf moved a little but held his ground. Finally, with an unutterable amount of pushing and pulling, Townsend again got his buffalo back to camp. But the infant would not be tractable. He butted anyone who came near, would not eat, and in general caused so much trouble that next morning Townsend turned the animal loose and watched him gallop away over the barren ridge.

The expedition pushed on more slowly now, often painfully in the stretches full of prickly pear cactus. As they left the buffalo country, food became scarce. Game of any sort was taken in desperation, whenever it could be found, and the men were never really filled. So needed was any sort of sustenance that it was difficult even to preserve a bird as a specimen. It was always looked at with hungry eyes, and Townsend knew he would lose it if he didn't skin it at once, then let the carcass be added to the pot. Sometimes it happened that he wasn't quite fast enough. Even his scientific friend, Nuttall, who he expected was above such things, and who wouldn't have thought of devouring his own cherished specimens even if he were starving, was caught in this contradictory act.

There had been little enough the night before. There was nothing at all for breakfast. Townsend had been out early and had shot a small owl which was new to him. He brought it back to camp and concealed it among his gear, intending to show it to Nuttall when he woke. Between them they might identify it. Then he went for a walk with the hope of finding something edible. When he recalled some of his dear grandmother's sumptuous breakfasts, not to mention her dinners and suppers, he wondered what he was doing here in a land beset with stark hunger. Then he would remember the birds he had found for science, and decided he could suffer a little.

In Nuttall's absence, he strolled along the stream back of camp and made a meal of sorts on wild rose buds. There were no birds, and it had apparently not occurred to him to eat the new owl. Full of rose buds but not really satisfied, he walked back to camp. There he found Captain Wyeth and Thomas Nuttall squatting beside a small fire. They were sucking the leg bones of a bird they had cooked. They had obviously not left any for him, and they had a guilty, cat-in-the-cream look when they saw him. As a horrid suspicion came into his mind he went hastily to check on his owl. It was missing. Its feathers, entrails, and head were in the bushes not far away. His new owl had lost its chance for immortality in the annals of science. Audubon would never paint this one! Hunger was too great even for a naturalist as dedicated as Thomas Nuttall to withstand; and to Captain Wyeth a bird was a bird. After that John Townsend took better care of his specimens.

The wet weather of the Northwest Pacific Coast descended on them as the expedition moved in canoes down the Columbia toward its ultimate goal at Fort Astoria. Day after day it rained; and, as if this were not enough, several of the canoes were upset in the rapids. The bales of specimens were soaked. The party made camp in the wind and driving rain. Nuttall was desperate at the state of his cherished specimens—before the expedition was over, he collected more than five hundred plants that were new to science. Now these that he had were soaked. As the rain ended, the job of drying out the papers containing the specimens was tedious and long. He had to open the packages and lay out the papers before an enormous fire, smoothing, drying them gently, rearranging them, specimen by specimen, nearly a thousand of them, while the great drops of perspiration rolled down his brow and his heart was filled with worry.

Townsend's bale of bird skins had been wetted, too, but they were easier to dry, though the atmosphere was so humid that he feared the skins and feathers might mold and spoil. The diligent efforts of the pair, however, remedied most of the damage, and the expedition continued down the Columbia to Fort Astoria near the coast. All the way, Townsend was amassing a growing store of information about western birds. To his collection of specimens for Audubon, he had added the common bush-tit, the chestnut-backed chickadee, Vaux's swift, the black-throated gray warbler, Audubon's warbler, the Oregon junco, green-tailed towhee, and many more, while Nuttall himself was finding species which were hitherto unknown.

Before they departed from Fort Astoria, Townsend was out on a walk when he heard a new song among the rocks and trees behind the fort. He followed the song, wondering; it was a dreamy, involved sort of melody, almost like that of a mockingbird, yet not that at all. It had a high-country sound, remote and pure and a little melancholy, with carefuly spaced phrasing. Stumbling, head up and scanning the trees, he climbed a rugged slope of rocks to where a dead cedar clung with most of its roots exposed and lichens thick and damp upon it in a gray-green upholstering.

In the top of the gray tree a gray bird sang—long tail down, beak in air. He called it the mountain mockingbird, but later it was given a more appropriate name, honoring the man who discovered it in its mountain haunts: Townsend's solitaire.

By September 17, 1834, they had reached the coast, collecting extensively from Fort Astoria to Fort Vancouver. The two then took passage on a ship bound for Hawaii. After their memorable experiences in this amazing land, they sailed for home and returned around Cape Horn with their cherished specimens.

Townsend and Nuttall happily presented to John James Audubon more than seventy birds that he had never seen before; they had brought him a magnificent treasure. The journey may have had its ludicrous moments, its uncomfortable ones, its hungry days; but Townsend had done a great thing for American ornithology, just as the indefatigable Nuttall had brought the beauty of prairie and mountain and Northwest Coast to the knowledge of the botanists.

In that same decade, more West Coast birds were added to the American catalogue when H.M.S. *Blossom*, under the command of Captain Beechey, cruised in a leisurely manner up the Pacific Coast, touching here and there up to and around Alaska. Captain Beechey mapped the sea route and shore line to Point Barrow, and left his mark in a map studded with places which he named *Beechey* and *Blossom*. He did not take with him one of the recognized naturalists, but his ship's physician, Dr. Collie, was much interested in birds. Wherever the ship stopped, the doctor hurried ashore. He was a careful collector; he wrote brief descriptions of birds, but was especially detailed in their anatomy and structural distinctions and peculiarities. The specimens were sent to Mr. N. A. Vigors, an English ornithologist, who studied them and then wrote about them in a brief volume, illustrated with plates drawn by several English artists and engravers. The collection, Vigors complained, was well enough in its way, but it was inconclusive. The birds had been picked up here and there, one at this port, one in another, sometimes widely separated. They had little value in telling anything connected about the wildlife of the West Coast of America and Mexico; they were only specimens, and he was rather scornful about it.

Nevertheless, Dr. Collie and Captain Beechey found some birds which neither Lewis and Clark, nor Townsend and Nuttall had found. At Monterey, California, the doctor, walking among the big pines, heard a small squeaking and a concerted, lowpitched chattering in the trees. He discovered troops of tiny gray and brown birds scouring the bark with a most minute attention, and going up, down, and sidewise with equal ease and aplomb. They were nut-hatches, the smallest in America. Finding the pygmy nuthatch was one of the accomplishments of Beechey's voyage in the good ship *Blossom.*

Another find was the strikingly beautiful black phoebe, which they discovered along the coastal cliffs where wild fuchsias hung thousands of carmine and purple pendants among dark green leaves with waxen red stems. The California jay was new. So were Beechey's jay, and a magnificent, long-tailed, long-crested, blue and white creature named for the doctor himself—Collie's magpie-jay—both of which were long believed to have been found in California but which had been collected in Mexico.

But not Lewis and Clark, nor Captain Cook, nor Townsend and Nuttall, nor Collie and Beechey in the Northwest, nor Swainson and Viellot and Bonaparte who collected in Mexico, had found all the birds of the American West. They had only opened more doors and trails to the naturalists who would follow.

One who took to the westward trail, in emulation of Townsend and Nuttall, was a young physician named Dr. William Gambel, aged twenty-two. It was that semi-recluse, Thomas Nuttall, who advised him to go to the Southwest to look for birds. Gambel set off in 1841 on a walking trip, following the Santa Fe Trail all the way to New Mexico and California. On an expedition whose itin-erary was but vaguely given, and on which he had no companions and was gone for four leisurely years, he found many wonders of which he had never dreamed. One was a funny little black-faced partridge in the desert, and others were an undescribed shrike, a chickadee with a black stripe through the eye, a new species of white-fronted goose, and a new sparrow. In 1848 he went back on another excursion, but died mysteriously en route in 1849. As his living memorial we have Gambel's quail, Gambel's sparrow, Gam-bel's white-fronted goose, Gambel's northern shrike, and the hand-some little mountain chickadee.

CHAPTER FOURTEEN

RAILROADS, BIRDS, AND BOUNDARIES

B Y the middle of the nineteenth century the boundaries of the United States and its territories had been settled—on paper, that is. After the war with Mexico, the United States owned the land north of the Rio Grande and westward at an uneven slant to the Gulf of California. The United States later negotiated the Gadsden Purchase to remove a corner of Mexico from Arizona and give to Arizona its present form. The new boundaries had to be surveyed, explored, and mapped.

In the 1850's, that decade of exploration of America west of the Mississippi, Americans also needed to know what they owned to the north. Canada lay nicely on the northern side of the Great Lakes and the St. Lawrence, but that stretch between Lake of the Woods and Vancouver Island was another matter. Here were no natural boundaries, only wilderness, or cactus flats, or high mountains, and it looked the same whether it was legally Canada or America. There was a good deal of controversy, polite and restrained most of the time, between the two countries, but it was clear that the boundaries needed to be defined before an international incident touched off something serious. Matters, in fact, had flamed to the cry of "Fifty-Four Forty or Fight!" during the Democratic campaign of 1844, as people demanded that the United States territory should extend to 54° 40′, the southern boundary of Alaska.

It had been a mix-up of territories and nations. Under the cession of 1824, Russia had relinquished all her claim to the territory south of 54° 40′ in North America. Great Britain in 1819 had had a quit-claim from Spain to all Spanish title to the Northwest Coast of Canada north of 42° latitude. The United States wanted what belonged to it, and so did Britain. A treaty compromising the whole thing was settled in 1846, making the 49th Parallel the new boundary between Canada and the United States. But this line unfortunately bisected San Juan Island and Vancouver Island at Puget Sound. It was here that the Pig War flared briefly.

A Canadian pig had trespassed on an American garden on San Juan Island. Insults flew, the situation grew tense, the militia was called out, and Britain and America on little San Juan almost came to war. The island, however, was amicably ceded to the United States, while Britain kept all of Vancouver Island. The international boundary in the Sound neatly passes between the two.

With the 49th Parallel settled upon as the line between the two countries, both nations needed to make a formal boundary. It would have no wall, no customhouses or inspection stations; there were no roads in most of it. But some sort of boundary was needed to satisfy the claims of future generations. Both sides agreed that it was too tough a terrain to attempt anything consecutive all the way across it. The great Douglas fir and spruce forests of the Cascades and the Rockies, whose summits were never without snow and whose seasons were a brief summer and a long winter, would not yield easily to the surveyor's chain and instruments. Thus it was agreed that in the survey an iron obelisk as a marker would be placed at various points, with the forest to be cleared for a space of twenty feet wide for a mile on either side; marks would also be placed at any settlement, road, or natural landmark.

The United States crew of the 49th Parallel Survey started work in 1857; the Canadians began the following year. It was a well-equipped crew on both sides, with not only surveyors, wood cutters, cooks, teamsters, etc., but naturalists, too. The American team also carried an artist who worked for eight months, sketching the country around the boundary markers and painting pictures of the wilderness landscape which no one had depicted until now.

With the Canadian surveyors went J. K. Lord, an ornithologist who lived the rough life of the surveying camps, tramped the high Cascades, and suffered the hardships of primitive living conditions while he collected birds. When the survey was finished, the Civil War was breaking, and funds were not at hand to publish the American report. The Canadian report, however, appeared several years later with Lord's catalogue of *Birds of the 49th Parallel Survey*.

A more comprehensive and longer survey was made on the Mexican boundary, and again the bird men went along. They were chiefly army officers who were fascinated by the birds found along the edge of Mexico and the southern reaches of the United States. Here was some of the most splendid and primitive landscape in America. The treaty and purchase from Mexico had added tremendous territory to the United States, including the Grand Canyon, the Painted Desert, Oak Creek Canyon, the Colorado River, the Rio Grande, the Gila, the San Juan, the Organ Pipe cactus country, the Joshua trees, the Coast Range, the redwoods and Sequoias, Yosemite and King's Canyon. It had also added a great unknown population of largely hostile Indians, and rattlesnakes, gila monsters, horned lizards, kangaroo rats, coyotes, peccaries, ring-tailed cats, tassel-eared squirrels, mule deer, cougars, and the beautiful, unknown birds of desert and mountain and mesa.

The Mexican Boundary Survey was a long-drawn-out affair swallowed in government red tape and payroll padding, rather badly handled by a well-meaning civilian appointee named John Bartlett of Rhode Island. Bartlett distinguished himself in the field of literature by compiling the classic *Bartlett's Quotations*, and later by writing a two-volume account of his Boundary Survey which he had developed into a heavily attended personal tour of Mexico and the Southwest. His only recommendation for this demanding position had been that he was tired of sedentary work and wanted to travel. He did—at the government's considerable expense. He hired several hundred men in the role of assistants, and assistants to assistants; quantities of baggage handlers, commissary men, even blacksmiths and tailors, as well as artists and naturalists, some of whom were experts from Germany.

After two years of rather aimless roaming that went far afield from the actual boundary he was supposed to have been surveying, he had accomplished very little of the latter but had gathered copious notes for his book of travels. The survey might have failed completely without the work of one of his topographical engineers, Captain A. R. Whipple, who did much of the actual surveying, and of Major William Emory, a highly competent topographical engineer who had worked on the boundary survey between Maine and Canada some years earlier.

A change in administration in Washington caused Bartlett to be suddenly recalled, leaving the whole expedition at a standstill in New Mexico. He had spent so much money, hired so many unnecessary people, gone so far out of his way, and bought so much equipment that he had a difficult time scraping together enough money to pay off his men.

In 1854, when the Gadsden Purchase in Arizona was completed, Major Emory was chosen as the best man to finish surveying the area and to carry the boundary across Arizona to the coast. Emory's report of the Mexican Boundary Survey, filling two large volumes and published in 1857, contained not only the survey and the topography, but a comprehensive report of the zoology and botany. It was well illustrated, well written, revelatory.

Even though, in 1854, the boundaries of the United States were finally established, little was known of what lay in the interior, between the 49th Parallel on the north to the Rio Grande and the Mexican boundary on the south. It was difficult to get to the Great West, let alone explore it. Stage coach travel was dangerous and hard; there was no water route except by way of Cape Horn or down to Nicaragua, then on foot across to the Pacific to meet a ship that was going to California. The gold strikes of 1848 and 1849, and the gold that was found on the 49th Parallel survey itself, were taking people to California. With railroads developing in the East, the government as well as the railroad interests knew that this could be the means to carry people easily and safely through the Indian country to the promised land of California, to the gold mines, and to Oregon.

At least one of the gold-seekers who arrived in the vicinity of the strike at Sutter's Mill was also looking for birds. He was John G. Bell, Audubon's taxidermist friend who had accompanied the latter's journey up the Missouri. Bell one day lifted his eyes from the stony streams to discover and collect two new birds. He sent them to John Cassin for names. One was the curious white-headed woodpecker of California and the other was the black-breasted woodpecker.

From what reports there were of the ruggedness of this western country, a railroad route seemed difficult to locate. Railroads were still in their infancy; locomotives could manage only the gentlest of grades, and they would have the Rocky Mountains and Sierra Nevadas to cross. The deep snows in the high mountains convinced railroad men anew that there could never be a northern route for rails. The Mexican Boundary Survey had blazed a trail from El Paso, Texas, to California, which was far more feasible. The Mormon Battalion had carved a wagon road through the desert going almost due west to the Rockies, which might take rails, too. Frémont's ill-starred mountain route was also a possibility.

The Pacific Railroad question became one of the vital causes in Washington, with many factions all crying to be heard. If the North had a railroad from Chicago to Oregon, what then would the South do? Sam Houston and Jefferson Davis wanted the southern route, by way of El Paso to San Diego, while Senator Thomas Hart Benton of Missouri cried out for a line to come through St.

Louis and cross the Rocky Mountains by way of Fremont's route of 1848. Chicago interests held out for the northern route.

To satisfy them all and find out what really was the best, safest, and most economical route, Secretary of War Jefferson Davis, under President Pierce, in 1853 sent out a number of groups of topographical engineers, crack graduates of West Point, to determine the best manner in which a railroad might get to the Pacific Ocean. They were basically to explore the northern trail, the Mormon Trail through Salt Lake City, the Benton route through Missouri, the 35th Parallel trail, and the southern trail. The expeditions, however, literally crisscrossed the West.

One ranged along the 47th Parallel from Vancouver through the Cascades, with Dr. J. G. Cooper as naturalist. The 38th and 39th Parallel routes under Captain Gunnison had a German naturalist named Kreuzfeldt who was killed by the Indians, and so, for that matter, was Gunnison himself. The 35th Parallel had two expeditions, one under Major Whipple and the other under Lieutenant Joseph Christmas Ives, while Dr. C. B. R. Kennerly was ornithologist. The California boundary was explored, the 32nd Parallel from Fort Yuma to El Paso, the Oregon line, the Yellowstone and Colorado Rivers, and much of Death Valley.

The surveys proved that the southern route would be best from the standpoint of distance and construction, as well as safest from the standpoint of weather and altitude. The Southern interests rejoiced, but the Northern interests yelled. They would not yield. The North must have a railroad. Expensive or not, the North would run a line to the Pacific. There were too many rising problems at hand in the mid-century; free states and slave states were contesting for the new territories, and secession was becoming more than just an ugly word. And, argued the North, if the South put through a railroad to California, soon all the western territories would be slave states. In the 'Fifties, these were fighting words.

In 1861, after much controversy, the Central Pacific Railroad of California was incorporated; it was later to become the Union

Pacific, with its miles of adventure while being laid through desert and mountain and Indian country. Eventually there were four Pacific railroads following the general routes of the four primary surveys—Northern Pacific, Central Pacific, Union Pacific, and Southern Pacific. And with the laying of the rails, the zoology, botany, and geology of the West came into the greater scope of American interest and knowledge. The twelve large volumes of the Pacific Railroad Surveys, with their beautifully illustrated reports of topography and natural history, revealed new secrets of the West. For years, bales of bird skins came to the Smithsonian Institution in Washington from the men of the surveys—John Cassin, Robert Ridgway, Dr. J. S. Newberry, Howard K. Stansbury, George Lawrence, Spencer F. Baird, Dr. C. B. R. Kennerly, Dr. A. L. Heerman, Dr. T. C. Henry, Dr. F. V. Hayden, Dr. J. G. Cooper, and many others.

One of the ornithologists on the surveys was only a boy. He was Robert Ridgway of Olney, Illinois, who had in his early childhood become imbued with the lure of birds. They fascinated him, and so did color. When he was still a child and had begun to paint bird portraits, he went to his father's drugstore to mix his own paints. From his puzzlement as to what to call the colors of birds, he developed a special subject which was later published as *A Nomenclature of Color for Naturalists*.

At seventeen, with an excellent record in ornithology already behind him, he was recommended by Professor Baird to the post of zoologist in the expedition of the United States Geological Survey of the 40th Parallel, lying between Sacramento and Salt Lake City. The real reason behind the expedition, or at least one of the reasons, was to locate a possible route for a railroad between the two cities. To young Ridgway, railroads were a minor item compared with birds. His zoological party and the geologists lived in a rarefied world of science and wonder far separated from iron rails and politics.

When Robert Ridgway disembarked at San Francisco in 1867, he was deeply disappointed. He was not sure what he had expected, but certainly he should have had an immediate sight of birds unknown to him in the East and Middle West. It was disillusioning. From the steamboat carrying him between San Francisco and Sacramento he saw only the familiar purple martins and cliff swallows. In the towns he heard no bird songs except the silly ecstasies of caged canary birds. As the boat steamed up the Sacramento, he stayed out on deck all day but saw only familiar species—coots scuttering to get out of the way, gallinules paddling over lily leaves in the shallows, ducks, a kingfisher perched on a willow overhanging the river, as kingfishers back on the Wabash had been doing all of his life. He might as well have stayed home.

But when he woke next morning in the inn at Sacramento, he got up in a hurry and leaped to his window. There were birds out there singing songs he had never heard before. It was a caroling and twittering, very musical, broken, sweet and continual. He looked down to the garden and saw small, sparrow-shaped birds hopping and flitting about—but not sparrows, not these! Though they had the familiar habits of the song sparrows in his mother's garden, they were far different, for these were pink and rosy, with red on the forehead and eyebrow and throat, the back and wings and tail streaked brown. The colors pleased him. He remembered that Say had found house finches or linnets in the Colorado foothills; these might be the same. *Burions,* the inn keeper told him, was their Mexican name. He felt he was really in the West now.

The itinerary of the survey, based on camps at specified spots along the route, offered weeks at a time for leisurely collecting and surveying. It began at Sacramento, went east through the foothills and pines of the Sierra Nevada range, then over the crest of the mountains and into Nevada, to the Big Bend of the Truckee River for a three-weeks' working camp. There was a side trip to Pyramid Lake and to the dry canyons of the Virginia Mountains.

It was all a fascination, even the discomforts of the alkali deserts which were ghastly to the young man brought up in the pleasant green country of Illinois. He had, besides, come down with malaria and was very ill, although feeling better between bouts. In late summer and early autumn the heat was unrelenting when they camped near the Humboldt Sink and its marshes. This was a miserable and unforgettable experience. Ridgway's report forgot to be impersonal and scientific. He was too young to overlook discomfort. He could remember only that the mosquitoes had come in such appalling hordes that they had actually extinguished the candles in the tents at night.

The marshes, stretching for miles, were covered with dense stands of tule rushes, except where the river would its sluggish route and expanded as a lake. These marshes were surrounded by alkali flats that in winter were fetid white mud but in summer were baked bone-dry and hard. All the hollows contained a deep deposit of white alkali. And from the Sink area, the desert stretched on and on to the rising wall of barren, purple-gray mountains, forbidding in the heat of day and mysteriously brooding at night. Even the sagebrush and greasewood were dry and parched and shattered off when touched. During the day the heat mirages shimmered across the alkali flats and sage desert in disquieting waves and dizzy quiverings which were exaggerated by the fevers of malaria.

The heat meanwhile sent up a stench from the putrid water of the marshes, filled as it was with decaying vegetation. By day the marshes reeked, and by night the mosquitoes attacked. It was all dreadful and unreal. A young man in the business of birds never knew what he could get himself into in the vigor of his enthusiasm until he took himself off on a government expedition.

There were few land birds in this vile place. Now and then a raven flapped croaking across the flats; or horned larks ran about oblivious of the heat; a few savannah sparrows were in the salt grass—nothing more. There were no songs, nothing but the grunts, whistles, screams, or pipings of the water birds that lived in the marsh. These were astonishingly numerous. He had never before seen so many, and they somewhat made up for the discomfort he was enduring.

Feverish, or shaking with chills, Ridgway would drag himself out of his tent and go to the edge of the stinking marshes to watch the odd little black-and-white stilts and the cinnamon-and-white avocets as they rose in flocks and flew about, yipping and crying, legs dangling, circling the marsh. Ill as he was, he never tired of watching them. As the avocets and stilts made their racket, the terns cackled and dived at him; sandpipers rose in swirling flocks and cut across the sunlight, turning so that white flashed on their underwings. The glossy ibises and herons took off in slower flight, and he saw willets, coots, plovers, grebes. He wished he had a boat, wished that he felt better. He would retire then, collapse on his cot, shaking with another bout of chills.

They gave up at Humboldt. Most of the other men at the camp had come down with malaria. They quit at the Oreana marshes, where in the miserable shack-town nearby the fever was even worse, and everyone there was desperately ill. If the surveying party was to be of any use, it must get away to higher country, to better air and water, away from those dastardly mosquitoes.

It was wonderful in the mountains. A brook of clear water ran tinkling over the rocks at night. The flow ceased during the heat of the day, but it was cool and clean and had no evil smells. Compared with the desert and the Humboldt Sink, the vegetation in the desert mountains seemed downright lush. Ridgway found wild cherry trees and dogwood, willows and clematis, junipers and pinyons and aspens. There were no large trees, but the small ones up here were certainly better than no trees at all. There were birds, too, birds that sang—titmice and vireos and rock wrens. Woodhouse's jays were "chacking" about and stealing food from the camp, and magpies slipped around to do the same. One day, to his surprise, a lone passenger pigeon flew through the camp, crossed the mountain, and was gone.

Leaving the mountains, the crews worked their way around in

a great circle over the desert and came back to Carson City for a winter base. It was neither a long nor a hard winter, and, with the coming of early spring, the expedition was again on its deliberate way. The route may have seemed meandering and aimless, but there was a great deal of unknown land to survey, mountains to chart, the whole area to be made clear on a map. The geologists had to collect fossils and minerals and write up their records, and the zoologists collected lizards and mammals and insects and birds. The party proceeded into the High Sierras to Lake Tahoe, and on through the great pines to Summit Meadows and Donner Lake Pass. It was an exhausting climb for men and animals; the rarefied air was difficult to breathe fully.

Around the camp the songs of unknown finches piped like small flutes in the twilight. They sounded to Ridgway at first like white-crowned sparrows, like those he had known in Illinois when they were migrating. When he shot one, he saw that it was different. He thought it must be the western variety called Gambel's sparrow. This has a pinkish beak, not yellow, and a white stripe over the eye beginning at the edge of the beak, not from the back of the eye as in the white-crown. But the bird in his hand seemed different in color. The feathers bore a purplish-ashy tinge, and the bend of the wings was distinctly yellowish. It *was* different. It was also very abundant in the meadows. Forgetting weariness, he walked about in the twilight, listening and watching. The singing continued as dusk came on, and he went back to supper. As he lay wrapped in his blankets in the cold mountain air, he heard the new sparrows still fluting at intervals throughout the night.

He would always remember Summit Meadows and Donner Pass because of this bird which, after he brought back his specimens and his descriptions to Professor Baird, was called Ridgway's sparrow. It was a subspecies, and it was his. Yet this distinction was taken away a good many years later. The 1957 edition of the American Ornithological Union's checklist, the *Who's Who of the Birds*, fails to recognize Ridgway's prize as a bona fide subspecies.

On this first expedition into the West, he discovered birds which were new to him; and to one who finds a bird for himself for the first time, it hardly matters that other men may have seen it also. This, for the moment, is his own discovery. Ridgway particularly liked the bold, pugnacious, western kingbirds, the species that Thomas Say called the Arkansaw flycatcher when he found it in Colorado in 1820. It was a big, rollicking, sulphur-bellied bird, gray-brown above, noisy and often seen. Whenever they set up a camp, the kingbirds were there sitting about on tent ropes or clothes lines.

In July Robert Ridgway was given a young kingbird by some of the Washoe Indians whom he had been questioning about their names for familiar birds. Ridgway was charmed with the gift and named the bird Chippy. The kingbird immediately became a great pet of the whole expedition, all of whose members united in catching grasshoppers and flies until the youngster was able to go out and catch them for himself. His appetite was tremendous. He could be quieted only by being literally stuffed with grasshoppers until the legs of the last one hung out of his beak. This quelled the incessant clamoring for about five minutes, after which he opened up and yelled for more. If only one person in the party had had to catch food for this insatiable grasshopper-trap, he would have been able to accomplish little else, but all took turns in bringing back food for the pet.

Astonished at the bird's capacity, and realizing that they were, after all, scientists in the pay of the government, not just bird-feeders, the men decided to keep a record of how many grasshoppers were fed to this one hungry bird. By evening, when notes were compared and grasshoppers tallied, it was found that one young kingbird had eaten no less than 120 of the insects. It was a relief to his foster fathers when Chippy could at last find his own provender. In a grasshopper-ridden West, the kingbird in numbers, they decided, could prove an effective check.

The bird was also an alarm clock. His loud, metallic twittering began early. If Ridgway, evidently his favorite, did not get up at once, the bird hopped the length of his chest, his claws catching in the rough wool blanket, and then walked with cold feet across his face. The bird liked human companionship so well that he preferred to go to sleep at night snuggled against a man's neck. When removed to the perch provided for him in the tent, he complained and flew back, until repeated removals convinced him that he had to stay put.

On expeditions the bird rode on Ridgway's shoulder, now and again flying out to somersault after a butterfly. If left behind, he hurriedly caught up, screeching and twittering. When Ridgway raised his gun to fire at something, the bird flew off his shoulder to wait until the jolt and noise were over.

One morning Chippy disappeared. There was no evidence to tell what had happened, nothing but the suspicious sight of a large hawk making off from the vicinity of the camp. Ridgway missed Chippy; they all did. Out of all the wonderful experiences of the survey, the pet flycatcher, perhaps—and the pelicans—were the outstanding events to be remembered.

The white pelicans nested at Pyramid Lake, forty-six miles northeast of Reno. Here were no chance strays, no small colony. As Ridgway—accompanied by the Indian Agent for this portion of Nevada, Mr. H. G. Parker, who had provided his boat for the excursion—descended the river toward the lake, the numbers of pelicans grew hourly. They flew past in groups; their nine-foot wingspread of dazzling white, accented with broad black tips, seemed enormous as they tilted past the boat. They coasted by in formations, or flew alone against a brilliant blue desert sky. When the boat reached the lake, drifting among the masses of tules, he could see beyond on the water hundreds of large birds. They floated like innumerable ships, some with their heads erect and yellow pouches shining, others resting with pouches collapsed and necks drawn in, rocking on the water which the wind was ruffling into low waves and swells.

The party landed three-fourths of a mile from the river's entrance and set up camp on the sandy shore. Now there were thousands of pelicans, not merely hundreds as he had thought at first. What he had seen earlier was nothing. The whole assemblage evidently roosted and nested on the island itself, about twelve miles away in the middle of the lake. All day birds were coming and going, flapping and sailing, each bird in the line alternating the flap and sail with the ones ahead and behind.

Soon after sunset the full moon rose. Its flooding illumination silvered the desert and rocks and gave the landscape a calm which the daytime heat did not possess. In the moonlight the kangaroo rats came out of their holes and leaped about almost as if they were airborne and had wings. The coyotes sang from the ridges; and the moonlight glittered over the placid surface of the lake. Ridgway and his companions left the camp by row boat and proceeded quietly through the magical moonlight to the island where the pelicans by this time were asleep.

It was ten o'clock at night, chill and still and eerie. It had been a long hard row of three hours to reach the island, whose great rocky pyramid gave the lake its name. The men muffled their oars as they approached; they tried to be very silent as they shoved the boat into the sand, but there must have been a watchman among the birds that slumbered there by thousands. With a sudden rushing and clattering and clashing of wings, the multitudes rose churning in confusion into the moonlight, until only the sick or old remained. The noise of the wings was so loud that the men could not hear themselves speak. Robert Ridgway did not wish to speak. He and the others sat in silent awe, watching this mammoth brigade of prehistoric-looking creatures leap into the ancient spell of moonlight.

With the inhabitants of the island largely out on the lake, the men hastily selected a spot apart from the roosting place to spread their blankets. They lay down and were quiet. As soon as they were settled, they could see the glint of white in the moonlight as the hordes came back, sideslipping, coasting down, circling, landing on the sand beach, uttering guttural comments, raising wings high, folding them, resting.

When Ridgway woke next morning in his dew-dampened blanket and raised his head to look down on the beach, he saw an unbelievable mass of great white birds. Not more than fifty yards away and extending out of sight around the shore, the entire beach was covered with them. It was as if they were snow, or a flock of sheep lying side by side. The birds swiveled pale eyes at the men as they quietly stood up, but when they walked slowly toward the pelicans, the birds began to walk away until they had all moved into the water. Some rose heavily into the air and came down on the water farther out. Their feathers early in the morning were dampened and this made flight difficult. But as the sun rose and their wings dried, the birds rose superbly into the air, formed long lines and circled the island, and sailed off to the tules to fish.

Robert Ridgway came back from this expedition of the Survey of the 40th Parallel a full-fledged naturalist and ornithologist with a growing prestige. He made many other surveys and explorations, became the leading ornithologist of the United States when Baird died, and finally was appointed Curator of Birds at the United States National Museum at Washington.

He was now a quiet, aging gentleman; he had a walrus mustache and thick lenses in his eyeglasses. He wore a vest with a gold watch chain across the front, and sat all day at a roll-top desk in the Smithsonian Institution, examining preserved bird skins, writing reports and books, and talking to visiting bird men. The days of excitement and exploration were over for him. He was being rewarded as America best knew how to reward an eminent ornithologist— at the Smithsonian. That was where Baird had gone, and others, when their great days of youth were over. It was fitting, most people thought. Yet these men must at times have longed for the old free days when there were new birds around every bend of the river and the chance of a discovery lay over every mountain trail and in every secret canyon. The discomforts of hunger and cold and heat and malaria and poor food and Indians were forgotten; they even took on an aura, when recalled, of glory quite out of reason with their reality. For these things meant vitality and adventure, when birds were birds, not dried, cotton-eyed specimens lined up precisely in trays and smelling of formaldehyde and mothballs.

CHAPTER FIFTEEN

BIRDS AND THE ARMY

THE Apaches had raided the outbuildings of Fort Whipple and had run off the beef cattle. A detachment of soldiers rode out the next day to retake the cattle and punish the Indians, but the latter jumped them, out in the chaparral, and one soldier was killed. The others, finding themselves far outnumbered, galloped back to the fort to report the disaster and get reinforcements. It was 1864, when the Apaches were a constant sore spot to the United States Army out in the precariously-held territory of Arizona.

A larger troop next day left Fort Whipple, rode down the steep, arid trail through the pines to the desert valley, and came suddenly and with horror upon the burned and dismembered body of the slain soldier. After the Apaches had departed, the wolves and coyotes had fought over the remains. What was left was sickening. It was also a grim warning of what could happen to any man there. The troop looked fearfully over their shoulders and wondered what might be hiding behind the pinyons and the palo verdes. It was too late for them to get back to the fort. They would have to camp here, after they had buried their unfortunate comrade's remains, and trust that the Indians did not return and find them.

Young Captain Elliott Coues, who was twenty-three, surgeon and physician at the fort, was with the party. He was usually a member of any foray or expedition because, besides being the one who sewed up wounds, ministered to fevers, doctored those who survived Indian attacks, and officiated at burials, Coues was a bird man. It was an invaluable hobby to one in his situation; it provided release and interest, a pursuit in which he could find escape from the tensions of the Indian troubles or from the boredom of long days when nothing at all was happening.

Here in this melancholy and ominous place, as the last afterglow of the sunset lit the tops of the palo verdes and gave even to the vicious chollas and dry little pinyon pines a deceptive charm and a velvety look, and while the men were gingerly gathering up the gruesome remains of the dead man, Dr. Coues heard a bird. His mind switched at once from the presence of disaster to the mystery of the song.

It was new to him, a plaintive fluting that was appropriate to the place and to the occasion. The bird sang softly while the burial was taking place, continuing until the night was quite dark. It was a satiny black creature, with silken crest, ruby eyes, and a graceful air. It was almost not a bird at all, but like some spirit, some creature of omen, either of good or evil; they could not tell. The men could not take their minds from it.

Coues knew now what it was. Swainson had found it in Mexico. Dr. Heermann, with the army in California, had found it in 1851. His friend, Colonel McCall, had seen it there also on a march between Vallecito and El Chino. While he and his men had stopped to rest beside a mountain stream, they had watched a dozen shining black-satin birds pitching about in the treetops after insects, or darting out and tumbling like acrobats in the air. One might have said that this strange black creature was a bird of the army.

But this was the first time young Dr. Coues had seen it—the elusive phainopepla or silken flycatcher, sometimes jokingly called by soldiers the Satin Sparrow. He thought he had glimpsed it before this. Once when he had observed a peculiarly silken bird, close enough to try for a shot, there had been strict orders not to shoot anything, for fear of the Indians' discovering their location. It was

that way now at the burial place encampment as they waited uneasily for the desert dawn. He dared not collect the bird, but somehow then he had no great wish to do so. The solemnity of the moment, the strange sensation of uneasiness, the feeling that the
Apaches were watching, while the ethereal bird sang in the darkness, kept him from it.

Elliott Coues was only one of the men sent into the Far West
by the United States Army or the Corps of Topographical Engineers in the 1850's, 1860's, and 1870's who were ornithologists.
There were a good many of them, and since the government encouraged their collecting wildlife specimens to further the knowledge of a virtually unknown area, the army's bird men were exceedingly active. Few, however, were as perceptive as Elliott Coues,
who knew how to take in the dramatic qualities of a scene, to sense
its beauty and atmosphere, as well as to spot an unusual bird in some
of the most impossible and Indian-infested terrain of the West.

There was a bird man in just about every one of the early army
groups and surveying parties in the West, at least one at each fort,
on each expedition. Their names ranged from Abert to Xantus, including the three C's—Cooper, Couch, and Coues; the four M's—
Mearns, Maynard, McCall, and McCown; also Bendire, Heermann,
Henry, Kennerly, Lawrence, Woodhouse, and a good many more.
All were expert ornithologists and all doing a good job at the same
time for the United States Army.

The era in which they throve was the era of the opening of the
West, the quelling of the Indians, the laying of railroads, and the
opening of wagon roads. The bird men were in at a pristine period
before physical changes had taken place in the landscape. But this
landscape in which they lived and fought and looked for birds was
not the kind to be easily changed by any amount of civilization,
except perhaps by the miracle of irrigation and the damming of the
Colorado. This was the wild Colorado River country, the Grand
Canyon, the San Juan "goosenecks," the San Francisco Mountains,
the Mojave Desert, Death Valley—and the arid lands and pine hills,

the high mountains, and the red and orange buttes and mesas and canyons of Utah, Texas, New Mexico, Arizona, and California.

There were birds out there, and to the bird men their own discomfort was of little importance in the face of what they were discovering. Many a time one of these men, situated in a dangerous or highly uncomfortable position, could find escape in watching birds, while his less inspired brethren could only curse and complain. Out in that heat and pain and thirst of the Indian country, birds could be the saving of a man's sanity.

Frequently it was the physician and surgeon assigned to an army post, a fort, or an expedition who was also the ornithologist. The aplomb with which one of these men avoided Indians and studied birds was unmatched except perhaps by the men of the Lewis and Clark and the Long expeditions, who, though not so much in danger of Indians, suffered horrible hardship, physical ailment and injury, indescribably poor food or none at all. Yet they calmly collected birds and plants and carefully described them in endless notebooks. Through their efforts and those of men on the railroad and boundary surveys and army locations, the whole great sum of wildlife between Canada and Mexico, west of the Mississippi, was largely discovered.

The birds of this huge area, therefore, were generally identified at or near army posts, forts, or encampments—Fort Randall, Fort Crook, Fort Riley, Fort Leavenworth, Fort Whipple, Fort Yuma, Fort Mojave, Fort Tejon, Fort Steilacoom, Ringgold Barracks, Cantonment Burgwyn. Here the army men found the birds which bear their names—Captain John Xantus at Fort Tejon, California, with his Xantus's hummingbird and a number of other new species; Lieutenant Charles Bendire, stationed in Texas and southern Arizona, finding the desert thrasher which bears his name; Lieutenant J. W. Abert leading the reconnaissance from Fort Leavenworth to San Diego in 1848, opening a trail and fighting Indians, and finding the sleek brown Abert towhee. Dr. R. W. Shufeldt found Shufeldt's junco; Dr. James C. Merrill found Merrill's pauraque; Lt.

Willis Wittich and his wife studied the birds of Oregon at Fort Klamath in 1879.

One February morning at sunrise in the Arizona desert, Colonel George McCall was half asleep on his horse. He and his men had been in the saddle since two hours before daylight. As his mount shied suddenly and stopped, he roused himself, looked ahead to see what had startled the horse, and saw a neat procession of blue quail, or scaled quail, crossing the trail. They were trotting along, he recounted later with pleasure, each with its white cottony plume spread out like a little fan or bonnet. The birds glanced over their shoulders at the horses, clucked at each other, and trotted on through the sage. McCall was evidently the discoverer of the blue quail, but because he did not shoot a specimen as proof, it was described much later by someone else.

He was now fully awake and looked about him while his men rubbed their eyes and decided to wake up. It was really a glorious morning. A heavy dew had congealed in frost, so that everything was a vast glitter of crystals in the sun. The mountains in the distance were shining. The plain, the desert, everything, had turned to diamond dust. The colonel, taking it all in, discovered behind them a mirage-lake spread out in deceptive wetness, but he knew that when they had come that way only a little while before, there had been no lake. He made full circle with his horse, and then, smiling at his men, they proceeded on their way. He hoped they would never forget, as he never would, that morning between Indian troubles when the blue quail woke them up.

Everywhere, under almost every circumstance, the army men found their birds. They were ornithological opportunists. Captain McCown found the black-headed gnatcatcher near Ringgold Barracks in Texas, and his McCown's longspur in Dakota territory, between battles with the Sioux. He was lucky; Sergeant John Feilner, who discovered the eggs and nest of the pygmy nuthatch and made other important birding news, had his life unceremoniously ended by those fierce Dakota Sioux. Dr. Kennerly and Dr.

Henry also lost their lives.

The Mexican jay was found in the arid tablelands near Puebla, Mexico, by an intrepid civilian who accompanied General Winfield Scott's troops to Monterrey. This civilian, William S. Pease, asked and somehow gained permission from the peppery general to go with the army during the final settling of the Mexican war. It was long before the surrender, before Mexico had relinquished Texas and Arizona and New Mexico, but Mr. Pease, with the calm and unfaltering enthusiasm of a true naturalist, trailed along with the army, stayed clear of any fighting engagements, dodged a certain amount of sniping and gunfire, and collected birds. He came back with a large and comprehensive list of Mexican and Texan birds, including the Mexican jay.

Captain Lorenzo Sitgreaves in 1854 took an expedition from Santo Domingo pueblo on the upper Rio Grande to the Zuñi Indian pueblo and then headed for the Colorado River. He had with him Lieutenant J. G. Parke and nineteen other men, including five soldiers, ten Mexican packers and *arriéros*, an artist named R. J. Kern, a guide named Antoine Leroux, and a physician who, of course, was also a naturalist, Dr. S. W. Woodhouse. They also had a flock of sheep as a walking food supply. The expedition had been delayed at the start because the commanding officer of New Mexico was about to make a foray against the Navajos, and if the Sitgreaves expedition followed in the wake of this avenging force, it would have some protection aside from its own small and very inadequate strength.

The party had reached Zuñi pueblo safely by September 1st, and then had another long delay because a military escort of thirty men which was to accompany them part of the way west had not arrived. Waiting until September 24, they consequently ate a good part of the provisions which had been brought along to supply the entire trip. At last they went on without the escort.

A military escort might have prevented some of the trouble they had with the Indians but could have done nothing to ease the difficulties of the country over which they traveled. Here was a murderous terrain—black-lava desert, the stretches of desolation around the meteor crater and Walnut Canyon, and then the San Francisco mountains, snow-capped and serene against a morning sky. Rough though the going might be, however, Dr. Woodhouse was always on the lookout for birds and spent his free time in ranging about the camps looking for something new. In the pines on the side of San Francisco peaks he found the beautiful rose-red hepatic tanager. While they camped at the base of Inscription Rock, where the old Spanish explorers had carved their names and dates, the sunset hours were alive with the scimitar wings of innumerable white-throated swifts which nested in crannies of the rocks. The Spanish no doubt saw them here, but it was Dr. Woodhouse of the Sitgreaves Expedition who had the pleasure of being their recognized discoverer.

By the time the expedition reached the Colorado River, the food situation had become serious. The sheep had been reduced to twenty; there was some emergency ration in the form of meat-biscuits, but nothing else. The men were growing desperately tired of the taste of mutton. Some of the sheep and mules, besides, were dying of the rigors of the journey; the feet of the survivors were so sore that they could hardly travel. Several mules had been lost one night in a canyon when a cougar had yelled from a nearby ledge and the animals had stampeded over the precipice. Because of the failure of the pack animals and the ultimate necessity of using some of the remaining mules for food, the equipment had to be abandoned along the great canyons of the thundering Colorado. Even the books belonging to Dr. Woodhouse had to be discarded; everything not vital to human safety was left behind. Somehow, painfully, and with a growing fear of never reaching civilization, lost as they were in the immense depths of the gorges of the Colorado, the men pushed on because they could not turn back. Their only hope now was to get to Camp Yuma where the Gila met the Colorado.

The Indians grew troublesome. They had heralded the party's

coming to the river by ominous signal fires on the towering cliffs. Now and again the Indians hiding on the rock walls shot arrows unexpectedly into the camp. Antoine Leroux was hit by three arrows in his head and wrist and was disabled for the remainder of the journey. Dr. Woodhouse, while sitting peaceably by the fire, trying not to think of how hungry he was and writing his notes for the day, was struck in the leg by an arrow. They could never see the assailants; only the arrows suddenly flashing among them.

Ultimately the group reached Camp Yuma, where they received food. They rested a few days and then continued with fresh equipment and supplies to San Diego. Dr. Woodhouse, meanwhile, though still limping from the disagreeable injury to his leg, continued to collect birds. To him is credited the Woodhouse's jay, found on this expedition, the rare black-capped vireo, and the new purple finch which he named for his ornithological friend, John Cassin.

Not all new birds were found under such distressing circumstances. Some were discovered casually and with no great strain or danger. Three warblers seen by men of the army are conspicuous on the bird lists among the masculine names of their finders. These three bear the names of Lucy, Grace, and Virginia. One feels suddenly rather sentimental, running across them. Who were Lucy, Grace, and Virginia, to have had warblers named for them?

Probably none of the three women ever saw their namesakes, at least in the wild, for women evidently did little birding in those days, especially in the Southwest. It was three army doctors who found these new species in a rough land and bestowed upon them their gentle names.

At Fort Burgwyn in northern New Mexico, Dr. W. W. Anderson, post physician, went out one day into the heat of the mesquite and chaparral country, up the arid slopes where the low, sprawling pinyon pines made little shade. While he ranged through some of this rocky terrain, dodging the low-slung pine branches and having to watch for rattlesnakes, he saw a small, flitting, white-and-gray bird with a red-brown cap and yellow throat and rump. He felt it was an unknown species but could not be sure. Bird books were few, and this area, ornithologically speaking, was virtually unknown. He knew he would have to shoot this tiny thing, carefully and without marring it, and take its measurements and color description before it faded. He would have to prepare the skin against decomposition and present it to the authorities at the Smithsonian Institution. If they agreed that it was, indeed, a new species, its name and description would be entered in the growing roster of American birds. The finder could offer a name; it might be changed years later by ornithological meddling or the correcting of nomenclature, but the finder had the privilege and pleasure of at least suggesting a name. Out of professional modesty and ethics he could not, of course, name it for himself. He might hope that one of his colleagues would do him the honor, but he himself could not. Sometimes ornithologists reciprocated nicely—you name your bird for me, I'll name my bird for you.

Dr. Anderson at Fort Burgwyn knew in sudden excitement that he surely had a new species. Because it delighted him immensely, he named it in honor of one about whom he felt much the same sentiments, his wife. The little bird was formally named Virginia's warbler by Professor Baird, and it bears that name today.

In the spring of 1861, Dr. J. G. Cooper was hunting birds around old Fort Mojave on the Arizona side of the Colorado River when he, too, found a warbler. It was, confusingly, rather like Virginia's warbler—gray on the back and wings, with a red-brown cap. But there was no yellow on the white throat, and the rump, instead of the yellow in the bird Anderson found, had the same red-brown as the cap. He named his bird for his good friend, Miss Lucy Baird, the daughter of Professor Baird. Lucy Baird was thirteen years old at the time and perhaps was the youngest person for whom a bird had ever been named.

Grace's warbler was discovered by Dr. Elliott Coues while

marching with the army over the mountains of New Mexico, bound for Fort Whipple, the new post in Arizona. The party was approaching the summit of Whipple's Pass in July, 1864—the pass and fort had been named for Major A. W. Whipple of the Mexican Boundary Survey—when Coues heard a bird which to him signaled immediate challenge and possible adventure. Whether or not it was a rest period for men and horses on the summit of the pass, or an overnight encampment, or whether he simply dropped out of the file and went in pursuit of the song, the report does not state. Ornithological records often would be far more interesting if they added some of these enlightening details. Nevertheless, near the site of old Fort Wingate, he tracked down the maker of the song and found a warbler. It was dark gray above, had white wing-bars, a white belly, a yellow throat marked with black streaks, and a yellow eye-ring.

He named the find for his sister Grace—"the name of one for whom my affection and respect keep pace with my appreciation of true loveliness of character." In later descriptions of the bird, he sometimes called it "my sister's warbler."

From Fort Whipple, his first western post, Coues ranged out on many a birding adventure; yet he had to keep constantly alert to the danger of Indians. The fort had been built in the mountains near what later became Prescott, Arizona, for the purpose of protecting men in the newly discovered gold mines from the irate Apaches.

Young Coues had a zest for excitement; the more excitement the better the birding. He would seldom let the smell of danger keep him for it. He said:

This shrubby hillside near Fort Whipple was a favorite resort of mine, not so much for what I expected to find there in the ornithological line, as for what I very sincerely hoped not to find in the way of the aborigines—for it was in full view of the fort, and much safer than the ravines on either side, where I had gone more than once to bring in the naked and still bleeding bodies of men killed by the Apaches.

This was in 1864–65, when the worst passions of both Red and White men were inflamed by atrocities exchanged in kind, and when practical ornithology in Arizona was a very precarious matter, always liable to sudden interruptions, and altogether too spicy for comfort. . . . My memory of many Arizona birds—in fact, my whole notion of the lives of some of them—is pervaded with local color . . . a crowded and strangely jumbled picture, while the swarthy savage crouches in the shadows of the background. They tell me things are better now—that the trails are seldom blood-stained. . . .

In another notation concerning the plumed quail, he added: "Here is plenty, at least, if not peace. Nothing mars the pleasures of the chase, but the chances of being chased. Were it not for Indians, we should have here the acme of Quail shooting."

From the comparatively comfortable climate of Fort Whipple in the mountains above 5,000 feet, Coues was transferred to Fort Yuma, which is still considered among the hottest and most uncomfortable spots in the United States. He may have disliked it thoroughly, but he made the best of it. Fort Yuma was situated on a bluff on the south side of the Colorado River, opposite the mouth of the Gila—a desolate spot that was often at the mercy of rising waters of the two rivers, as well as the heat and insects. Fort Yuma, however, was in touch with the outside world; steamboats with spluttering engines and smacking stern wheels often came up from the Gulf of California to bring supplies and passengers. It was, in fact, a jumping-off place for the gold mines of Arizona.

Dr. Coues, finding Fort Yuma very different indeed from his experiences in the mountains, discovered that the birds of Fort Yuma and Fort Whipple were also almost entirely different—"total strangers to each other."

The two rivers made a marshy stretch below the Yuma bluffs, a seemingly incongruous swampland in an arid country; but swamps they were, and the ornithologist was there whenever he could get away and when the heat permitted. To bypass the latter, he liked to rise very early and leave the fort as a cool, pearly light came over the desert. At that hour it was only ninety degrees after a day which may have been 115 degrees in the shade—if shade there was. The temperature would probably be up to a hundred by the time he returned for breakfast.

He followed the trail along the bluff and descended on a well-worn path made by cattle and Indians, leading to the thickets and willows of the bottomland. These were not amiable thickets to push through, for in Arizona there were few specimens of vegetation without thorns. Even the oak leaves had spines, and so did the mimosas, the acacias, the mesquites, the cat-claw, and the cacti. There were great piles of driftwood to climb over, and he had to be wary of snakes. He stayed on cattle paths until they grew too muddy.

At dawn this was a bird-filled place. Coveys of plumed quail, calling in soft, clinking conversations to each other, their slender headpieces nodding as they walked, trooped along the half-covered places. Lieutenant Abert's towhees rustled in the tangles, and the orange-crowned warblers which Thomas Say had discovered in Colorado flitted in the willows. He watched as they delicately sipped dew from the channeled leaves.

Coues continued through the fetid swamp and spiny tangles until the ground became so mucky that he had to leap from log to log. He was already dripping with perspiration. As he pushed through the thickets, a flock of wood ibises rose from the marsh pools, croaking as they climbed into the air. This was what he had come for. He needed ibis skins for his collection; so he followed, with great discomfort, wetness, and mosquitoes, and got into sucking mud. He was scratched, muddy, wet, swearing. But he brought down two of the coveted birds, retrieved them with difficulty from the swamp, and escaped from the place while mosquitoes gathered so thickly on him that his eyebrows were furred with them.

By the time he had cleaned up for breakfast, the thermometer was a trifle over a hundred. The soaring sun was a scalding glare. After he had carefully measured his birds, he skinned, salted, and put them away. Then Coues knew that he had the whole unbearable day to worry through until night began to cool the air again. There was nothing doing at the fort; the Indians were apparently too hot to feel irritable. He tended the few patients he had and wished he had some ice for the fever patients. Then, half undressed, sweating, he sought the veranda on the shady side of his quarters. He wished he could go birding again, but it was just too hot.

Then before his half-glazed eyes rose a long white line, dimly seen at first because of the heat waves shimmering between him and it. He blinked and sat up straighter. Out of the gray-green woods above the swamp the wood ibises were leaving their steaming retreat for the cooler layers of the upper air. The long flocks and lines drew nearer and passed over the fort, circling, soaring, floating, in a brilliant white that was almost translucent against the deep blue of the sky, the black wing tips and black heads inked in contrast to sky and plumage. It took some flapping at first until they got onto the columns of the thermals formed by the heated desert air; then the big birds soared without having to flap. They spiraled, they rose, they drifted, sometimes in formation, sometimes breaking up in a wide flock. It was a beautiful thing to watch, and his mind forgot his own discomfort. Coues found that this flight of the ibises happened each day shortly after noon; it was something to wait for, to time the deliberate passage of the sun over the sky.

Sometimes when he was out with the army in pursuit of the Apaches or Yumas or Yavapais, there was no shade anywhere and even the nights were less than comfortable. He remembered the night he spent on the Mojave Desert at a place called Soda Lake, east of Cajon Pass—one of the most uncomfortable nights he ever endured. Late in October it was, with a full moon that made a pallid, eerie light over a scene that held only death and desolation. The desert was still heated from the day yet swimming in the deceptive coolness of moonlight, broken here and there with clumps of dried creosote bush, greasewood and sage, scattered yuccas, sotol, and ocotillo—none of them kindly plants, all armed in defense of the desert.

The party had come along a trail that was strewn with the bleached and well picked skeletons of horses and cows of wagon trains, animals that had perished under the heat and thirst of the desert. The men had seen at the foot of some cliffs the heads, horns, and ribs of bighorn sheep, shot by earlier travelers, but in the moonlight the white bones appeared twice their normal size and unearthly in the glare. It was like some impossible landscape on the dead face of the moon. Everywhere was whiteness—the bones, the moonlight, the chalk-white sea of soda and salt where the lake had evaporated or sunk into the sand, leaving only its sediments. The Soda Lake was dry except at the center, where the dark green stalks of tules stood up quite black in contrast. There was a little water out where they grew, but it was too nauseous to drink. Even when boiled it was disgusting to use for tea or cooking.

The horses, like the men, were exhausted. That evening one unfortunate mare had given birth to a foal and lay groaning where she had fallen. There was nothing for the animals to drink except that foul stuff out in the tules.

The men made a poor meal. Nothing tasted right. The meat was growing putrid; the water was sickening; weevils were in the flour. Sleep was almost impossible, for although the men in fury and in cursing desperation wrapped themselves completely in their blankets, the bloodthirsty swarms of large mosquitoes came from the stagnant pools and somehow found all the vulnerable spots. They could even bite through an army blanket. The air seemed filled with the shrillings of millions of voracious insects. For days afterward the men's hands and faces were sore and swollen from the bites.

It was as depressing a night, perhaps, as men ever spent on the American desert. But that intrepid bird man, Elliott Coues, managed to ignore the mosquitoes, the hunger, the thirst, the uneasiness, and the general discomfort long enough to be entertained by some birds. He watched mallards and teal fly in and plummet into the tules. Marsh wrens perched sidewise on the bending stalks and seesawed back and forth to the tune of their thin, whirring songs. As dark came, the wrens grew quiet, and so did the ducks. The frogs then set up a basso concerto that served not at all to drown out the falsettos of the mosquitoes.

Then from the middle of the marsh came the loud *crik-crik-crik-k-k-k-k* of a Virginia rail, wide awake in the moonlight. Another answered, and another, until there was a wonderful racket of rails calling and cackling. Listening to the night voices, trying to think beyond the present, wondering what birds he might see next day, Elliott Coues still found the night at Soda Lake to be inordinately long.

This was a great period for ornithologists, if they survived the rigors of birding in the Great West. It was an exciting and challenging sport, because an ornithologist could become just as bloody a corpse when the Apaches or the Sioux had finished with him as any enlisted man whose thoughts never rose to the heights of birds. Always to be recalled by the cocky were poor Sergeant Feilner, Dr. Kennerly, and Dr. Henry, to name a few, all of whom had been promising bird men and all slain by the Indians.

But Elliott Coues was one who miraculously survived in spite of the risks he took in the name of ornithology. The army, however, in spite of offering him new fields of discovery, continually got in the way of his scholarly endeavor in the East. He had been made Professor of Zoology and Comparative Anatomy at Norwich University in Vermont when, in 1873, he was ordered out with the U.S. Northern Boundary Survey Commission. By 1876 he was made Secretary and Naturalist of the Surveys, but then he was sent to Arizona again on frontier duty, with so little freedom to collect birds or write that next year he resigned from the army. He devoted the remainder of his life to birds—teaching at Columbia University, working at the Smithsonian, becoming President of the American Ornithological Union, and writing many authoritative books on birds. He died in 1899 at the age of fifty-seven.

CHAPTER SIXTEEN

FRANKLIN, RICHARDSON, AND THE CALL OF THE NORTH

THE mewing of the *whiskey-john-eesh* was so sudden and loud in the overwhelming silence that the men in the canoe started and glanced at each other nervously. They had not realized that it would be quite like this in the great North, this dreadful, brooding silence that made the ears ring for want of any other sounds but one's own voice and the swish of a paddle. It was a relief when the occasional birds flitting along the banks now and again chose to say something. The *whiskey-john-eesh*, or Canada jays, had been following them for some time. They were large and plump and fluffy, with a black cap placed low on the back of the head, pleasant-looking, agreeable birds. John Richardson said of them: ". . . it is the only inhabitant of those silent and pathless forests which, trusting in the generosity of man, fearlessly approaches him; and its visits were, therefore, always hailed by us with satisfaction."

Dr. John Richardson was the ornithologist as well as physician in Captain John Franklin's expedition to explore part of the North where few white men had gone since young Samuel Hearne in 1772 had traveled with the Eskimos and discovered the Barren

Grounds. Hearne himself, a naturalist and artist, had described many birds between Hudson Bay and the Coppermine River. But because his report had been tantalizingly and obviously incomplete, John Richardson welcomed the invitation to go with Franklin.

The Arctic was the mysterious goal of many birds that migrated northward in spring, then vanished until they returned southward in autumn with the young which had been hatched somewhere in the unknown vastness of tundra and marsh. Except for Hearne's reports, and those of David Douglas on the West Coast, there was little knowledge of the wildlife of this area. So, to find out more about it and to map and explore as much of the region as he could, Captain Franklin's small expedition set sail from England in 1819. In his party there were, in addition to Richardson, two midshipmen who went along to make drawings and maps—George Back and Robert Hood—who were also amateur naturalists.

It had all looked jolly and rather simple when viewed from England, or even from the deck of the ship as it made a safe landing at York Factory on the western side of Hudson Bay, on August 11, 1819. This point was the jumping-off place, the doorway to where the real adventure began. To Richardson, collecting birds in the Arctic also began here with the beautiful goshawk, the specimen from which William Swainson later painted a portrait to illustrate this species in the book on which he and Richardson collaborated.

Perhaps part of John Franklin's ultimate tragedy was his poor timing. Autumn should have seemed an inappropriate season for an expedition to head into the Arctic on foot and by canoe, at a time when the birds themselves were clearing out and the breath of winter was already a warning in the air. Yet, on September 9, in a boat given them by the Governor of the Hudson's Bay Company at York Factory, the expedition started up the Nelson River, bound, by many difficult portages from river to lake to river, to reach the Saskatchewan and the Hudson Bay post called Cumberland House, situated close by on Cumberland Lake.

None of this suicidal trip was easy, and it began at once to get

tough. The river was so low that the men frequently had to pull
the boat along, meanwhile slipping and stumbling and falling in
the mud of the banks, whose crumbling bluffs also endangered
them. Snow fell heavily on the 17th, blurring with menace the remaining pale yellow leaves of aspens and willows along the river.

It was a strange, silent, winter-waiting land. The aspens' color
seemed uncommonly bright against the dark green of the spruces
and the purple-red of the red-stemmed dogwood canes. Now and
again the party came upon aftermath blooms of yellow cinquefoil
on the higher bank. They were as welcome as the first roses in
England. But over all was the oppressive quiet of that great land,
with only the mewing and twittering of the *whiskey-john-eesh*
breaking the silence.

The days were hard, and they were slow. If they made sixteen
miles in a day, they had done well. They did not dwell on how in-
terminably far it was to the Coppermine River and to the rim of the
Arctic Ocean. At the nightly camps there was time to collect a few
specimens and for Richardson and Back to prepare them for shipment to England. On November 23, they thankfully reached Cumberland House. Primitive as it was, this was a haven from the great
force of winter which was already upon them. The Governor invited the party to remain there until spring; he warned them against
continuing now. Even the fur men did not often start north in
winter.

But Captain Franklin could not rest while the North lay out
there waiting for him. He would proceed with part of the group
by dog sled and snowshoes, while Dr. Richardson and Mr. Hood
remained behind at Cumberland House to collect birds which might
be far more readily sent back to England's waiting ornithologists
from this point than from later places in the great unknown journey
to the Arctic Sea. They would join the others at Fort Chipewyan on
Lake Athabaska in the spring. The great northern lakes were arranged in a convenient chain slanting northwest, some with a fort
as a way station. Above Cumberland Lake lay Lake Athabaska,

then Great Slave Lake, then Great Bear Lake two hundred miles below the Arctic Ocean.

The intrepid Franklin set off in January, 1820, with his crew and headed north by dog sled through country which was perhaps more easily traversed in this manner than in summer, on foot or by canoe, when there would be the incessant need for portaging the innumerable lakes and marshes. The cold was now tremendous, and food was not always easily found. The Franklin party, however, without too much hardship, traveled north 857 miles and reached Fort Chipewyan on March 26.

It was still deep winter. Snow had blown in massive drifts against the walls of the fort. The temperature lay far below zero, as if it could never rise again. Yet, on April 8, the Indians in great excitement pointed to the gray sky, talking delightedly about something they were seeing up there. And Franklin, looking up, saw a flock of geese flying northwest. At the sound of their faint gabbling he knew a lift of spirits as great as those of the Indians, who were like new men now that the geese were coming back.

Then the weather grew stormy, snow fell heavily again, and there were no birds until the swans came over on the 15th. At the same time, the snow began visibly to waste away from the south slopes of the hills and from the surface of the lake ice. Nightly, the aurora borealis was wonderfully brilliant. The first houseflies appeared in the fort by the first of May, and the ice went out of the river.

Meanwhile, 857 miles away at Cumberland House, John Richardson had been watching the weather. Cliff swallows appeared, and other birds were daily arriving around the buildings. On a spruce tip in a swamp one day he had seen a trim bird that called a monotonous *pep-pep-pep-pep-pep* as long as he was in the vicinity, and had a pleasant sort of *cheer-cheer* song besides. When he brought it down, he found he had an olive-green creature nearly as large as a robin, with a fluff of white on either side—the olive-sided flycatcher, a bird of the northern swamps and bogs. He found black-billed magpies around Cumberland House, magpies quite different from the yellow-billed kind seen by Lewis and Clark farther south. He discovered the white-tailed ptarmigan, and heard flocks of black and white lark buntings singing in the Saskatchewan sunlight on the thawing prairie. He prepared and packed up all his specimens found thus far and left them to be sent back to England. Whatever happened to the expedition and whatever else he should chance to find, these at least would be safe.

Richardson and Hood set off for Fort Chipewyan where the whole group was thankfully reunited at last. Richardson was relieved to know that Franklin had survived that lone trek into the great cold; he had often wondered about him in the long silent months when Arctic winds had thrown blizzard drifts in a blinding smother as high as the roof of the house.

Proceeding, the expedition reached Fort Providence where some twenty men were added to the party—mainly French-Canadian voyageurs and half-breeds who came on as hunters, workmen, canoe-men, and interpreters. Most of them were faithful and eager, especially at the beginning, and were capable of prodigious amounts of work. Some stayed with the party through all the terrible times that came later. One, however, the half-breed Michel, an interpreter and a man whom both Franklin and Richardson personally liked, almost cost the expedition the lives of the leaders themselves.

They set out for Great Slave Lake, then worked a slow route north and northwest by way of Great Bear Lake, with the intention of reaching the shores of the Arctic Ocean where the Coppermine River flows into what was later called Coronation Gulf. It was an immense, trackless country that seemed endless to traverse. Yet along the way John Richardson now and again collected a bird specimen and prepared it during the evening's camp. Most of his discoveries, however, took place near the forts and Hudson's Bay posts, where there was leisure enough for this pursuit. He was finding some of the species which much later would honor the leaders of the expedition—Franklin's grouse, Richardson's grouse, Franklin's gull, and Richardson's owl. This latter was the little bird the Montagnais Indians called *phillip-pile-tschsh,* the Water-dripping Owl, which, they said, had challenged the voice of the waterfall and, in reproof, had been made small by the Great Spirit, with a high-pitched, bell-like voice. But the Crees called it the Death-bird, *Cheepai-peethees,* and believed that whoever heard the little owl's melancholy whistle must whistle back at once. If the owl replied, all was well, but if it did not, the man thus ignored would die.

There was much to do, and a short summer in which to do it. The way had to be mapped and pictures drawn; food had to be obtained daily by the hunters, and it was sometimes difficult to find. Soon it had grown so late in the season that they knew they would never get safely to the Arctic Ocean and back again that year. The warm season was so short, the distances so long.

At the southwest end of Great Bear Lake they built Fort Franklin for winter quarters. The French-Canadians could build a house in quick time; they were eager fellows, and experts. They hewed timber, cut logs, and built a house fifty feet long and twenty-four feet wide, containing a hall, three bedrooms, a kitchen, and big fireplaces. Later the men added the niceties of bedsteads, tables, and chairs. But unfortunately, the winter winds were soon whistling with vigor through the cracks between the logs. The clay beside the lake had been too cold to stick when they had tried to chink the logs with it. The men finally doused water over the whole exterior of the house, and thus sealed it up in ice. Soon the great dryness of the cold caused the ice to disappear, and the wind came through as freely as before. Nevertheless, it was far better than being outside when the temperature reached sixty degrees below zero. The chimneys drew well, and the fireplaces were a luxury when the wind was a demon and the North a menace.

The next spring, when the belated thaw came at last, the mosquitoes returned and the geese arrived. Dr. Richardson discovered the Arctic bluebird, blue as a summer sky, hovering around the fort. By July the expedition again was on its way to the Arctic

Ocean, with Dr. Richardson going on ahead so that he would have more time to hunt for birds, plants, and mineral specimens. He was first to arrive on a barren, wind-swept promontory of utmost bleakness, and to stand at last, shading his eyes against the hard light, above an ocean filled with broken ice as far as he could see. The great loneliness and the great mystery of the Arctic for a long moment were his.

To some of the others, when they arrived, the Arctic was terrifying. The Indians who had promised to assist as guides and hunters began to desert, and several of the French-Canadians were afraid to stay in this forsaken land of ice. They wanted to leave, and had to be watched to make sure they did not slip off. Yet they were afraid to go alone—where would they go in all that vastness? And they had heard gruesome tales of what Eskimos did to men that they captured.

Ignoring the cowards and complainers, the leaders set about exploring the shores on foot and by canoe, and gave names to rivers and capes and points. They went north to the Melville Peninsula where Richardson found a small, exquisite gull, the Ross's gull, with bluish wings and back and rose-pink breast. He named it for Sir James Clark Ross, eminent British navigator in the Arctic. The black-and-white duck with a white crescent on its purple-black head he named Barrow's goldeneye, for his friend, Sir John Barrow—"as a tribute to Mr. Barrow's varied talents, and his unwearied exertions for the promotion of science." Later, when Richardson's and Swainson's book was being written, Mr. Swainson rather acidly remarked that naming new birds for just anyone who might have contributed some iota of encouragement to science was all too common a practice and he did not hold with it, though grudgingly admitting that John Barrow might possibly deserve this current honor.

While the pack ice menaced, they ranged along the shores. As the supply of food grew scarce, the men grew more afraid. They had premonitions of all the game leaving the coast, and the noise of the ice kept them constantly uneasy. For a time their fears were relieved and their stomachs filled when a large polar bear was killed —a trifle fishy-tasting, Franklin thought, but to hungry men it was certainly palatable.

Franklin named a cape for his friend, John Barrow, then named a stopping place Turnagain Point, whence they headed back to the mainland. By August 14 the eider ducks were beginning to stream southward in tremendous flocks. The pack ice was up against the shore. The navigation season was over.

Up until this point, when it was time to leave the shores of the Arctic Ocean, the expedition had been successful. Not too many hardships had been endured. They had always managed to shoot some game before anyone was really too desperately hungry; in fact, if the French-Canadians did not like the idea of eating the meat of seal, for instance, they disdainfully rejected it. They could be very dainty about their eating if there was any choice and if they were not too hungry.

But supplies were now undeniably scarce, and game was leaving the shores with a finality which meant that winter was alarmingly close. Franklin had stayed a little too long in the fascinating country as he tried to ferret a way among the numerous islands and land masses in the ice-clogged sea, looking for a northwest passage. He had stayed too long. They could not now return by the much longer and more circuitous route down the Coppermine to Fort Franklin. After a conference, Richardson and Franklin decided in desperation to cross through the Barren Grounds at a slant southeast to reach Fort Enterprise. So that there would be enough food on hand when the party arrived, they sent ahead some of the remaining Indians to inform the men at the fort. Then began the incredibly terrible journey to reach the fort.

The Barren Grounds over which they traveled were composed of low, rocky tundra with no elevations except occasional cliffs to break the force of wind and cold. There was insufficient wood to make fire to cook what little food could be found. Starvation was a perpetual and desperate presence. Franklin himself had a fainting fit from exhaustion and hunger. Richardson was emaciated and gaunt. The hunters came back without meat. Now and again they shot ptarmigan, but there was never enough. It was learned later that the reason several of the hunters maintained their own strength so well was that they kept a supply of gunpowder and balls for themselves, often shot partridges or other meat and cooked and ate it before returning empty-handed to the starving party.

Blizzards followed the beating rains across the Barren Grounds and blurred their gray monotony. Ice that formed on tundra pools was not yet thick enough to risk their crossing on it. Yet, when it seemed that all was surely lost and they would starve, someone always managed to shoot a reindeer or a fox. They ate it all—everything—entrails, ears, lungs, and they cracked the bones for the marrow. In between meat meals they subsisted meagerly on rock tripe, a particularly nauseous lichen covering the rocks of the tundra with a black scaliness. It had nourishment when boiled, with what little meat they had, to a slimy, loathsome porridge. It helped to keep them alive, though some of the men became ill every time they ate it.

If they saw birds now, it was purely from the standpoint of using them for food. The white-tailed ptarmigan which Richardson had discovered was still present as a welcome food, but there was little else, very little. Dr. Richardson regretfully had to leave behind a bundle of bird and plant specimens because he was too tired and weak to carry them any farther, and he would not ask the men to carry anything for him. Piece by piece the equipment, the tents, the specimens, were all discarded on the trackless, snow-covered Barren Grounds. It was no longer a time to think of science; it was a matter of maintaining life itself.

Painfully, horribly, the men struggled on. They were reduced to eating deerskin from which the hair was singed off; reduced to scavenging the already gnawed and picked carcasses of long-dead reindeer which the wolves had killed and eaten months before.

When one of these treasures was come upon, the men pounded the bones between two rocks to get out the acrid, black marrow. It excoriated their lips and tongues. They boiled moccasin leather. For a time, this and the rock tripe were all they had.

The lack of food made the cold harder to endure. Dr. Richardson noted that when they had had something to eat, they slept warm at night even though the cold was intense and the wind a punishment; but when they had nothing, no amount of covering or fire seem to warm them. Yet, each time that energy and hope seemed lowest, and the Barren Grounds endless and revengeful, they again managed to kill enough small game to reanimate their failing spirits and feeble bodies.

When things were at the lowest ebb and Hood was ill and could go no farther, two of the French-Canadians did not come back to the camp from their day's hunt. Those who went out to search for them declared that the pair could not be found. But Michel, who continued in an astonishingly well-nourished condition, next day asked to borrow an ax. When he came back he had some chunks of frozen meat which he said came from a dead wolf. The men at the camp, without questioning or caring as long as it was edible, cooked and ate the meat. Not until later did Franklin and Richardson realize that it had undoubtedly come from the two missing men.

Hood could not continue until he had rested for a while and had gained a little strength. With the last tent set up in the comparative shelter of some low spruces, he was left with Dr. Richardson, Michel, and some of the others. Franklin determined to push on to the fort, which was believed to be not much farther distant. He would send back help. And while the party was thus separated and consequently weakened in strength against an enemy which was stronger even than that of hunger and cold, Michel, the villain, determined to be the only survivor. Coming unseen into the tent, he shot Hood in the back of the head.

Richardson heard the shot and hurried to where Hood had been lying ill, and found him face down, dead. Michel told an implausible tale of having seen Hood shoot himself. But when Richardson in grief examined his dead friend and saw that the ball had entered at the back of the head at a slant, he looked up suddenly and saw such evil in Michel's eyes that he knew with grim certainty that none of them would now be safe. If only help might come quickly from the fort!

The next day John Richardson discovered Michel aiming his gun coldly and steadily at another member of the party. Richardson himself was so weak that he could scarcely lift his own gun, but he knew he must do it. Leaning there on his elbow, and trembling, he brought the piece up high enough and shot Michel cleanly through the heart. Richardson, the gentle bird man, the physician pledged to save lives, lay back on the ground, faint and ill. He had killed a man. But if he had not, that man would have destroyed them all.

Help did not come. Feeling that something terrible must have gone wrong, Richardson and the survivors from the camp dragged themselves at last to Fort Enterprise.

When they first caught sight of the bleak fort on the wind-swept, snow-drifted landscape, they knew with a sinking feeling that something was very wrong. Only a feeble wisp of smoke issued from one chimney; there was no sign of life anywhere. The windows were bare and open, with no parchment left in them to keep out the cold and wind. The temperature was twenty degrees below zero . . . and a premonition of doom settled upon John Richardson as he came up to the sagging door of the fort. Inside he found John Franklin and the others. Two of them were dead. The others seemed close to it.

Franklin aroused himself enough to whisper to Richardson the explanation of what had happened. They had come to the fort, had found it deserted—the windows open, as cold inside as out. They had scavenged bits of deerskin, some old bones . . . it was the end. There was no hope now.

But it was still not quite the end; not quite. The Indians who, long before, had been sent ahead to Fort Enterprise to prepare the way, finding it empty, had gone on to the next fort, all the way to Fort Chipewyan, for help and food. They got back several days after Richardson and the others arrived.

The Indians brought meat and tea and bread. They were shocked at the white men's debilitation, were tender as mothers with young children in caring for them. They removed the dead bodies, built up the fires, brewed tea and broth and cooked the meat. The starving men were so feeble that they could not at first feed themselves. The Indians fed them gently. Then the men ate too much and were violently ill in consequence. It had been so long since their stomachs had held much of anything; it would take time to get used to eating again.

The Indians stayed with them. They patched up the windows, shut out some of the cold, nursed the white men until they could travel again, and finally got them to Fort Chipewyan. The ordeal was over. In the spring they went on and rejoined the ship at York Factory.

From the hardships and physical debility and loss of life which took place on this calamitous expedition, one would think that John Franklin and John Richardson would have had enough of the Arctic, but the North had worked its insidious spell. Unpleasant though it might be, it called, and they returned. There were lands that Franklin determined to explore more fully, now that he had the measure of the North, and there were a great many more birds for Richardson. He could not forget those abandoned specimens on the Barren Grounds; he needed to re-collect what he had lost. So they went back.

This time, in 1825, with the experience of the first expedition clearly in mind, they came better equipped, the planning was wiser, and precautions were taken against starvation and illness. From Hudson Bay the party again set off on much the same route as before to the Coppermine River. They spent the winter at Fort Franklin, which was still standing, and went down the Mackenzie River to see the northern terminus of the Rocky Mountains. They continued to Point Franklin westward on the Arctic Ocean, but did not see the ship they had half-way expected.

This was the *Blossom*, commanded by Captain Beechey, coming the long way around to probe into the Arctic Ocean as far as he could, mapping and charting, looking for that still-hoped-for passage. If Franklin's party had met the *Blossom*, some of them might have gone back to England with it. But the Arctic Ocean was empty of sails; there were only the jostling sea ice, the white bears, walruses, and seals, the king eiders, Ross's gulls, white geese, and now and again some Eskimos.

Failing to meet the *Blossom*, the men went by canoe in the other direction—eastward among the islands and land masses in the Gulf of Bothnia near Baffinland. It was not easy; the Arctic was never easy. But it was bearable, and they almost always had enough to eat.

Richardson returned to England with many more new birds. He had at the same time gathered a tremendous amount of knowledge on the breeding birds in the Arctic. Later, much of this material was used in the splendid book which he and William Swainson wrote, entitled *Fauna Boreali-Americana*—for many years the guidebook and source of authority about Canadian and Arctic birds.

On May 26, 1845, John Franklin, who had become Sir John Franklin, but without Sir John Richardson, set off again for the Arctic. He was confident now that he could find the way from the North Atlantic to the North Pacific via the Arctic Ocean. With two sturdy vessels equipped and designed to withstand the pressure of ice, and with 140 men in the party, he headed for the North. From his past experiences he knew exactly what to do and where he wanted to go; with his present equipment and knowledge, there could only be success for an expedition which would add new information about the tantalizing North and would blaze the hoped-for route of the Northwest Passage.

There was, therefore, no real reason why the expedition should fail. The ships reached Whalefish Islands in Baffin Bay on July 12, 1845, from which point they sent back letters via a whaler heading for England . . . and Sir John Franklin and his 140 men were never seen or heard from again. They had vanished.

The North had not, after all, been conquered. It had only been waiting, like a monster in a cave, to pounce. The North had let them get back to civilization that first time, when there had been every reason why Franklin and Richardson and the others should have left their bones on the tundra; had let them come back a second time and gain confidence in a successful and far easier trip. But on the third journey something happened. John Franklin and his men simply dropped out of existence. Evidence of their first winter's camp was discovered by searching parties. The Eskimos told of finding the remains of a party of white men, all dead; only forty of them, however, who had evidently suffered terribly and died in their remote camping place in the Arctic. But that accounted for only forty, and no one could say what had happened to the other hundred.

The mystery of what befell Sir John Franklin sparked further Arctic exploration. Ship after ship went out to search for him in the wilderness of the Arctic Ocean and around Baffin Bay. Some expeditions went over land, as Dr. John Rae did, up to Repulse Bay. It was he who received word of the remains at the death camp. But there was no real proof, no explanation.

Although the Franklin expedition dropped from sight in 1846, expeditions almost ten years later, including one of which his old friend Sir John Barrow, was a member were still going out with the search as an excuse. They brought back, if not news, information which continued to increase the world's knowledge of the Arctic and its wildlife, even more than Franklin himself had done.

Sir John Richardson, knowing the Arctic as well as anyone, finally sailed with Captain Sir Edward Belcher on the H.M.S. *Assistance* in 1852–54, on the last of the voyages to hunt for the missing men. And, as always, the now elderly Richardson was still collecting birds.

CHAPTER SEVENTEEN

THE TELEGRAPH TRAIL

THE Atlantic cable had snapped again. Men in discouragement said that a cable would never be successfully laid across the depths of rugged sea bottom from America to England. There was too much water, the Atlantic floor was too unknown, and the breaking of the cable once again proved that America and England could never be connected by wire.

It was then, in 1864, that the Western Union Telegraph Company, looking keenly at the map of the northwestern part of the American continent, and thinking of what had been suggested by a certain United States commercial agent in Siberia, decided that if the cable could not be laid to Europe, still a telegraph line might be sent to Russia. In that direction there was little break in the two land masses. There was only Bering Strait to cross. The line then could be carried through Siberia to St. Petersburg, which had direct connections with European points. It might seem the long way around, but at least the lines would be visible, would be above ground, and any difficulties encountered would not be those of ocean depths.

Permission was obtained by President Lincoln from Czar Alexander II of Russia. The Czar apparently was agreeable to the whole plan, which included bringing the lines up through Russian America, the common designation for Alaska. The Americans would install the telegraph wires as far as the Amur River; Russia would take them from there.

Queen Victoria graciously granted permission to set poles and string wires through British Columbia. Papers were signed, and on December 6, 1864, Abraham Lincoln in a message to Congress spoke of the new overland telegraph's having been undertaken "with the cordial good will and support as well of this government as of those of Great Britain and Russia."

The way from Puget Sound to Bering Strait lay through some of the most rugged wilderness terrain on the American continent, and some of the least known. To prepare the way and study the topography and natural history—long before a pole could be set or wire strung—a survey of the Russian-American territory was needed. The little-known Yukon River would have to be explored and mapped. There had to be some concrete knowledge of the geology and zoology, as well as of the people.

Young, exuberant Robert Kennicott was the man for the job. Selected as Chief of Explorations, Kennicott agreed to go to Alaska only if he were permitted to choose his own assistants, who would collect natural history specimens for the Chicago Academy of Sciences and the Smithsonian Institution. This was granted. To Robert Kennicott, lean, dark, and handsome, aged twenty-nine, and to the six young scientists he chose, it seemed almost too good to be true.

Robert Kennicott had already lived an exciting, full life in the field of natural science. Often frail in body, he was strong and active in mind, and full of an enthusiasm which was infectious to those around him. He loved a song, a joke, an unexplored country, and the sight of a new bird. Because of ill health in his youth, he had not been able to complete his formal education; but under his father, a physician in Northfield, Illinois, and with special tutoring elsewhere, he went far ahead in the delights of natural history. He studied ornithology with the celebrated Dr. J. E. Kirtland in Cincinnati, for whom the rare Kirtland's warbler was named by his friend, Professor Baird. It was Dr. Kirtland who sent Kennicott to Spencer F. Baird, who was now Secretary of the Smithsonian Institution and the friend of every aspiring young naturalist. Baird was continually alert for promising young men of ability and enthusiasm to whom a bird was adventure, and new forests, new waters, and new specimens were reason enough to face any hardship.

Because everything in the natural world fascinated Kennicott, he believed that the Middle West needed museums of natural history to preserve and display that wild life so that everyone could see and know it. When the newly formed Northwestern University planned a museum according to his ideas, he was engaged to make a collection of plants and animals to stock it. He was its first curator, as well as its chief collector and inspiration.

He collected extensively in his home territory around Lake Michigan and on the prairies. Then, feeling that a museum should be wider-spread than this, should represent a broader scope of wild life, he took himself alone to the North, carrying as little equipment as possible. He was only seventeen; the world was his.

It was a primitive life, and he loved it. He slept on the ground, rolled in a blanket, and lived on game, tea, and crackers. He traveled the old Red River road, northwest, narrowly missing being attacked by Indians who had shortly before massacred members of a party on that same precarious route. He joined a group of Red River carts going north, and went beyond Lake Winnipeg. It was an unforgettable journey, filled with the excitement of new country, from which he brought back no less than 2,500 zoological specimens: birds, mammals, insects, reptiles, and fish.

It seemed to his friends, to whom his outgoing nature and affectionate, selfless disposition were a delight, that he had no sooner come home than he was making plans to go off again to his beloved North. He had covered only a tiny part of it, and he had to go back.

Since Sir John Richardson had collected birds in Saskatchewan and the Arctic, little if anything had been done in that area. Sir

John had not gone into Russian-America at all. Little knowledge had come out of it in the years since Franklin's expeditions—chiefly from the fur traders and the Russians, or from explorers who had only touched at the coasts and brought back a few tantalizing specimens.

Leaving a steamer which had taken him to Fort William on the north shore of Lake Superior, Kennicott traveled with French-Canadian canoe men in a brigade going to the Hudson's Bay Company at Lake Winnipeg. The big Chippewa canoes were thirty-six feet long and four feet wide, each capable of carrying three thousand pounds of freight, manned by eight Indians paddling forty strokes to the minute, twelve to fifteen hours a day, with only brief breaks. Their stamina astounded him. The trip was really too rapid for a man who had to satisfy himself with observing everything he could see from the canoe and collecting quickly during the brief stops.

There were portages; he was thankful for these, but there were few other delays. They reached Lake Winnipeg and Norway House, the Hudson's Bay post at the north end of the lake, and then he went on alone, following much the same route taken by Franklin and Richardson up the Saskatchewan to Cumberland House. He was beset with mosquitoes; he camped on wet ground. He reached Lake Athabaska and Fort Resolution at the mouth of the Slave River, and then the headwaters of the Mackenzie River, which flows into the Arctic Ocean. He was a long, long way from Chicago.

With side trips into cold of sixty-two degrees below zero, he spent the winter at Fort Simpson on the Mackenzie, went down to Fort Liard, southward, hunting, studying Indian languages, and then walked back to Fort Simpson in nine days. He was forcing himself at times beyond endurance, but short rests satisfied him. There was much to see, to learn, to accomplish. Knowing, as his friends did later, that he had a bad heart, Kennicott was certainly daring providence.

From the Mackenzie in the summer he crossed the mountains into Russian territory and went on through the rough country to the Porcupine River, a branch of the Yukon. There he obtained a canoe and went down the Yukon itself to Fort Yukon, where he spent the long winter of 1860–61. There was no real daylight; the flaring of the northern lights illuminated the dark sky and cast a strange purple and pink shine over the snow. He learned to adapt to the Arctic night, which was not really dark. He learned how to manipulate a dog team. His dogs responded to him; he loved them. It was a joy to see them trotting fast, with heads and ears and tails up, tongues out, coming up to the fort or galloping with a fine flourish out to La Pierre House.

Nothing seemed too hard, too cold, too dangerous to Kennicott when he was doing what he loved, and everything he found in the North was soul-stirring and a challenge. He did not mind being away from home at Christmas, and spent it memorably on the trail. The temperature held at forty degrees below zero and the snow was deep and powdery on the mountain slopes as he returned from the fort at Peel's River with his dogs and a load of furs, and half a dozen French-Canadians similarly occupied. On Christmas morning, 1861, they were crossing a high range, and all paused at the summit to get their breath before the swift descent over the dry snow in cold that seared the lungs.

Christmas. He thought of Christmas in Chicago. It was certainly another world, and he laughed. He wished he could at least smoke a cigar in honor of the holiday, but he couldn't do that, it was just too cold. So to the astonishment of the fur men and the dogs, he simply yelled instead, "Merry Christmas!" He shouted it to the brittle trees and the cold dark sky and the depths of snow with the strange illumination from northern lights. The fur men grinned and answered with their "*Joyeux Noel!*" The yelling roused the dogs and they were up, tails wagging, ready to go—and off they all went, with Kennicott leading the way on the runners of his sled, singing *La Claire Fontaine* at the top of his voice. The fur men joined in and the dogs barked and leaped ahead with a will. He thought the dogs really liked it; he often sang when he was out with them and noticed that they always worked better than if he was glum. So they all raced down the mountainside on Christmas day, in a land where it was midnight at noonday, and reached the next fort by that night.

Another summer of collecting and another winter in the North, and he started for home. He had been sending his collections back by anyone who was going that way. He reached Chicago in October, 1862.

He had started something in that northern wilderness. No one had ever seen his like up there. His enthusiasm for collecting specimens had aroused an urge to do likewise in men he had met and lived with on the Hudson's Bay posts—even in the fur men. He had encouraged them to send their collections to him at the Smithsonian. His friend, William Healy Dall, said of him:

> The advent of Kennicott, young, joyous, full of news of the outside world, ready to engage in any of their expeditions or activities and to take hardships without grumbling was an event in their lives. When he taught them how to make bird-skins and collect Natural History objects and showed them how, by means of their collections, their names would become known in the civilized world and even printed in books, they seized on the project with enthusiasm. . . . For more than ten years, collections poured into Washington from the North until those who had been inspired by Kennicott retired from active service.

In 1864, the newly formed Chicago Academy of Sciences bestowed upon him the first curatorship. But what he liked best was going out to collect, especially in his beloved North country.

This, then, was the logical man to be selected to go to Russian-America as Chief of Exploration, to blaze the way for the Telegraph Trail. He had served a few months in the Civil War and now as Major he accepted the new position. His six assistants all made names for themselves later on in natural history. They were J. T. Rothrock, botanist; William H. Dall, H. W. Elliott, Charles Pease (who had discovered the rare Kirtland's warbler in 1851), Henry M. Bannister, and Ferdinand Bischoff, zoologists and geologists; and G. W. Maynard, who come on as a volunteer and general naturalist. They were all in their twenties, all excited, all filled with boundless enthusiasm and energy, and ready to do anything Kennicott suggested.

The Civil War was nearing its end when they steamed out of New York harbor on March 21, 1865, and sailed to Nicaragua. Disembarking, they walked or rode or poled a boat across the isthmus—fascinated by the jungles en route—to take ship, the *America*, on the other side. This was a good deal faster than having to travel around the Horn and up the coast of South America.

As they proceeded up the Pacific coast they passed a steamer from San Francisco—it was April 23—which came close enough to shout the news: Richmond had been taken, the war was over, and President Lincoln had been assassinated. The shocked hearers sent out a small boat to get the latest San Francisco newspapers, and for the rest of the day the ship held an excited and saddened group. As young Henry Bannister said: "It would not have been safe for any one to have uttered any secession sentiments aboard of the *America* at that time."

At San Francisco there was a long halt for outfitting and a transfer to a different ship. While they were there, Kennicott became suddenly ill in his hotel room. He was gasping for breath, his lips blue, his face white. They forced brandy down his throat and he came out of the attack, but he was ill and weak for several days. He had not really recovered when he insisted that the expedition proceed. His friends were deeply worried about him, but he persuaded them he was really quite all right. His cheerfulness returned, he smiled again that cajoling smile, and he looked himself at last.

The construction crew, meanwhile, was already working north from Puget Sound, finding the easiest grades, clearing the great trees of coast spruce and white cedar, cutting and trimming poles, digging holes, setting poles, stringing lines—mile by mile by mile.

Kennicott's party went at once to St. Michael's in Russian America, located on the coast above the Aleutians and not far below the Arctic Circle. Preliminary explorations were made, and then a base was settled at St. Michael's. Henry Bannister, aged twenty-one, was left in charge of supplies; he was to carry on the meteorological observations and collect birds for the Smithsonian. Young Henry did not have the physical stamina to endure the heavy going and hardship in the back country. Although his feelings were hurt at being left on the coast, where life was inordinately dull, and although he did not have enough to read, he filled his part on the expedition.

The exploring group, meanwhile, went out to Unalakleet, on Norton Sound sixty miles above St. Michael's, from which point they separated into two parties. Kennicott led one party across the rough portage of about a hundred miles to Nulato—a small Russian trading village five hundred miles up the Yukon River from St. Michael's, but only a fifth of that distance from Norton Sound. It was a possibility as a direction over which to carry the telegraph lines. From Nulato, Kennicott was to proceed up the Yukon and explore its headwaters, then make contact with the construction crew coming up from the south. There had been word of their progress; they were coming astonishingly fast, considering the kind of country in which they were working. They were to meet Kennicott and his men somewhere on the watershed between the Yukon and the Frazer.

The other group, under William H. Dall, was exploring the portage between the Yukon and Bering Strait, working out a trail over which the telegraph line would be taken, and collecting birds, plants, and mammals as they worked. Kennicott saw that a house was built at Unalakleet on the coast for the party's winter quarters; winter was always quick in coming to the Arctic and there was very little time to work in the short summer. With three men, then, he made his way over the portage to Nulato, according to plan, and the four took winter quarters there.

With the return of the geese and the arrival of the eider ducks and gulls in late April, spring came. There were loons on the open waters, thrushes singing in the leafing willows. Henry Bannister at St. Michael's, William Dall at Unalakleet, and Robert Kennicott at Nulato were out daily watching for the arrival of birds, looking for new ones, noting what kinds were beginning to nest. Among these three ornithological experts, not much would be missed.

Henry Bannister, moodily ranging along the shore and into the tundra back of St. Michael's in search of anything to break the monotony of life in this remote outpost of nowhere, saw a little greenish-yellow bird dive into the Labrador tea bushes. His boredom vanished, he followed, and although the little creature slipped about fluidly and almost eluded him entirely, he managed to get his bird. It was a warbler, yet even smaller, he thought, than most warblers he had known; it was something like a kinglet, but it wasn't a kinglet, either. He prepared the skin and tried to find out more about his bird. It would probably have to wait for Kennicott or even for Professor Baird to identify it.

William Dall, hunting along the coast, found an owl different from any he had ever known; it seemed to be a cross between the screech owl and the long-eared owl, and was a splendidly handsome specimen. He felt that Kennicott would be most pleased with this discovery, which was undoubtedly a new species.

Kennicott and his companions at Nulato had endured the long winter, had gone out with the Indians into the grim mountains to the west of the village and had sought for a pass leading to the coast. The mountains were a vast array of height and rock and snow so formidably aligned that he could not see how a telegraph line might be put through without the greatest effort and hardship.

Kennicott worked long hours and often did not rest well at night.

His dark eyes sometimes looked enormous in a face whose bones were showing under the skin. As spring came slowly, with mud on the river bank and skeins of geese in the sky, he seemed more like himself. He joked, laughed, sometimes burst into song as he liked to do. But after a long trip into the unrelenting mountains which even springtime could not soften, he looked unwell. He went to bed early the night of May 12, 1866. The others were worried about him. Some time in the night Robert Kennicott got out of bed, lit a lamp, and spent a long time writing careful directions to his successor, who would have to finish the expedition in case something happened to him. He did not want affairs left disordered, their value lost.

Up early the next day, he went out into the spring chill along the Yukon River and began to mark lines on the mud, indicating the arrangement of the mountains and trying to figure where a pass would be as seen from here. He used his compass and marked the figures on the pliable mud before they were transferred to his notebook.

When he did not come in to breakfast, the men scattered to search. They found him face down on the Yukon shore, dead.

It was a great grief to his friends, who had loved him. Word came to Henry Bannister at St. Michael's, to Ferdinand Bischoff at Sitka, to William Dall out at Unalakleet. The heart of the expedition had gone.

But Kennicott's work had not ended. Following his written directions, his associates under Dall continued the exploration of the Yukon River; the peninsula from the head of Norton Sound to Bering Strait was explored, and so was the stretch between Norton Sound and Nulato, though they never found the easy passage Kennicott had sought.

Meanwhile, part of the telegraph crew had been working across Bering Strait, heading slowly toward the Amur River with the lines. It was from this point that the Russians would continue to St. Petersburg. The Americans had accomplished a good deal. They were progressing over the difficult Arctic landscape and with some satisfaction were flying the United States flag as they went—perhaps the only time this flag was ever flown for so long in Russia.

Then the blow fell. Belatedly, the word came that Cyrus Field had actually succeeded in laying the Atlantic cable. Queen Victoria and President Johnson had sent congratulatory messages to each other. There was no need now for the Western Union Telegraph's lines to Russia. The project, with its millions of dollars of expense and its glowing enthusiasm, was dropped. Later, some of the Alaskan Indians were discovered using discarded coils of telegraph wire as a framework for their skin-covered houses.

Kennicott was gone. The Telegraph Trail had all been a useless business. His friends might have wondered bitterly whether he would have died so tragically and so young if he had not gone to Alaska on that fruitless expedition. Yet much of value remained. The reports went to the Smithsonian. Professor Baird, who was the government's consultant on exploration, had them available when William Seward was groping for the right answer to the question of purchasing Alaska for the United States. The reports of Dall, Bischoff, and Bannister, and the latter's presence in Washington at that crucial time, turned the tide of opinion toward buying the land which was facetiously known as "Uncle Sam's Ice Box" and "Seward's Folly"—land popularly supposed to be occupied solely by walruses, Eskimos, and perpetual snow and ice. Henry Bannister went with Spencer Baird to the hearing and presented his facts to Senator Sumner and Secretary Seward. The purchase of Alaska went through.

Robert Kennicott left his mark on the landscape and in the files of zoological literature. The little bird which Henry Bannister had found on the tundra back of St. Michael's was named Kennicott's Arctic warbler. A sharp-tailed grouse found by Kennicott at Great Slave Lake in 1861 also bears his name as discoverer, and the owl found by Bischoff near Sitka became known as Kennicott's screech owl. The name was bestowed by Daniel Giraud Elliot, who said:

In bestowing on this Owl the name which I trust it is ever destined to bear, I simply express the desire which I am sure is felt by all ornithologists, to render honor to him who, combining the intrepidity of the explorer with the enthusiasm of a naturalist, twice penetrated the forbidding cheerless districts of the far north, in order to extend the knowledge of his favorite science; and who perished in his early manhood, in the full tide of usefulness, on the banks of the Yukon.

The fine specimen of Kennicott's owl which was sent by Dall to the Chicago Academy of Sciences was borrowed by Elliot when he was preparing his magnificent books on the birds discovered after Audubon and Wilson. This portrait was painted by A. Wolf in London, who returned the owl—in time for it to be consumed in the Chicago Fire.

Through Kennicott and his companions, Alaska's wildlife was extensively explored. Dall's sheep were discovered, and 212 species of birds were collected and their habits and distribution studied. This was all virtually new material. After these reports were in, more was known by Americans about a relatively unknown and very newly acquired territory than in all its history before this time. Robert Kennicott and the Telegraph Trail had served their purpose.

CHAPTER EIGHTEEN

THE CRUISE
OF THE CORWIN

AGAINST the heavy sheathing and the icebreaker bow of the revenue cutter *Corwin*, the pack ice crunched and resounded and broke away. Then it built up an all but impervious barrier which threatened to squeeze the *Corwin* in a grip that would crush her sides, smash her decks, knock down her masts, and set her crew on the ice, if they were lucky enough to get there before the ship sank, to make their way back to land if they could. That was what had happened to the *Jeannette* the year before. Only thirteen out of thirty-four men had finally reached civilization after a desperate retreat across the ice, and it was primarily to hunt for traces of the rest that the *Corwin* was on this cruise into the Arctic. Two whalers also were missing, and news was sought of any survivors.

The *Corwin*, a trim little steam vessel 137 feet along, which also carried sails for emergencies, was a government ship with a duty to perform in patrolling the seal and otter islands in the Pribilovs against illegal hunting, and to hunt for men set on the ice by a ship's disaster. She also did her share in exploring Arctic natural history—on most voyages at least one naturalist was aboard. The ill-fated *Jeannette* had had one also, who desperately had held on to his newly found bird specimens as he made his way across the ice.

On the *Corwin's* 1881 voyage in search of the *Jeannette,* John Muir had come aboard at San Francisco to make geological and glaciological studies and to collect plants. And at St. Michael's, Alaska, a man had been watching for days for the arrival of the ship bearing his friend Muir, who had never had what he liked to call the "house habit," but was more comfortable in the wild mountains, among pines, far away from people. It was strange to think of John Muir on a ship in the Arctic. Yet the Arctic was a wilderness of the worst sort, and it fascinated him. He had left his young wife behind when the Arctic called.

On the bleak shore with the unpainted frame buildings behind him, the towers of the weathered gray Russian church standing against the backdrop of the dark mountains, and the tundra stretching between town and mountains, Edward M. Nelson waved a greeting to the *Corwin.* He could see Muir on the bow, whiskers blowing in the wind, telescope in hand, surveying him and the shores. Trust Muir to have come well equipped with everything he needed!

While the *Corwin* was loading coal and supplies for the extended cruise northward into the ice, Nelson and Muir went out to the tundra for a field trip. They had an exciting time sinking knee-deep in the sphagnum and among plants which the delighted Muir called a "spongy plush." He dug down through the vegetation and found permafrost and ice only a little way below. The ice itself lay on a bedrock of black lava.

The two collected vigorously in the short time they had. The tundra came into bloom in those several days before they sailed. There were andromeda and bearberry and cassiope and twinflower, primroses and bluebells and alp-lilies. The white-crowned sparrows piped along the edges of the Labrador tea bushes, and the Siberian wagtails in their spectacular black-and-white plumage were parading in their long-strided gait along the shores. The two naturalists disliked to leave, but the ship was departing for further adventure in lands even more remote than the tundra at St. Michael's.

The *Corwin* moved into the ice. Over the northern horizon they saw the strange, lightly shimmering, yellow-white glow of the distant iceblink telling of the pack ice beyond the Arctic Circle. Floating ice was growing more dense, yet it parted as the sturdy ship nosed through. Near Herald Island it was so heavy that they came to an abrupt halt many times. With ice masses jammed high all about them, higher than the decks and spilling over on them, it would seem that they were stuck for good. Yet before the pressure grew too great, there would be an opening, a lead, and the ship would shove through, backing and pushing, backing again for a run, the engines grinding and black smoke pouring. They would get through at last. But always with them was the knowledge that it was here, near Herald Island, that the *Jeannette* had been crushed and gone down.

Near the island the ice was solid, old, and very dense, as if it had been there forever. This was as close as the *Corwin* could come to the bleak contours of this lone Arctic island.

The principal reason for attempting a landing here at all was to look for evidence of any survivors from the *Jeannette*. It was the logical place for them to seek haven; or they might have left a cairn and a message in case they had been taken off by Eskimo *bidarka*. To Muir and Nelson, the stop at Herald Island was an unparalleled chance to look for the birds and flowers of an uninhabited, unexplored island.

As the ship halted at the edge of the solid ice, the whole island ahead seemed to be a vast aviary swarming with birds. The two naturalists were reminded of what Baron Nordenskiold had written during his voyage of the *Vega:*

It is not the larger inhabitants of the Polar regions, such as the whale, walrus, bear, and seal, which first attract the explorer's attention, but the innumerable flocks of birds that swarm around the Polar traveller

during the long summer day of the North. And this is especially striking about any of the islands which birds—the gulls, guillemots, and
auks—seek as breeding places. The islands of Bering Straits resemble
enormous bee-hives, about which the birds swarm in countless numbers, filling the air with their swiftly moving forms in every direction,
and the waters are covered with them all about the islands, while every
jutting point and place where foothold can be obtained is taken possession of by them for breeding places.

Sheer above the narrow beach, crowded with rocks and ice, the
shaly cliffs rose a thousand feet from the sea. A massive snowbank
slanted up at one place; the rest was a grim jumble of ice, deep gul-
lies, and nearly perpendicular cliffs. But when the *Corwin* stopped
and permission was given to go ashore, the men could not get to
this forbidding place fast enough. The island had been discovered
in 1849 by Captain Kellett and named for his ship, the *Herald*, but
he had not landed, and no one, it was believed, had ever been there
before. The men of the *Corwin* were making history and each
wanted to be the first to stand on the summit of the brooding, wind-
swept cliffs. Muir and Nelson, however, had their own plans and
left the crew who, in their hurry, had some narrow escapes from
falling into crevasses as they went across the sea ice to the island.

On the beach the crew had to go down into a steep ravine before they could commence the climb up the cliffs. The men slipped
and fell; those who were ahead sent down avalanches of loose shale
onto those below. The ones above got stuck on a ledge and could
neither go up nor down. When the captain in disgust ordered them
to return, the ones below had to stand clear of the landslide each
man made as he came down through the shale.

But Muir had known mountains before. With his telescope he
had examined the island and had seen the great snowbank. Therefore, when he and Nelson with their collecting equipment went
cautiously across the sea ice to the island, it was to the snow area
that they headed. Muir had brought an ax. Neatly cutting steps in
the packed snow, the pair mounted with ease to the top of the
island. Up there, and on all the ledges on the far sides of the island—

everywhere—they found birds.

Birds! Neither had ever before seen so many in one place. Every rocky projection was covered with eggs and brooding birds— white gulls, black, penguin-like murres, guillemots, and auks, with little chubby black-and-white auklets and murrelets. There were curious tufted puffins with enormous red-and-orange beaks and a pair of yellow plumes on either side of the head. As the men walked among them, or peered down at them from the top of the cliff, the birds rose in a deafening clamor of wing-beats and shrill cackles and cries; then they swept back and forth before returning in a great surge to their eggs.

The top of the island was covered with four-inch dwarf willows hugging the rock in the endless cold and wind. Among them the flocks of snow buntings flew and sang, and there were small flowers that charmed Muir. It was astonishing how much life existed on an island which from the ship had appeared to be nothing more than barren, purple-black rock jutting from the deadly ice.

White Arctic foxes were abundant and unafraid—not belligerent, only intensely curious. They sat about watching the two men, came close, sniffing, retreating a little distance again to watch. When Edward Nelson laid down his notebook, a fox slipped in and ran off with it to its burrow before he could retrieve it. With some difficulty, they captured a young fox and took it back with them to the ship, where it became very tame and confiding.

Muir and Nelson explored until two o'clock in the morning. There was no real darkness and it was difficult to realize what time it was. While Nelson was off along the bird ledges, Muir had stood alone at midnight on the highest point of Herald Island. It was one of the most impressive hours of his life.

The enormous silence pressed down on that whole vast, virgin landscape, while the sun lying near the horizon reddened the masses of ice in the frozen ocean—with the dim blue bulk of mysterious Wrangell Island a hundred miles away on the horizon.

There was no sign that any other men, certainly no one from

the *Jeannette*, had ever been there. It was as if the two were the first and the last men ever to stand on Herald Island. Then Muir looked out to the open water and with a jolt he saw the *Corwin* steaming off into the loose ice.

It was not possible. The captain had assured them that he was not going to leave until tomorrow. Or had time escaped them in their preoccupation with the island? Nelson, who also had seen the *Corwin* sailing off, hastily joined Muir. Both knew some disquieting feelings of alarm. Herald Island was not the place they would choose to be marooned.

Carrying their specimens, they went back to the beach where, after several hours of waiting, they saw the ship return and signal them to come aboard. The captain had simply reconnoitered the island and had had no intentions of abandoning them. But it was extremely good to be back in a warm cabin, with a bunk, and food, and comforts. The bleak summit of Herald Island with its white foxes and its millions of screaming, flying, odorous birds was certainly not the place for an extended stay.

They watched the shape of Wrangell Island draw nearer and take on character. The water was open enough for the *Corwin* to steam in fairly close for a brief stop so that the men could go ashore in the small boats. The captain went also and claimed Wrangell Island for the United States, planting the flag in the whipping Arctic wind. But no sooner had this ceremony been completed and Muir and Nelson had begun to get their bearings for an extended exploration than they were all called back to the ship. There had been a sudden change in the ice conditions. A strong tide was surging the massive chunks into the lately open water, so that the ship could not stay long in safety and it was risky even for the small boats to come back.

Muir complained with some heat that there was too little time to see or collect much of anything in this unexplored place, and Nelson himself had found nothing new among birds in his brief excursion. It was a great disappointment, and they looked back longingly as the boats took them off and away forever from Wrangell Island. Then a sailor in the same boat with Nelson touched him hesitantly on the shoulder and gave him a dead bird.

The man had a sheepish expression. He said he knew it wasn't much of a bird. He and the others had been somewhat infected by the naturalists' zeal for collecting and had realized that a new specimen was evidently the fondest wish of these two important gentlemen from the world of science. To the sailors, the relative value of plant, bird, or mammal was quite unknown.

The sailor had picked up the dried mummy of a bird on the rocks of Wrangell's harsh beach and his fellows had dared him to give it to the "bird man" and see what he would say to a gift like this useless thing. All were taken aback by Nelson's delight. This was one of the greatest prizes of the entire cruise of the *Corwin*, at least from the standpoint of ornithology.

It was the crested shrike, an Asiatic bird. Carefully preserved in alcohol, it was brought back to the Smithsonian Institution, where Robert Ridgway painted a picture of it as it may have been in life. He depicted it perched on a piece of driftwood, which Edward Nelson had said he had seen floating off Wrangell; driftwood was rare in the ice pack, but he had found some there. In the background is forbidding Wrangell itself, taken from the sketch which John Muir made from the ship before they departed.

Edward Nelson, the man who had discovered Nelson's sparrow in the Calumet marshes near Chicago in 1875, was a member of the U.S. Signal Corps and had been stationed for a year at St. Michael's, Alaska, during which time the cruise of the *Corwin* was the highlight of his experiences. He was an expert naturalist who roamed the tundra and the stunted forests around Norton Sound and found many new birds. There were several kinds of ptarmigan and other grouse in the area, and among these he located the species which is now called Nelson's ptarmigan. He also found Nelson's downy woodpecker, Nelson's gull, and the first known sharp-tailed sandpipers recorded on the coast of North America. To a bird in flight, the forty-mile stretch between Siberia and Alaska is nothing. Thus the Northwest coast knows many Siberian species, and no doubt many American birds cross to the west and mingle with Asiatic fauna.

Another species he found on that trip was the spoon-billed sandpiper, which had been collected very seldom before, and only at one other time on the American coast. It had first been found here by the ship named the *Plover*, during the summer of 1849 on a search for Sir John Franklin. Franklin's friend, Sir John Barrow, for whom he had named Cape Barrow and also remembered by the duck known as Barrow's goldeneye, had been aboard, hoping to find his friend. Instead, he had brought back a collection of birds which went to the Oxford Museum. The curious spoon-billed sandpiper, however, was quite disbelieved. No one had ever seen a sandpiper with its beak flattened preposterously at the ends like a little spoon. Besides, the bird seemed to have no hind toes—something decidedly unusual. This, ornithologists jeered with scientific scorn and a cold opinion of any man who would stoop so low, must be a *Tringa* sandpiper with the beak remodeled by means of hot water and a little manipulation, and the hind toes cut off. Sir John Barrow was accused of nature-faking.

But Nelson found the sandpiper of contention alive and fully believable. It was a beautiful, brown-breasted bird with a rust-brown head streaked with black, and that curious, flattened, ice-cream-spoon beak. The hind toes, however, were not really missing; they were only very tiny and useless. This and the other species which he collected on the cruise of the *Corwin* went back to Washington with Nelson, where Ridgway painted portraits of most of them.

In 1884 the *Corwin* went back to the Arctic to investigate new volcanic disturbances in the Aleutians, also to check up on the seal islands and punish any known instances of poaching. The vessel was to look for stranded crews of whaling ships lost in the ice and carry on some natural history exploration. On this trip there were no trained naturalists aboard, but the assistant engineer, Samuel McLenegan, evidently was an amateur naturalist of no little ability and enthusiasm. To him, at any rate, though rather against his will at first, was delegated the job of keeping notes and collecting specimens of birds, mammals, fishes, rocks, minerals, and plants for the National Museum, on a special exploring expedition which was sent off by the *Corwin* while the ship went on about its other duties.

The Kowak River (on today's maps given as the Kobuk) was one of the large unknown rivers of northwestern Alaska. It lay a few miles north of the Arctic Circle. The Indians had told of it, so that its presence, but little else, had been known for thirty years. No white man had ever explored it or had seen more than its many mouths at the muddy delta on Hotham Inlet, Kotzebue Sound.

In this remote spot the *Corwin* let off young Sam McLenegan and four other men, with Lieutenant J. C. Cantwell as leader of the party. They had a supply of food and a little steam launch that looked like a child's rather crude version of a steamboat, and two canoes, one of them covered with skin. They were told to be back at the point on Hotham Bay opposite the mouths of the Kowak at a specified time in order to be picked up. And, if something happened to the *Corwin* up in the ice, as it well might, they were to make their way back, somehow, to San Francisco by the first vessel that would take them. To be abandoned here in the Alaskan wilderness was not a very happy thought. They consoled themselves with the fact that the *Corwin* had always weathered the ice and would surely be back for them.

It was July 7, 1884, as the *Corwin* steamed around the cape and was gone, leaving the six men, including a miner named Miller who was going upriver and a native interpreter named André, with the inadequate boats and a small amount of coal for the launch. They confidently hoped to find coal seams somewhere up the river. If not, they would have to use wood as fuel, or simply abandon the launch and proceed in the skin boat and the canoe.

It was, from the start, a wild and dangerous river, often rushing over rocks and great rack-heaps of driftwood caught on shoals. Giant furrows had been plowed by the ice in the banks. The party had to pass beneath several miles of ice cliffs standing two hundred feet high, from which huge chunks were constantly breaking off in the warmth of the ninety-degree sun and plunging with great splashes into the river. With difficulty the men stayed clear of the cliffs, for a strong current continually tried to sweep them under the standing ice walls.

Beyond the region of the ice they came into a beautifully idyllic valley whose rocky beaches provided good camping places, with an alluring stretch of fir and pine wilderness beyond. The trip now became a delightful excursion for the six. The *Corwin* and the rigors and disciplines of the Arctic Ocean seemed far away and unreal. Reality was here with a camp fire and trout broiling over the coals, the smell of coffee and bacon in the air, bread baking, and six men in congenial accord.

It would have been perfect if the mosquitoes had not been so bad. Alaskan mosquitoes have always been noted for their extraordinary vigor and venom. More than any other discomfort, far worse than the cold, these insects have always been the hardest trial for explorers to endure. Although the heat went up to ninety degrees by day and it was bitterly cold at night, nothing deterred the mosquitoes. The faces of the men in the party were almost unrecognizable with welts. Sometimes when a man was chopping wood, he suddenly halted, dropped his ax, rubbed his blood-covered face in anguish, and plunged into the river to escape the maddening horde. The men made cloth hoods for themselves as the Indians did, but they found them of little use.

There were heavy rains. The river rose, then dropped quickly, leaving much trash ashore. There was more and more trouble with the launch, whose boiler wasn't working right. For a time the men took turns pulling the balky craft. Then it was decided that the

After Dr. Samuel W. Woodhouse, U. S. Army, discovered the black-capped vireo in Texas in 1851, it was believed to be a lost species, until in the 1870's when W. H. Werner collected a pair and painted them as seen at the first nest ever discovered. (*Bull. Nuttall Ornithological Club, 1879.*)

The elusive phainopepla, the silken or black flycatcher, or "satin sparrow,"
was discovered in the Southwest and frequently observed there by men
of the army. (Painting by Cassin in his *Illustrations of the Birds of California*, etc., 1856.)

John Richardson named Ross's gull in honor of the Arctic explorer and British navigator, Sir James Clark Ross, top. (*Point Barrow Expedition, 1881*, Government Printing Office.)
When young William Gambel took a four-year bird walk on the Santa Fé Trail, he discovered Gambel's quail, bottom. (Portrait by Geo. G. White, in *Illustrations of Birds*, Cassin, 1856.)

John Richardson in the Arctic found a small owl called "Death-bird" by the Crees. Believed to be a European species, Tengmalm's owl, it proved to be a new kind, now known as Richardson's owl. (Painted by William Swainson for *Fauna Boreali-Americana*, by Swainson and Richardson, 1831.)

Franklin's grouse, top, and Richardson's grouse, bottom, served more than any other creatures to keep alive the starving Franklin Arctic Expedition, 1819–20. (Painted by William Swainson, *Fauna Boreali-Americana*, 1831.)

This specimen of Kennicott's owl, discovered in Alaska in 1866, was sent to the Chicago Academy of Sciences, which then loaned it to Daniel Giraud Elliot. The owl was shipped to London to be painted by J. Wolf, and was returned to America in time to be consumed in the Chicago Fire. (*Birds of America, Discovered After Audubon and Wilson*, Elliot, 1869.)

Prize of the 1881 cruise of the Revenue Cutter *Corwin* was the crested shrike from Wrangell Island. The portrait was painted by Robert Ridgway in Washington, with a background derived from sketches made by John Muir on the cruise. (*Cruise of the Corwin, 1881*, Government Printing Office.)

On Otter Island in the Arctic, the *Corwin* obtained the first specimens of young auks and auklets ever collected. Clumsy, comical, and fluffy, these infants had their portraits painted by Robert Ridgway, for use in the government's report, *The Cruise of the Corwin*, 1884.

launch could go no farther. Sam McLenegan and Mr. Miller would stay with it and repair it if possible. Cantwell and the others went on with the skin boat to explore the region of the mysterious Jade Mountain and try to find the headwaters of the Kowak. The Indians had said rather vaguely that there was a great waterfall far up the river; the men wanted to see that, too.

McLenegan saw them on their way, then turned to listen to the gray-cheeked thrushes singing their reedy songs in the alders. He discovered almost at the same moment the presence of enormous mammoth tusks and bones embedded in the eroded river bank. The tusks were impressive; when he measured several he found they were eight inches in diameter. They were much too heavy to carry to the coast.

The upbound party came upon a village of Indians along the river who told them about a lake and offered to go along and show them the way. This side trip was more work than the results were worth, for the men returned wearily to the river, knowing they were now 125 miles from the launch, and had five days' provisions left. The skin boat was leaking, having been snagged when they had unwisely dragged it through the bushes in search of the lake. It had to be dried out before it could be repaired.

Taking advantage of this delay, the energetic Mr. Cantwell went off to explore the beautiful green peak called the Jade Mountain, which loomed on the horizon about twelve miles from the camp. He took his interpreter, André, and an Indian called Natorak, but the other Indians who had accompanied them from the villages below refused to go. They said their shaman forbade it, for the Jade Mountain was the home of a devil which would catch and eat them if they went there. They shook their heads at the rash explorers and predicted that no good would come of it.

But Cantwell was determined. The mountain called, and he went. The devil on the Jade Mountain, however, must have been working his spell, because it was one of the worst trips the young man had ever endured. The way at first lay across the soft, yielding tundra and through shallow lagoons and bogs, around lakes and dense thickets of tangled willows and aspens, then through long stretches of pine forest of great antiquity where fallen trees caused them constantly to turn aside, almost doubling their distance, or else climb over them with attendant bruises and contusions. At one moment they were exposed to the burning heat of the Arctic summer sun, and the next they were floundering, plunging, struggling waist-deep in dark brown pools of stagnant water in a spruce swamp, to which the light of day doubtless never penetrated.

A galloping white-water river swept around the base of the Jade Mountain, separating it from another high peak in the same range of mountains. The bed of the river was filled with rocks in huge heaps which had been piled up like beaver dams by the ice.

André and Cantwell hunted for greenstones from the mountain, but Natorak's heart failed him and he would neither go further nor touch the fatal green rocks which were the property of the evil spirit on the mountain. So they left him to make a fire and cook supper while they explored upstream. They found the greenstones everywhere—a kind of nephrite, not true jade. Prehistoric people in Alaska had used it for amulets and symbolic figures, but no one until now had known where it originated.

The two collected a number of very heavy rocks and divided the specimens into packs convenient for three people to carry. It was hot; they were worn out. After supper, fighting mosquitoes, they went to sleep. They had not realized it was so late; light stayed bright in the Arctic in late July. It was nearly midnight before the sun dipped out of sight, and it was back again by half-past three.

When the first faint gleams of light came from the sky behind the mountain—the air was cold, and the hot tea and hot bread baked on a stick roused the men—they were on their way. Each carried a load of greenstones; even Natorak had been persuaded with some effort to do his part. André, also carried the whole camp outfit dangling from his belt or strapped to his shoulders, yet even with the addition of a load of rocks, he frolicked like a colt in the brisk early morning, sometimes chasing down a bear trail and then charging back up the slope with the greatest vigor and joy.

This was not exactly Mr. Cantwell's mood. He was still stiff and sore from the previous day's exertions, and after the first five miles he began to regret having collected so many geological specimens. By the time the three got back into the pine forest, the mosquitoes and deer flies attacked with a violence which Cantwell later declared was utterly beyond description. After two hours of suffering they came out into the tundra where there was at least a fresh breeze; they threw themselves down and buried their faces in the moss and grass until the wind had blown away the insects.

Cantwell was overtired and suffering from insect bites and the nervous exhaustion brought on by their incessant pricking. He was almost insensible by 5 p.m. when they dragged into camp. His boots were worn through and his feet were so lacerated and swollen that André had to cut away the uppers to get them off. He knew he could not explore any farther and doubted if he could even make it back by canoe to the launch. He sent one of the Indians down the river with a note to Samuel McLenegan to come at once and get him.

Next day they all looked hourly for the launch, but it did not come. Nor did it come the next. About noon, they saw a canoe and the Indian with a message from Sam. There had been severe boiler trouble, he explained. He had worked all night on the tubes and had had to plug six of them, but the launch was not working well. If they were to get back to the coast in it, they must not try the strain of an upriver trip. From what he could learn from the Indian, the skin boat was not disabled, nor was Cantwell, and he urged him to come in it and meet him at the launch, if at all possible.

Cantwell was feeling a good deal better by then. He ordered camp broken and they set off down the river to the launch.

Meanwhile, Sam McLenegan, aside from repairing boilers, had been birding. He had not collected specimens of everything he saw, thus defying the National Museum and Professor Baird. Sam was an amateur, not a scientist, and he felt such a warm sympathy for many birds that he could not be induced to take their lives, even for science. If science didn't accept his word for having seen them, it could forget it. So this assistant engineer, repairer of boilers, conscientiously listed birds, described them and where he found them. He wrote of the gray-cheeked thrush:

Among the tangled and almost impenetrable forests of the interior we often hear the sound of sweet melody. As we stop almost involuntarily and listen to the clear, sweet tones our tired frame seems quickened to a new life. Like the weary traveler who kneels over the clear spring to quench his thirst in the cool waters below, we feel revived. The feeble pulse becomes stronger, the eye becomes brighter, and we listen with bated breath to the strange melody of the forest.

He found robins, too, with delight in seeing something from home. And Hudsonian chickadees—they were playing about in the lichen-hung spruces just above his head when he was repairing the boiler. They were too friendly, he said, too brave for him to presume to take their lives.

He recorded eighty-three species, from the thrush to the loon. The loons he heard often in that wilderness, their wild cry in the stillness filling him with an indescribable loneliness.

Though many were a great delight to him, none of his finds was new to science. But the value of his observations, as well as those of other expeditions on which no new species were found, was not so much in newness or rarity as in slowly adding to an understanding of known species. To learn where each bird spent the summer, over how wide a range; to find out its nesting habits, its abundance, and its food, was the purpose. Many more men and many more expeditions were needed before the habits of each American bird were known. The *Corwin* and its naturalists had added a tremendous fund of knowledge to the ornithology of Alaska and the North American Arctic.

CHAPTER NINETEEN

GOOSE CHASE

O N an October day the brilliant deep blue of the sky is cloud-less, unmarked, glittering with sunshine. Strands of floating silk of young ballooning spiders move on the wind. Migrant sparrows fill the roadside weeds; a hawk or two, or half a dozen of them at a time, drift over the sky, circle lazily, are finally out of sight before more come along. Then out of that transcendent blue comes a strangely resonant, bell-like tinkling—broken, high-pitched tones that seem to be everywhere yet nowheere. Very high, very brilliant in that light of October, a scattered flock of white birds with black wing-tips, and gray birds with white heads, pattern the sky. The snow geese and blue geese are going south.

They had nested in the Arctic, had bedded their eggs in down-filled nests on the mosses of the tundra. In that little-explored, wet wilderness of the Far North many birds nest. It is the place into which the snow geese and the blue geese, migrating northward each spring, once vanished and were lost to knowledge until suddenly on an October day they came south. Southampton Island in Hudson Bay was discovered to be a favorite place for the lesser snow geese to nest. That much was known. But no one knew where the blue goose nested, nor did anyone know where the little white Ross's goose raised its young. There was so much territory up there, and there were no roads and but little open water during much of the year. Although the snow geese and the blue geese often traveled together in migration, and spent their winters together along the sea marshes of the Barataria country and the Gulf of Mexico in Louisiana, somewhere in the North they separated along either side of Hudson Bay. The blue geese disappeared and were not to be found nesting with the snows.

The blue goose had been known since it had been identified by Edwards from a specimen brought to him from Hudson Bay in the mid-eighteenth century. Pallas had discovered the snow goose some years later. The blue goose had a blue-gray body with black barring on the dark breast and wings, and a distinctive white head, the white extending part-way down the neck. There was also some white on the wings. The beak was pink and so were the feet. It was altogether a most unusually marked bird, and it was far from small.

Blue geese were too large to disappear easily. As they fed on a gravel shore they were, it is true, well concealed in their surroundings, but as soon as they put up their heads to query the vicinity for danger, the white stood forth brightly. Yet, although the blue geese appeared in the United States in company with the snow geese, flying together in a distinctive undulation of flight which gave them both the name of "wavies"—a flickering flight, as of white paper fluttering down from the upper sky—they separated somewhere en route to their nesting grounds. When the blues and snows went north in spring, lingering along Lake Traverse between Minnesota and South Dakota until June when the ice had finally gone out of the Arctic bays and tundra pools, the blues simply vanished into the mystery of the great North. The mystery was long unsolved, as noted by the authority, A. C. Bent, in 1925:

To find the breeding resorts of the blue goose is one of the most alluring of the unsolved problems in American ornithology. It is really surprising that such a large and conspicuous species, which is numerically so abundant, can disappear so completely during the breeding season.

Even the Eskimos could not tell, or, if they could, they did not. They knew where *Khanġuk,* the snow geese, nested, but not the blue ones.

The riddle of the blue goose sent one man on a goose chase that lasted nearly seven years and covered more than thirty thousand miles of impossible country—the broad, chill, soggy marshland and tundra of the great North. It took him over the sticky mud flats along Hudson Bay and the Arctic Ocean; into a land of sudden moods of weather, few of which were good, ranging from snow squalls to rainstorms. There was always and forever the punishment of the wind.

The Department of the Interior in Canada had decided to solve the puzzle of the blue goose. Although the world would continue very well without this knowledge, man's yearning for truth makes him seek the answers to riddles and puzzles. As long as one of these remains, he is challenged. The siren call of birds still leads many a man into the pathways of adventure.

J. Dewey Soper, an official of the Department of the Interior in Canada, made it his task to find this solution. His time to explore the tundra wastes was limited; the summer was short, but there was the advantage of almost twenty-four hours of daylight, and that could prolong the hunt. Much of it was done by air, much by canoe and Eskimo kayak and larger boat in the wild gray-blue waters of Hudson Bay. Dodging icebergs and floating masses of ice, he visited Ellesmere Island, and Devon Island, and the tremendous shoreline of Baffin Island. He found many snow geese and eider ducks, Arctic foxes and jaegers and terns and curlews. But there were no elusive white heads above blue-gray necks and bodies. Season after season went by, and the great expanse of water and snow and tundra, marsh and mud flat, seemed endless and unrewarding. Somewhere, somewhere, the blue geese nested.

In 1929, Dewey Soper reached the east shore of Bowman Bay, in Foxe Basin. It was a polar panorama that looked very much like what he had been exploring for so many years. It was bitterly cold, even though it was summer. There was perpetual ice in Foxe Basin; and there were reeking mud flats fetid with goose droppings and littered with feathers. Leaden skies let down snow in unexpected gusts, and the sun had no real warmth in it. But something different could be seen in this landscape—white heads and gray bodies. There were *blue geese* and their downy young on those mud flats! They had been cornered at last.

Dewey Soper in jubilation went back to Ottawa with this gap filled in American ornithology. Just the next year, not knowing as yet of this accomplishment, the United States ornithologist, George Miksch Sutton, on his own expedition and for the same purpose of discovery, came to Baffin Bay. There on Cape Kendal, Southampton Island, almost six hundred miles west of the place where Soper had found his blue geese, Sutton also found them nesting. Both the blues and the snows were nesting together, and some of them were evidently interbreeding. He thought with joy that he had been the one to solve the riddle, and later sadly discovered that he had not been the first. He had, however, added much to the knowledge of the blue goose and its range.

Canada had another goose chase a few years later. There was still that other species hiding its nesting place in utmost secrecy— the Ross's goose of California, the smallest of the family. It is mallard-duck size and all white except for the black primaries—in fact, much like a miniature snow goose. It winters on the California coast, but nothing at all was known about where it nested. It was suspected that this, like the blues and snows and the big emperor geese, went into the unexplored areas of the Arctic, where they would be virtually impossible to locate.

The little Ross's goose had been discovered in 1861 by Bernard Rogan Ross, who was the Chief Factor of the Hudson's Bay Company at Fort Resolution, far up on the Great Slave Lake in upper Canada. He was interested in birds and natural science, and was a correspondent of the Smithsonian Institution at Washington. Therefore, when he shot a small white goose which he felt cer-

tain was a new species, he sent it to the Smithsonian. There John
Cassin named it Ross's goose in his honor. Its finder had discovered
no nests; all he had thus far contributed was the bird itself.

It became something of a contest, then, for each subsequent factor at the Company's remote post to find where Barney Ross's
goose had its nest. None of them succeeded. The years went on,
and the Ross's goose continued to bring forth its young in absolute
secret.

Late in June, 1940, Angus Gavin and Ernest Donovan of the
Hudson's Bay Company set out by canoe from Perry River Post,
on Flagstaff Island, to make another search for the goose. They
were seventy-five miles north of the Arctic Circle, so in that season they had unbounded daylight. They had not, therefore, started
out until four in the afternoon. The two sat in the middle of the
canoe, with Eskimos paddling fore and aft.

For a change, the weather was perfect. They could not recall
when there had been a finer day in all that cantankerous country,
in a landscape that was mostly water, marsh, ice, mud, and sky.
The river had many bends, and around each one lay possible adventure and excitement—perhaps even the elusive Ross's goose.
Hordes of nesting ducks and honking Canada geese rose from the
flats; there was the constant singing of the longspurs and the joyous
trilling of plovers and curlews. Flocks of plovers and sandpipers
sprang up in a flurry of wings as the quiet canoe went by in the
marshes, flew circling and crying, sunlight flashing on their wings,
and then settled again.

The river became more rough. It was filled with rapids at intervals, splashing blue and white water over rocks. Careful paddling
took them speedily through the white water and into calmer
stretches, until they reached plunging rapids of more than a mile.
This was hard, skillful work to navigate, breathtaking to the two
white men but commonplace to the impassive Eskimos. They simply said nothing, and paddled.

When they again slid into calm water they saw a small white

goose with black wing-tips, standing poised on a mud flat. Another white goose flew quickly above the canoe. And suddenly, with no more ado, they had reached their goal.

They had been paddling all night and had not realized it. After the briefest swing out of sight, the sun was up again and the waters were turning pink and apricot and yellow. The colors splashed on the lovely white creature that winged toward the lake which lay ahead.

The lake was a mirror, and over it Ross's geese were flying wherever the astonished men gazed. This was wonderful, this was marvelous, this was what they and their predecessors had hoped for almost seventy-nine years. On the first of three islands which they visited they found about fifty pairs nesting, separated by only a few feet. Other islands sheltered them, too, hundreds of them. The two had found the private world of Ross's goose.

Gavin and Donovan wanted to get back quickly and tell the news at the post. Old Barney Ross had been vindicated. Hudson's Bay men had done it again, and on Dominion Day at that.

Yet, as in the mystery of the blue goose, the Ross's goose riddle, if fate had only worked it that way, might have been solved by a man from the United States. Charles E. Gilham of the Fish and Wildlife Service of the U.S. Department of the Interior had been coming into the North to make surveys of the status of migratory waterfowl, beginning in 1935. He returned during the next several years for the survey, which covered a vast and wild territory of unbelievable scope.

In 1939 he came by plane and flew over the Perry River, where one year later Gavin and Donovan were paddling to their rendezvous with the geese. But the ice conditions were bad and he could not come down for a landing. He had simply looked down and had seen countless white birds in the marshes and in the mazes of water mirroring the sky. He could not tell from his height in the plane whether he was seeing geese or swans or gulls.

He had to find out. The question haunted him. Next year he

again chartered a plane for a trip into the Perry River country, determined to find out what the birds were that he had seen so tantalizingly down there. But the day before departure his pilot died of a heart attack. The trip was canceled. He hoped he could do it the next year, but before he got back to civilization the word had come that the Hudson's Bay men had found Ross's goose—on those same Perry River marshes.

To fill the open niches of knowledge is man's perennial urge. It is this which drives him insatiably to conquer and then perversely to yearn for the days when all was not known or conquered or catalogued. The finding of the blue goose's nesting place was one milestone that filled one gap of knowledge, and so was the triumph over the Ross's goose. But they were not the only remaining mysteries of the North. A few years later another puzzle was solved and more new information obtained about a bird which Audubon had discovered ninety years before.

The eggs of Harris's sparrow were the Grail this time. George Miksch Sutton, on his way home in the fall of 1930 after finding the blue geese on Southampton Island, knew he felt the incurable lure of the tundra in his veins. It was a pleasantly consuming disease, this Arctic-hopping, this wilderness-roaming. Some men have been affected by the attraction of jungles, others by the North; the one environment is tangled and dense and dangerous, the other is open and bleak but also dangerous. The tundra wilderness has a call that is not to be denied.

When George Sutton was in Churchill, Manitoba, on the southwestern side of Hudson Bay, waiting for the one-train-a-week back to civilization, he saw flocks of Harris's sparrows in the spruces and Labrador tea bushes. That meant they had no doubt nested here. This, in fact, was well known to ornithologists. The nest of Harris's sparrow had been located in 1907 by Ernest Thompson Seton near Great Slave Lake. But although this much was known and, some years later, the young birds themselves were found, no one—not even residents at Churchill—had ever seen the eggs of the Harris's sparrow. To a person who is not an ornithologist, this astonishing lack has less than any meaning at all. What does it matter that no one knows what color are the eggs of a particular kind of insignificant bird that chooses to come to a forsaken tundra in summer? Who cares?

Some men did care, and this was a challenge. The more difficult such a challenge is, and the longer it takes to conquer the problem, the greater the excitement and zeal to solve it. It becomes an almost feverish contest among the scientists who want nothing more in life than to have had the honor of being the first to reach this goal.

In September, 1930, George Miksch Sutton took up the challenge. When the train from Winnipeg came back to Churchill next spring, Sutton and three friends stepped down into the deep snow. It was May 24, 1931, and the sub-Arctic landscape looked like midwinter. The Churchill River was frozen far back from its entry in the bay, and the bay itself was a tremendous expanse of broken ice, icebergs that shot sparks in the sun, or ice masses that bobbed soddenly with the wind and waves under low and menacing clouds.

The four—George Sutton, Olin Sewall Pettingill, Bert Lloyd, and John Bonner Semple, all from Cornell University—found lodgings at the construction camp of the Department of Railways and Canals. The Harris's sparrows themselves had not yet arrived.

Waiting, the men ranged out into the thawing world of the tundra, which was rapidly changing from the look of winter to the aspect of early spring. Migrant birds were appearing daily. On the 27th the Harris's sparrows came in. It was much too soon for any nesting or laying of eggs, but the four wanted to be on hand to see them when they did come. The provoking thing about eggs was that they don't stay that way past a certain time—and young Harris's sparrows were no novelty to ornithologists.

The four men had busy, full, rather exhaustingly long days, days marked by the strange singing and howling concert of the Eskimo dogs at sundown, the sounds of birds coming over in the brief darkness, and the caroling of the Harris's sparrows at dawn. Far out on the horizon the pale yellow-white glow of the iceblink reminded the men that they were not very far from the Arctic Circle.

They were up at dawn with the construction crew and ate with them. Then they walked or rode out to the spruce woods, six miles or more, and slogged through the spongy tundra, explored the low, wild spruce woods, and got wet to the knees in the muskeg. They took a lunch along and sat on a dry spot to eat, while all around them the birds sang and flew and prepared to build their nests— the pipits, mounting like skylarks into the sky to hang high, singing, on beating wings; the white-crowned sparrows piping in the bog laurel; the curlews and horned larks and longspurs all tinkling and whistling. And the Harris's sparrows, those big handsome sparrows with black head and throat, white breast, and gray-and-brown back and wings, were singing from the spruce tips. The measured, meditative, often melancholy notes challenged other singing males across the landscape. But there were no nests visible, no eggs.

Suddenly the situation changed and became a contest. A week after the Cornell quartet arrived, there came four Canadian ornithologists with the identical purpose to accomplish for the honor of Canadian ornithology. This immediately put a different face on the matter. It might have been an amiable race before, to see which of the Cornell men would have the honor of presenting the news to the scientific world, but now it was an international challenge which brought an urgent sense of hurry to the Sutton crew.

They had been decently quiet as they ranged the tundra and the tea tangles, poking around muskeg potholes in the search for a nest. Now the Canadians went about the same area, beating on pans and tin trays to make a noise that would scare up the birds and thus reveal the whereabouts of the nest. When at times the two groups met in the hunt, they were polite and blandly noncommittal. But both sides knew very well that neither had as yet found the eggs, and the time was growing very short.

On June 16, George Sutton went out alone. He felt rather dis-

couraged as he ranged out once more through the muskeg, with
its stunted spruces and entangling thickets of Labrador tea and
laurel at the edges of the wetter places. The tea—the hardy rhododendron of the North—was now in bloom, full of fragrant white
clusters of blossoms above the leathery leaves with their rolled-
under edges and furry white or brown undersides. Its fragrance
and charm were everywhere. So were the color of the low pink
bog laurel and the pale pink bells of bog rosemary in the sogginess
of the sphagnum. Mosquitoes rose in swarms to torment him; the
deer flies were beginning their assaults in the warming sunshine.
But the birds sang, the sparrows piped, the sun felt good on his
back, and he was growing utterly sick at heart to think how this
mission had probably failed.

Then a slender dark bird slipped out almost from under his feet
and flew anxiously to a spruce. Bending over, and sinking almost
to his knees in the sphagnum while he tried to ignore the mosquitoes, Sutton parted the branches of Labrador tea and saw the nest.
There were four green-blue eggs.

It was, as he wrote later in his book, *Birds in the Wilderness*, an
almost holy moment. Finding the Grail could hardly have been
more uplifting.

. . . . A thrill the like of which I had never felt before passed through
me. And I talked aloud! "Here," I said. "Here in this beautiful place!"
At my fingertips lay treasures that were beyond price. Mine was Man's
first glimpse of the eggs of the Harris's Sparrow, in the lovely bird's
wilderness home. The sixteen days' search had become a victory for
the Americans!

CHAPTER TWENTY

THE LAST NEW BIRD

FOR a long time, America was too close to the wilderness to appreciate its wildlife. Birds were part of that often repugnant forest, swamp, plain, or mountain which spelled danger, discomfort, hunger, or death. Birds, if large enough, were something to be shot for food; or, if small, to be ignored. They were simply part of the furniture of the forest and considered to be of little good to anyone but poets and scientists.

Gradually, as the wilderness drew back, man, growing gentler, began to yearn for it. The farther it went from him, the more he perversely seemed to crave it. This became the heritage of all Americans. Though at first they may have hated the wilderness, they might, once they had conquered it, wish to keep part of it with them—not too close, but held at a safe distance to be there when, like Antaeus, they needed to renew their strength by touching and knowing the earth and its creatures again. There came a change toward the study of birds, quite apart from the scientific pursuits of the ornithologists who had been exceedingly busy during the nineteenth century in discovering almost all of the birds known to inhabit North America.

As early as the 1840's a new trend had begun in the understanding of birds and other wildlife. Henry David Thoreau was one of its originators—one whose voice has carried far and clear through the woods of time to the landscape of today. Thoreau did not profess to be a scientific ornithologist. He was a naturalist and a philosopher to whom birds were simply part of the society of woods and fields, and he liked to look at them and think of them as friends. In birds he found comparisons with human characteristics, yet he did not personify them as some of his followers did. Instead, he interpreted in birds some of the traits of human beings in order to point up human character.

He liked owls, and said:

I rejoice that there are owls. Let them do the idiotic and maniacal hooting for men. It is a sound admirably suited to swamps and twilight woods which no day illustrates, suggesting a vast and undeveloped nature which men have not recognized. They represent the stark twilight and unsatisfied thoughts which all have. All day the sun has shone on the surface of some savage swamp, where the single spruce stands hung with usnea lichens and small hawks circulate about and the chickadee lisps amid the evergreens, and the partridge and rabbit skulk beneath; but now a more dismal and fitting day dawns, and a different race of creatures awakes to express the meaning of Nature there.

He relished the crying of the little screech owls:

I love to hear their wailing, their doleful responses, trilled along the woodside; reminding me sometimes of music and singing birds; as if it were the dark and tearful side of music, and regrets and sighs that would fain be sung. . . . They give me a new sense of the variety and capacity of that nature which is our common dwelling.

He passed through the transition of most Americans from the gun to observation, and, going even farther, to philosophical interpretation.

As for fowling, during the last years that I carried a gun my excuse was that I was studying ornithology, and sought only new or rare birds. But I confess that I am now inclined to think that there is a finer way of studying ornithology than this. It requires so much closer attention to the habits of the birds, that, if for that reason only, I have been willing to omit the gun. . . .

Then he added:

No human being, past the thoughtless age of boyhood, will wantonly murder any creature which holds its life by the same tenure that he does . . . [and still later] . . . Everything is better off alive than dead, men, and moose, and pine trees. . . .

He was the kind of man on whom the chickadees would alight, and who could, without being maudlin, talk to loons and robins, with no loss of dignity on either side.

I once had a sparrow alight on my shoulder for a moment while I was hoeing in a village garden, and I felt that I was more distinguished by that circumstance than I should have been by any epaulet I could have worn.

Nine years after Thoreau's untimely death at forty-five, a small volume was published which in its quiet yet powerful way lifted up the torch that he had dropped. John Burroughs was a thoughtful man who, some said, had inherited Thoreau's mantle. It was, perhaps, not so much an inheritance as a reassertion of the goodness of nature and the abiding interest and meaning which more and more people were beginning to find in the out-of-doors. Burroughs wrote at a time when men were leaving behind their pioneer instincts and were growing increasingly excited about the esthetic and spiritual interpretation of nature.

John Burroughs was one of the first of the nature men who made the out-of-doors popular, who opened the door to the woods to many a man and woman, boy and girl, not alone of his generation but for many years afterward. His writings are perhaps not as profound as those of Thoreau, and this may be one of the reasons why so many people read them with appreciation and inspiration, as if what he said applied directly and individually to them. His *Wake Robin* was published in 1871; his other books came at intervals, none of them pretentious, but all of them exerting a powerful leverage on public interest and opinion. He said, in his preface to the first edition of *Wake Robin:*

This is mainly a book about the Birds, or more properly an invitation to the study of Ornithology, and the purpose of the author will be carried out in proportion as it awakens and stimulates the interest of the reader in this branch of Natural History.

Though written less in the spirit of exact science than with the freedom of love and old acquaintance, yet I have in no instance taken liberties with facts, or allowed my imagination to influence me to the extent of giving a false impression or a wrong coloring. I have reaped my harvest more in the woods than in the study; what I offer, in fact, is a careful and conscientious record of actual observations and experiences, and it is true as it stands written, every word of it. But what has interested me most in Ornithology is the pursuit, the chase, the discovery; that part of it which is akin to hunting, fishing, and wild sports, and which I could carry with me in my eye and ear wherever I went.

He was well acquainted with the northern woods. Camping in the Adirondacks in 1863, he wrote: "curious, above all else, to know what birds I should find in these solitudes,—what new ones, and what ones already known to me." He found the hermit thrush—

> In the primal forest's hush,
> Listen! . . . the hermit thrush!

and he listened, awed, to the winter wren's fairy music-box cascading liquid notes in an incredible gush of song in the dark hemlock woods. But he found not too many species of birds in the forests. He was somewhat disappointed, and then he was surprised when he went to live in Washington, D.C., that fall, to find more kinds of birds in the city than in the wilderness.

There were, indeed, a great many birds in Washington. They compensated for his having to earn his living there. Nature was never far from him or out of his thoughts. After he had attended the inauguration ceremonies of President Lincoln on March 4, 1865, Burroughs left the crowds and went out for his first excursion of the season.

Less than two miles from the White House and the tall, sad man who had just vowed to "bind up the nation's wounds . . . to do all which may achieve and cherish a just and lasting peace," Burroughs found a quiet woods. There he heard white-throated sparrows piping as he had heard them in the mountains, saw a mourning-cloak butterfly flitting in the warming sunshine, found the first bluets in bloom, and heard a spring peeper trying his whistle in a sunny puddle. It was spring in Washington, and Burroughs was savoring every fleeting quality in it.

He was for a time still of the old school of ornithology. This was his recipe for learning to know the birds:

First find your bird; observe its ways, its song, its calls, its flight, its haunts; then shoot it (not ogle it with a glass), and compare with Audubon. In this way the feathered kingdom may soon be conquered.

But in a later edition of *Wake Robin*, he added a revelatory footnote: "My later experiences have led me to prefer a small field-glass to a gun." Unconsciously, perhaps, John Burroughs had opened the way to the out-of-doors for the generations who would follow him, minus guns and bearing binoculars, along its mossy trails and stony shores.

Perhaps it was Chester A. Reed in the early twentieth century who helped most to encourage this change. His small pocket volume was the first popular bird book. There had been little or nothing before this which one might carry in his pocket when he went out with his field glass to look at birds, as Burroughs had recommended. It was no wonder the bird men of the past had needed to shoot a bird and bring it home in order to find its name. They could scarcely have carried with them the great tomes of Catesby, Wilson, or Audubon. But Reed's pocket guides, one for land birds and one for the water and game birds, while far from perfect, solved the problem beautifully. Inexpensive, easy to carry, easy to use, the Reed *Bird Guides* were very likely responsible for bringing more people to the enjoyment of birds in the first quarter of the twentieth century than any factor—until Roger Tory Peterson in 1934 and 1941 produced an even more usable and accurate pair of guides.

As the National Audubon Society and the Boy Scouts of America made the collecting of birds' eggs and dead bodies unpopular, birding with book and binoculars quickly replaced it. Then, in place of the bird man's gun, came the camera. Photographing birds required nerve, aim, concentration, and dedication. It was never easy, and it was a perpetual challenge. Bird photography took a retired banker, Charles A. Broley, into the tops of tall dead trees in Florida to photograph and band nesting bald eagles. It took Robert Allen into the mangrove swamps to photograph the elusive roseate spoonbills; George Sutton to the Arctic and to Mexico; Robert Cushman Murphy to the southern oceans; Olin Sewall Pettingill to the Falklands.

Photography has lured many another man and many a camera to strange places—Karl Maslowski, Roger Peterson, Allan Cruikshank, Elliot Porter, A. A. Allen, Walter Breckenridge, Paul Zaul, Murl Deusing, Cleveland Grant, John Gerard, and many more—into a swamp to photograph ducks, to a cliff's rim to photograph duck hawks, or to a bird-blind forty feet in the air, exposed to heat and mosquitoes and other torment, to photograph herons or hawks or owls or woodpeckers. It is a good deal more complicated and more demanding than collecting with a gun, and it followed casual gunning as a natural order of sequence among men and birds.

Then an added refinement and a new zest were added to birding when men went out with microphones to capture bird songs on records. It became the absorbing aim of Albert R. Brand and Arthur A. Allen of Cornell University to record the voices of all American birds while they were still with us, particularly those which were in danger of becoming extinct. This pioneering expedition, like none ever known before, was sponsored by the American Museum of Natural History and Cornell University.

With motion picture cameras, a sound truck, and large parabolic reflectors to funnel sound into the microphones as birds moved about, the expedition took off in 1935 on a trip of fifteen thousand miles. Paul Kellogg of Cornell was sound technician and George

Sutton was artist. James Tanner, a graduate student in ornithology, was assistant in photography and sound recording, and a general handy man who provided unquenchable amounts of enthusiasm when it began to flag in the older members of the party. Mr. Brand and Dr. Allen controlled the route and procedure of this unique expedition.

The first project was to record the voices of the nearly extinct ivory-billed woodpeckers. Dr. Allen had seen them in 1924 in certain remote swamps in central Florida. There was no way of knowing whether the big woodpeckers were still in existence. A species so near extinction could have died out in that time. In Florida the sound truck went into the swamps which were suspected of concealing the rare birds; when it bogged down the men walked and waded. But they had no luck. No ivory-bills could be located. The ornithologists realized that they might even now be too late to record the voices of these birds.

In late March of 1935 the crew started for Louisiana where, in deep swamp forests along the Tensas River, someone in 1932 had reported having seen ivory-bills. This was in northern Louisiana, almost due west of Vicksburg, Mississippi. The truck went as far as it could until deep water barred the way. The road, what there was of it, lay submerged in a spring flood. Yet the region was too alluring and too promising to give up now. Here was an unbroken forest stretching eighteen miles in one direction and thirty miles in another. Somewhere in there, among the buttressed cypresses and big tupelos and gums, in a swamp spilling over with spring song, ivory-billed woodpeckers might possibly be nesting.

There is more than one way to navigate high water. The men left the sound equipment and truck in a comparatively dry place and then went in on foot to explore. They borrowed a pirogue from a Cajun and paddled among the cypresses—listening, looking, wondering.

It was like a jungle, a wet world filled with singing prothonotary warblers, the buzzing calls of parula warblers, the explosive comments of the white-eyed vireos, the loud caroling of Carolina wrens and the staccato hammering of woodpeckers—but not the sounds that were so keenly sought. Spring migration was in full swing and the treetops were alive with northbound, singing birds. Down at the level of the swamp, water snakes, some of them cottonmouth moccasins, sunning themselves, were draped on bare branches and dead wood over the brown water. Turtles, sometimes piled up three deep, made their retreat when the questing piroque approached too close. Now and then an alligator submerged in the dark water.

Seven miles from the road, and after three days of exploring, they found the ivory-billed woodpeckers. Incredible, rare, magnificent, prehistoric-looking—there they were, nesting in a cypress. It was an historic moment which very easily might never be repeated. In the days of Catesby, Audubon, Wilson, and Du Pratz, the ivory-bills were noticeable and to be commented upon, but they were not considered particularly rare. Yet, it is probable that they were never as abundant as the red-headed woodpecker or even the big pileated, which comes closer to the magnificence and size of the ivory-bill, but which does not have the peculiar demands for subsistence of the latter.

The ivory-billed woodpecker is twenty inches long. The male has a brilliant scarlet crest standing straight back in line with the ivory-white beak, which is like a great blunt chisel. A long white stripe down the side of the black head, neck, and back joins the white patches on the wings. The breast, tail, and the rest of the wing-surface are glossy black. The ivory-bill is unique. We will never see his like again.

Each pair of ivory-bills needs about six square miles of primeval forest in which to subsist. In a similar space, Dr. Allen estimated that perhaps 126 pairs of red-bellied woodpeckers might find home and food and room to fly, or thirty-six pairs of the big pileated woodpeckers. The ivory-bill evidently requires as a food source those trees which have been dead for only two or three years. When the first insects get into the outer wood and their borers chew tunnels under the bark, the tree is ready for the ivory-billed woodpecker. With a wooden sound of wings and a *clunk!* the bird claps against the resonate side of the dead trunk. Then there is a heavy thumping, like an ax on a log, and great slabs of bark are torn away and flung to the ground as the bird goes after the fat white grubs that lie beneath. When the woodpecker is finished with a tree, it moves on to another, leaving the barked tree for the red-heads to hammer, the red-bellies to pound, the pileateds to chop. Into abandoned holes may come chickadees and prothonotary warblers to nest. Flying squirrels or screech owls may take over the cavity.

Since the ivory-billed woodpecker requires the peculiar situation of newly-dead trees in a primeval forest, an area of some size can, therefore, support only a few. There simply are not enough or ever were enough of its special grubs to feed more than a limited population of ivory-bills.

No one knew these facts until Dr. Allen's expedition with the sound equipment went into the Louisiana swamps. The young graduate student from Cornell, James Tanner, returned later to pursue the study. He had become imbued with that feeling of conquest, that search for adventure and the spirit of dedication of a man pioneering in science. He determined to learn all there was to know about the ivory-billed woodpeckers before they became extinct. James Tanner devoted three years of his life to the project. He traveled more than forty-five thousand miles—on foot, by car, on horseback, by boat—into nearly all the southern forests where ivory-bills either had been reported or in which he suspected they might still live.

But back to Dr. Allen's expedition in 1935, with the sound truck still at the edge of the swamp, seven miles from the nest of the ivory-billed woodpeckers. A sound truck with 1,800 pounds of equipment does not easily navigate a swampy terrain which has recently had an additional supply of water from the spring rise.

They drove back, therefore, to the nearest town and obtained the cooperation of the mayor and the sheriff. The truck was dismantled, and everything in it was set up in the bed of an old, unpainted, solid, and serviceable farm wagon. After the precious contents were bolted firmly in place, the wagon was hitched to four mules. The animals plodded down the dirt road to the edge of the swamp; they kept on going. While the wagon groaned and rocked and sucked at the muddy depths, and while the owners of all that expensive and highly cherished equipment no doubt held their collective breaths, the wagon finally reached the spot where there was comparatively solid ground, only three hundred feet from the nest of what might possibly be the last pair of ivory-billed woodpeckers in the world.

The men set up camp. To make a dry base on which to put the tents and mosquito netting, they cut piles of palmetto fans and stacked them crisscross in a kind of thatch or flooring at the base of a huge water oak whose roots offered some solidity in a soaked terrain. A 24-power binocular on a tripod, like a telescope, was set up and a camp chair was placed before the eye piece. The lens was focused on the nest hole so that attention could be paid to whatever was going on up there, while the microphone with its "sound mirror" faithfully recorded the calls, the talking, the guttural sounds that came from the cavity.

The men were there for eight days. When the woodpeckers became accustomed to human presence, a blind was built in a neighboring tree; it was set up level with the nest and not more than twenty feet away from the opening through which the adult birds flew several times a day.

The whole experience was something which none of the four would ever forget. They made the recording for posterity. Then they went back to town, reassembled the sound truck, and set off for Oklahoma to record the booming of the lesser prairie chickens on a spring dawn, and for Colorado to photograph and record the golden eagles and many other western birds.

By the time the summer's adventure was over, they had exposed almost ten miles of film and had recorded the voices of more than one hundred species of American birds. Yet this was only the beginning. The Foundation which was formed as a result of the expedition resolved to record the voices of all the birds in America. But it was the ivory-billed woodpeckers, perhaps more than any other birds studied and recorded, which held the greatest thrill and meaning to the men who started the expedition.

To have it all finished, done with, collected, catalogued, labeled, everything put in its proper niche—there is a melancholy finality in the phrase: *finished*. Completion does not always bring with it a feeling of triumph or the true meaning of success. In many pursuits the delight is in the doing: in the painting of a picture, not in looking at the finished art; in the writing, not the reading, of the published book; in the seeking, not in the total finding. There has to be some reward for the doing, but often this is the experience itself, with more pleasure in the retrospect than in the completion. It is rather sad to have finished a thing. It will be sad when the last new bird in America has been found, collected, catalogued, niched.

Naturalists believed that this end had been reached in 1918, when A. H. Howell, strolling on the sandbur stretches of the coastal prairie along the southwest coast of Florida, saw a dusky little bird slip out of one clump of sea-oats and skitter across the crest of sand into another. Howell was a bird man, trained, quick of eye, his mind an orderly catalogue of known birds. His discovery was not, however, a known bird; it was the Cape Sable seaside sparrow, whose range is restricted to about six miles of shore and sand prairie in the extreme southwestern tip of Florida.

After this event, Dr. Frank M. Chapman, that eminent and much beloved ornithologist, with the finality of closing a large volume, heavily and with regret, stated that the Cape Sable seaside sparrow is "not only the latest but probably the last new species of bird to be found in eastern North America."

In spite of that statement, the half-way expectation and hope in the ornithological mind, as well as the secret hope of nearly everyone who goes out on a spring morning with his binoculars and his *Guide,* is that maybe—just perhaps—a new bird hitherto unknown may come across his field of vision. On May 30, 1939, this happened to two young men out looking for birds in the eastern part of West Virginia. It was mountainous terrain, covered with a mixed woods of oak and pine. The date was a trifle late for migrants to be passing through, but it was a good day to go out, and they went.

The two were J. Lloyd Poland and Karl W. Haller. They knew birds. So when they heard a different sort of song they immediately were alert. They thought it sounded somewhat like the rising buzz of the parula warbler, but with a subtle difference, a sort of double-parula buzz. When they secured the mysterious singer, they were even more puzzled. They knew it was neither a parula warbler nor the yellow-throated; yet it had characteristics of both.

In a family of birds that are noted for their sleek forms, rapid motion, and bright colors, this warbler was superb. The throat was orange-gold, shading to a white belly. The back and wings were blue-gray; the wings had two white bars and sharp black markings. There was a white eyebrow and eye-ring on a black cheek which extended in a black streak into the gold and white below. A new warbler with a double-parula song—the news was electrifying to ornithologists. Study collections in museums and universities were examined to see if a similar bird had ever been collected before. It had not. Yet the eastern states had been so thoroughly studied, from Catesby to the present day, by capable, thorough, expert ornithologists, that it seemed incredible that a new species should have been found here—within less than a hundred miles, in fact, of the Smithsonian Institution in Washington.

In following years, several more of the new birds were seen.

They were now named Sutton's warbler, in honor of the man who has painted birds, taught ornithology, studied birds, written about birds, and explored for birds with unflagging zest and enthusiasm. Although it has been found a number of times, the veracity of Sutton's warbler (which is probably a hybrid between the parula and the yellow-throated warblers) is still being argued.

But to the two young men who had heard that strange and different song in the hills of West Virginia, it will always be their own new bird, their great adventure, *their* warbler. And as it happened to them, it can happen to anyone with a keen eye and a discerning ear; to anyone with persistence, and the urge to follow adventure into the woods and hills of America.

On an April morning in 1952, when William H. Drury, Jr., with Allen Morgan and Richard Stackpole, of Cambridge, Massachusetts, got up before sunrise and started out on a birding expedition in Sudbury Valley, they had no idea of finding a new bird.

As the sun came up in the chill, exciting, April dawn, into a world filled with music and motion and sunshine, and the full flush of spring, they scanned a pond for ducks and possible newly-arrived waders. Instead of ducks, they saw a dark, heron-like bird with a down-curved beak such as no heron ever had. They hastily set up their telescope on shore. One of the men thumbed through pages of herons and ibises—yes, that was an ibis out there, the glossy ibis. This was marvelous. Ibises, they knew, had almost never been seen in Massachusetts—the last one had been found 102 years before, back in 1850.

Taking wing, the ibis flew with its legs dangling and its bent-down beak outstretched. This was an exhilarating start to a wonderful day. It was hardly worth while looking for anything else; nothing more could approach this splendid record.

Then up in a feed-lot near a barn above the pond, Morgan saw a flash of white. He thought at first that a large white hen or a turkey had flown down among the cows, but this bird was neither hen nor turkey. It was like a heron, but rather plump and squat. Moreover, it was early in the season for egrets to have come to New England; snowy egrets and American egrets had longer legs and slimmer forms than this. There was certainly something odd about it. . . .

William Drury had been in Guiana several years before and had seen cattle egrets following after South American cattle, and although he could hardly believe his own identification, he began to think that this was, most preposterously, a cattle egret. A closer examination showed the unmistakable wash of creamy buff on shoulders, head, and back—no native American egret or heron had that distinction.

One cattle egret—native of India, Spain, South America—in a Massachusetts cow-lot! It was a new bird for North America, but the only way they could possibly prove this fact was to shoot the bird before it got away. Morgan had a Federal collecting permit; his gun was in the car. First, however, they found a telephone and called Ludlow Griscom, the great field ornithologist, to tell him the news. He sent them back in a hurry to collect the bird before it got away. He would see it later.

At the cow-lot, Morgan attempted several shots but missed the heron as well as the cows; shooting among the latter was a touchy business. The bird flew away. The men followed at a fast and dizzy clip in their car. They knew that cattle egrets are lured to the presence of cows which, as the animals walk about, stir up insects for the birds to eat.

The egret had gone. At the next farm they found neither cows nor heron. Although it must have seemed to the frantic trio that days had elapsed since they first saw the new bird, it was only six o'clock in the morning. They had been up for hours and, like most birders, considered that everyone else had been up for hours, too. They telephoned to a friend who had a private airplane. The friend, no doubt awakened from his Sunday sleep, was instantly aroused by the news.

By means of the plane, the egret was at last located. The plane circled as low as possible; the information was shouted down to the men in the slowly following car. They left their vehicle and skulked behind a tractor, finally drew a bead on their bird—and it was theirs, in the name of science. It was then, and not until then, that the cattle egret was legally added to the birds of North America.

By 1953, more cattle egrets had been found in many places, and they were discovered to be nesting in Florida and Louisiana. A man in Florida calmly said that he had been seeing them since the early 1940's, but had not reported them because he thought they had probably escaped from captivity.

In Florida in 1955, still another flurry of excitement rose among ornithologists. A new bird had been seen. Hurricanes being what they are, and Florida being situated where it is, it is no new thing for tropical birds to appear and then vanish. They are misplaced individuals and seldom survive for very long.

Nevertheless, there was a new oriole in southern Florida, and people were seeing not one, but many of them. Miami's interested and intelligent bird enthusiasts observed a brilliant bird which was eating loquats, a bird that did not tally with any picture in any bird book at hand. It didn't appear to be a stray from Texas or California. The Fish and Wildlife Service in Washington received calls. A dead oriole, killed accidentally, was sent for examination and identification.

This was the spotted-breasted oriole of Central America and southern Mexico, a splendid orange-gold creature with black and white wings and tail, a black patch on the throat and around the eye, and a few black speckles near the shoulder. The orange-yellow crown distinguished it from the American orioles. The song was brilliant and glorious. Now nesting in Miami and southern Florida, the spotted-breasted oriole is accepted as a new member of the North American bird residents.

Was this the last new bird? It is not likely. At any moment now, perhaps today, perhaps tomorrow, the next new bird will be discovered. The chance of such an event keeps alive the zest of birding adventure.

Adventuring with birds means many things to many people. It may mean that first time when cedar waxwings on a winter day suddenly gathered in a juniper tree in the garden; or the vacation trip when the water ouzel sang beside a mountain stream; or the boat trip out to Bonaventure Island to see thousands of gannets, as Audubon saw them in 1833. It may mean the presence of an oriole in the front-yard elm; or loons crying in the moonlight above a northern lake; or gulls along a shore. There are as many splendid personal experiences to be had as there are birds to be found.

For a bird is not like other animals. It is unique. It, alone of wild creatures, is clothed in feathers whose colors are often resplendent and often deceiving, their pattern a marvel of symmetry, arrangement, and design, for concealment or display. It is as hard to understand a feather as it is to understand the bird itself; or its song, which may be pitched so high that only part of it is heard. One listens wistfully, wondering what else might be heard if human hearing were not limited.

Although the song of the bird may be a mystery, *why* it sings is not half so puzzling as *how* it sings. Flight is a mystery, too, for although insects have perfected it, none can compete with the hummingbird's incomparable performance. Birds on the wing have their own distinctive modes of flying—gulls drifting in translucent white, almost motionless, high in an ultramarine sky above a sea; a tern flying from the Arctic to the Antarctic and back again, seventeen thousand miles round trip each year; the strange nuptial flight of the woodcock on an April evening, a bird which, by all the laws of aerodynamics, should never be able even to get off the ground. Feathers, flight, song—these are the bird, yet there is something else which makes the whole bird, and that is the greatest mystery and source of adventure of all.

This is what brings men and women and young people to the woods and waters, year after year, spring after spring, often for a lifetime, to look for birds, to study them, to wonder about them. Although the big adventures and the great discoveries may all be done, that heritage from the past is part of our whole resource of knowledge today. This is the heritage which resulted from the adventure, pain, hunger, disappointment, despair, and death, and the ultimate triumph of truth, among those men who, from the ancient Hopewellians to the present, were the finders of our American birds.

BIBLIOGRAPHY

CHAPTER ONE: FIFTEEN HUNDRED YEARS AGO THERE WAS A RAVEN

The Rutherford Mound, Hardin County, Illinois, by Melvin L. Fowler. Illinois State Museum, Scientific Papers, Vol. VII, No. 1. 1957.

American Indian Ways of Life, by Thorne Deuel. Illinois State Museum, *Story of Illinois Series,* No. 9. 1958.

The Piasa Bird: Fact or Fiction? by Wayne C. Temple. *Journal of the Illinois State Historical Society,* Vol. XLIX, No. 3, Autumn 1956, pp. 308–327.

Modoc Rock Shelter, Preliminary Report, by Melvin L. Fowler and Howard D. Winters. Faunal analysis by Paul W. Parmalee. Illinois State Museum, *Report of Investigations,* No. 4, 1956.

Hopewellian Communities in Illinois, by Thorne Deuel. Illinois State Museum, Scientific Papers, Vol. V, 1952.

CHAPTER TWO: COLUMBUS

Voyages to Vinland, The First American Saga, translated and interpreted by Einer Haugen. University of Wisconsin, 1942.

Journal of the First Voyage of Columbus. Original Manuscripts of Early American History, Vol. 2.

BIBLIOGRAPHY

Admiral of the Ocean Sea, by Samuel Eliot Morison. Little, Brown and Company, Boston, 1942.

CHAPTER THREE: MARK CATESBY

Spanish Exporation of the Southwest, by R. G. Thwaites, in *Early Western Travels.* A. H. Clark Company, Cleveland, 1906.

Narratives of Early Virginia, Observations of George Percy, in *Original Narratives of Early American History.* Scribner's, New York, 1906.

Narratives of Early Virginia, Captain John Smith, 1612.

Original Narratives of Early American History, Scribner's, New York, 1906.

Natural History of Carolina, Mark Catesby. London, 1771.

Mark Catesby, by G. F. Frick. University of Illinois Press, 1961.

CHAPTER FOUR: THE LURE OF LOUISIANA

History of Louisiana, of the Western Parts of Virginia and Carolina, by Antoine Simon Le Page Du Pratz. London, 1774. Annotated edition, Pelican Press, Inc., New Orleans.

CHAPTER FIVE: GEORG WILHELM STELLER

Steller of the North, by Ann and Myron Sutton. Rand, McNally, Chicago, 1961.

Touched with Fire, Alaska's George William Steller, by Margaret E. Bell. William Morrow and Company, New York, 1960.

Birds of the World, by Oliver Austin, Jr. Golden Press, New York, 1961. *Lives of Celebrated Travellers* (Peter Simon Pallas), by James Augustus St. John, Vol. 3, Harpers, New York, 1868.

CHAPTER SIX: WILLIAM BARTRAM

Travels of William Bartram, ed. by Mark Van Doren. Dover Publications, New York, 1928.

BIBLIOGRAPHY

CHAPTER SEVEN: CAPTAIN COOK, JOHN LEDYARD, AND THE THRUSH OF NOOTKA SOUND

Voyages of Captain James Cook, 2 vols. London, 1784.

Passage to Glory: John Ledyard's America, by Helen Augur. Doubleday, New York, 1946.

Captain Cook's America, by E. M. Halliday. *American Heritage,* Vol. XIII, No. 1, December 1961.

CHAPTER EIGHT: LEWIS AND CLARK

Original Journals of Lewis and Clark, 7 vs. Antiquarian Press, New York, 1959.

The Natural History of the Lewis and Clark Expedition, by Raymond Darwin Burroughs. Michigan State University Press, 1961.

Trail of Lewis and Clark, 2 volumes, by Olin D. Wheeler. G. P. Putnam's Sons, New York, 1926.

CHAPTER NINE: THE YELLOWSTONE EXPEDITION

Expeditions of Zebulon Pike, ed. by Elliott Coues, 2 vols. Francis P. Harper, New York, 1895.

S. H. Long's Expedition to the Rocky Mountains, Early Western Travels, by R. G. Thwaites, Arthur H. Clark Co., 1905.

American Ornithology, by Wilson and Bonaparte. Philadelphia, 1828.

CHAPTER TEN: ALEXANDER WILSON

American Ornithology, by Wilson and Bonaparte. Original edition, Philadelphia, 1808.

CHAPTER ELEVEN: JOHN JAMES AUDUBON

Birds of America, by John James Audubon. Macmillan Company, New York, 1937.

BIBLIOGRAPHY

Audubon and His Journals, ed. by M. R. Audubon, 2 vols. Scribner's, New York, 1897.

Audubon and the Wild Swans, Journal of Illinois State Historical Society, June, 1942.

Up the Missouri with Audubon, by Edward Harris, ed. by John Francis Mc-Dermott. University of Oklahoma Press, 1951.

CHAPTER TWELVE: PRINCE MAXIMILIAN OF WIED

Maximilian's Travels in the Interior of North America, 1832–34, *Early Western Travels*, by R. G. Thwaites.

CHAPTER THIRTEEN: TOWNSEND, NUTTALL, AND THE WEST-WARD TRAIL

Narrative of a Journey Across the Rocky Mountains, by John Kirk Townsend, 1839, *Early Western Travels*, by R. G. Thwaites.

Manual of the Ornithology of the United States and Canada, Thomas Nuttall. 1832.

History of the Pacific Northwest, by George W. Fuller. Knopf, New York, 1931.

CHAPTER FOURTEEN: RAILROADS, BIRDS, AND BOUNDARIES

Personal Narrative of Exploration and Incidents in Texas, New Mexico, California, Sonora and Chihuahua, by John Russell Bartlett. D. Appleton, New York, 1854.

The Great Reconnaissance, by Edward S. Wallace. Little, Brown and Co., Boston and Toronto, 1955.

Building the Pacific Railway, by Edwin L. Sabin. J. B. Lippincott Company, Philadelphia, 1919.

Illustrated Birds of California, Texas, Oregon, British and Russian America, a general synopsis of North American Ornithology after Audubon, by John Cassin. 1856.

Death Valley Expedition, U.S. Biological Survey, *North American Fauna*, No. 7, 1891, by Frank Stephens.

BIBLIOGRAPHY

U.S. Geological Exploration of the 40th Parallel, Part III: Ornithology, by Robert Ridgway, 1877.

Reports of Explorations and Surveys for a Railroad from the Mississippi River to the Pacific Ocean, 1858, 12 vols., by Baird, Cassin, and Lawrence, Washington, D.C.

Birds of North America, discovered after Audubon and Wilson, by Daniel Giraud Elliot. London, 1869.

Exploration and Survey of the Valley of the Great Salt Lake of Utah, Including a Reconnaissance of a New Route Through the Rocky Mountains, by Howard K. Stansbury, 1853, Washington, D.C.

CHAPTER FIFTEEN: BIRDS AND THE ARMY

Report of Exploration down the Zuni and Colorado Rivers, by Captain Lorenzo L. Sitgreaves. Washington, D.C., 1854.

Report of the Colorado River of the West, 1857–58, by Lieutenant Joseph C. Ives, Corps of Topographical Engineers.

North American Birds, Charles Bendire. Govt. Printing Office, 1895.

Birds of the Colorado Valley, by Elliott Coues. U.S. Geological Survey, F. V. Hayden, 1878.

Birds of the Northwest, a Handbook of Ornithology, by Elliott Coues. U.S. Geological Survey of the Territories, F. V. Hayden, 1874.

Illustrated Birds of California, Texas, Oregon, British and Russian America, by John Cassin. 1856.

CHAPTER SIXTEEN: FRANKLIN, RICHARDSON, AND THE CALL OF
THE NORTH

Ornithology of Beechey's Voyage of the Blossom. N. A. Vigors, London, 1839.

Thirty Years in the Arctic Regions, by Sir John Franklin. Geo. Cooper Publ., New York, 1859.

Fauna Boreali-Americana, by William Swainson and John Richardson; Part Second, The Birds. London, 1831.

BIBLIOGRAPHY

Journey from Prince of Wales's Fort in Hudson's Bay to the Northern Ocean, 1769, 1770, 1771, 1772, by Samuel Hearne. Macmillan Company, London, 1958.

CHAPTER SEVENTEEN: THE TELEGRAPH TRAIL

The First Scientific Exploration of Russian America and the Purchase of Alaska, by James Alton James. Northwestern University Press, 1942.

International Polar Expedition to Point Barrow, Alaska. Washington, 1885.
Birds of North America, discovered after Audubon and Wilson, by Daniel Giraud Elliot. London, 1869.

CHAPTER EIGHTEEN: THE CRUISE OF THE CORWIN

Report of the Cruise of the Revenue Steamer Corwin in the Arctic Ocean, 1881–1884, 4 vols., Washington, D.C.

The Cruise of the Corwin, by John Muir. Houghton Mifflin Company, Boston, 1917.

CHAPTER NINETEEN: GOOSE CHASE

Birds in the Wilderness, by George Miksch Sutton, Macmillan Company, New York, 1936.

Ducks, Geese and Swans of North America, by F. H. Kortright. American Wildlife Institute, 1943.

Solving the Blue Goose Mystery, Saturday Evening Post, July 16, 1932.

CHAPTER TWENTY: THE LAST NEW BIRD

Birds Over America, by Roger Tory Peterson. Dodd, Mead & Company, New York, 1948.

National Geographic Magazine: Hunting the Voices of Vanishing Birds, by Arthur A. Allen, June 1937; *A New Bird Immigrant Arrives,* by Roger Tory Peterson, August 1954; *An Exotic New Oriole Settles in Florida,* by Charles M. Brookfield and Oliver Griswold, February 1956.

BIBLIOGRAPHY

Wake Robin, by John Burroughs. Houghton Mifflin Company, Boston, 1871.

Walden and other writings of Henry David Thoreau, edited, with biographical introduction, by Brooks Atkinson. Random House, Modern Library, New York, 1950.

INDEX

Abert, J. W., 178
Abert's Towhee, 178, 186
Alaska, 39, 44, 70, 160, 205-216
Albatross, Steller's, 52
Aleutians, 47, 65, 70, 224
Allen, A. A., 246
Allen, Robert, 246
Alligators, 53, 57-62
Alpine flowers, 100, 101, 218
Alton, Illinois, 7
America (ship), 211
American Ornithologists Union, 38, 169, 189
American Ornithology (Wilson), 112
Anderson, Dr. W. W., 182
Anderson, Dr. William, 63
Anhinga, 61
Antelope, 150
Apache Indians, 175
Arctic regions, 195, 204, 233
Arctic Ocean, 195, 208
Arkansas River, 104
Army and birds, 175
Assiniboine (steamboat), 139, 144
Atlantic Cable, 205
Audubon, John James, 119-135, 156; along Ohio River, 3, 121, 129; at St. Louis, 130; hunts buffalo, 119; hunts swans, 123; in Labrador, 129; meets Wilson, 116; on steamboat, 129-132
Avocets, 168

Bachman, John, 125
Back, George, 191
Baird, Spencer F., 134, 165, 207
Baird's Sparrow, 134
Baldwin, Dr. William, 92
Banks, Sir Joseph, 69
Bannister, H. M., 211
Barren Grounds, 197
Barrow, Sir John, 196, 224
Barrow's Goldeneye, 196
Bartlett, John, 161
Bartram, John, 55
Bartram, William, 53-62, 109
Beechey, Captain, 157
Beechey's Jay, 157
Bell, J. G., 129, 132, 163
Bell's Vireo, 132
Bendire, Captain Charles, 178
Bendire's Thrasher, 178
Bent, A. C., 232
Bering, Vitus, 39, 43
Bering Island, 48
Bering Strait, 206
Bibliography by chapters, 258-264
Biddle, John, 92
Bird Rock, 126

267

Birds, Arctic, 220-221
Birds in the Wilderness (Sutton), 240
Birds of America (Audubon), 126
Bischoff, Ferdinand, 211
Bitterroot River, 86
Blossom (ship), 157, 202
Bluebird, Arctic, 195
Bodmer, Charles, 136, 139
Bolshaya River, 50
Booby, 12
Bonaparte, Prince Lucian, 102, 118
Boundary Survey, Canadian, 159-160
Boundary Survey, Mexican, 161
Boy Scouts of America, 246
Brand, Albert R., 246
Breckenridge, Walter A., 246
Broley, Charles A., 246
Buffalo, 79, 97, 133, 139, 153
Bunting, Lazuli, 98
Burroughs, John, 243

Cache Creek, Illinois, 121
Cairo Point, 92
Cameahwait, Chief, 84
Cantwell, Lt. J. C., 225-229
Cascaes, Portugal, 19
Cassin, John, 163
Catesby, Mark, 20-29, 110
Catherine, Empress, 40
Catherine the Great, 71
Chapman, Dr. Frank M., 251
Charbonneau, Toussaint, 81, 144
Charleston, South Carolina, 56
Chat, Yellow-breasted, 25
Chicago Academy of Sciences, 210, 216
Chickadee, Hudsonian, 230
Chickadee, Rocky Mountain, 158
Chouteau, Pierre, 130
Churchill, Manitoba, 237
Clark, George Rogers, 73

Clark, William, 75-90
Clark's Nutcracker, 85
Cock-of-the-Plains, 89
Collie, Dr., 157
Collie's Magpie-Jay, 157
Colorado River, 177, 185
Columbia River, 75, 88, 156
Columbine, Rocky Mountain, 99
Columbus, Christopher, 10-19
Condor, California, 89
Cook, Captain James, 63-70
Cooper, Dr. J. G., 164, 183
Coppermine River, 70, 191
Cormorant, Spectacled, 49
Cornell University, 238, 246
Corwin (ship), 217-230
Coues, Dr. Elliott, 175, 183
Council Bluffs, Iowa, 78, 95
Crane, Whooping, 26
Cruikshank, Allan, 246
Cruise of the Corwin, 217-230
Crying Bird, 54
Cumberland House, Sask., 191

Dall, William H., 210
Dall's Sheep, 216
Davis, Jefferson, 163, 164
Death Valley, 177
Deusing, Murl, 246
Discovery (ship), 65
Die Bestiis Marinis (Steller), 49
Donovan, Ernest, 235
Dowitcher, Long-billed, 95
Dreidoppel, 136
Drury, William H., 253
Duck, Bemaculated, 125
Duck, Wood, 36
Du Pratz, Antoine, 30

Early Archaic Hunters, 3
Egret, Cattle, 254
Eider, Steller's, 49
Elliot, Daniel Giraud, 216

Emory, Major William, 162
Empress Anna Ivanova, 41
Empress Catherine, 40
Empress Elizaveta Petrovna, 50
Engineer Cantonment, 95
Ericson, Leif, 10

Falcon pipe, 5
Fauna Boreali-Americana (Swainson), 202
Feilner, Sgt. John, 179
"Fifty-Four Forty or Fight," 159
Finch, House, 98, 166
Flicker, Red-shafted, 69
Florida, 53
Flycatcher, Olive-sided, 193
Flycatcher, Scissor-tailed, 102
Flycatcher, Small-headed, 125
Fort Astoria, 156
Fort Burgwyn, 182
Fort Chipewyan, 193
Fort Clark, 143
Fort Clatsop, 88
Fort Enterprise, 200
Fort Franklin, 195, 202
Fort Klamath, 179
Fort Mandan, 81
Fort McKenzie, 139
Fort Osage, 93
Fort Rosalie, 32
Fort Smith, 106
Fort Union, 132, 139
Fort Vancouver, 156
Fort Whipple, 175, 184
Fort Yuma, 181, 185
Fortieth Parallel Survey, 165
Forty-Ninth Parallel Survey, 160
Foxes, Arctic, 48, 221
Franklin, Captain John, 190-204
Franklin's Grouse, 194
Franklin's Gull, 195

Gadsden Purchase, 159, 162

Gallant (steamboat), 129
Gambel, William, 158
Gambel's Quail, 158
Gambel's Sparrow, 158
Gannets, 126-127
Gavin, Angus, 235
Gaviota Pass, 20
Gerard, John, 246
Gilham, Charles E., 236
Gnatcatcher, Black-headed, 179
Gold Rush, 163
Goose, Blue, 231
Goose, Ross, 234-236
Goose, Snow, 68, 231, 233
Goose Chase, 231-236
Grace's Warbler, 182, 184
Great Bear Lake, 194-195
Great Falls of the Missouri, 84
Great Slave Lake, 194
Griscom, Ludlow, 254
Grouse, Dusky, 99
Grouse, Franklin's, 194
Grouse, Richardson's, 194
Grouse, Ruffed, 27, 110
Grouse, Sage, 89
Gull, Franklin's, 195
Gull, Ross, 196

Haller, Karl W., 252
Harris, Edward, 129, 131
Harris's Sparrow, 131, 237-240
Harris's Sparrow, search for eggs, 237-240
Hawaii, 66, 70, 156
Hearne, Samuel, 190
Heerman, Dr. A. K., 176
Henry, Dr. T. C., 179
Heron, Great White, 124
Hood, Robert, 191
Hopewellian people, 1
Howell, A. H., 251
Hudson Bay, 191, 233
Hudson's Bay Company, 191, 234

Humboldt Sink, 67
Hummingbird, Ruby-throated, 37
Hummingbird, Rufous, 69

Ibis, Glossy, 253
Ibis, White, 61
Ibis, Wood, 186
Independence, Missouri, 78, 148
Inscription Rock, 181
Ives, Lt. J. C., 165

Jade Mountain, 227
James, Dr. Edwin, 96, 99-102
Jay, Beechey's, 157
Jay, Black-headed, 47, 87
Jay, California, 158
Jay, Canada, 190
Jay, Maximilian's, 141
Jay, Mexican, 180
Jay, Pinyon, 142
Jay, Rocky Mountain, 87
Jay, Steller's, 46, 118
Jay, Woodhouse's, 168
Jeannette (ship), 217
Jefferson, Pres. Thomas; Ledyard
    expedition, 70; Lewis and Clark
    expedition, 73; with Wilson, 111
Jessup, Augustus E., 92

Kamchatka, 41, 42
Kansa Indians, 93
Karlsevni, Thorfinn, 10
Kayak Island, 45
Kellet, Captain, 220
Kellogg, Paul, 246
Kennerly, Dr. C. B. R., 179
Kennicott, Robert, 205-216
Kennicott's Arctic Warbler, 215
Kennicott's Screech Owl, 216
Kennicott's Sharp-tailed Grouse,
    215
Kingbird, Western, 102, 170-171
Kingfisher, 36, 120

Kirtland, Dr. J. E., 206
Kirtland Warbler, 206, 211
Kowak River, Alaska, 225

Labrador, 129
Lake Winnipeg, 208
Lark Bunting, 194
Last New Bird, 241
Law, John, 30
Lawson, John, 25
Ledyard, John, 63-72
Lewis and Clark Expedition, 74-90
Lewis, Meriwether, 75-90, 137
Lewis's Woodpecker, 85
Limpkin, 54
Lincoln, Pres. Abraham, 206, 211,
    244
Lincoln's Second Inaugural, 244
Lincoln's Sparrow, 128, 131
Linnaeus, Karl, 29
Lloyd, Bert, 238
Lolo Trail, 85
Long, Major S. H., 91-106
Long's Peak, 98
Loon, 230
Lord, J. K., 161
Louisiana, Lure of, 30-38
Louisiana Purchase, 75
Lucy's Warbler, 183

Mackenzie River, 70
Magpie, Black-billed, 194
Magpie, Yellow-billed, 79, 82
Mandan Indians, 81
Maria's River, 83
Marion (ship), 124
Marquette and Jolliet, 8
Maslowski, Karl, 246
Maximilian, Prince of Wied, 136
Maximilian's Jay, 141
McCall, Col. George, 176, 179
McCown, Captain, 179
McCown's Longspur, 179

McLenegan, Samuel, 225-230
Meadowlark, Western, 132
Merrill, Dr. J. C., 178
Merrill's Pauraque, 178
Mexico, War with, 180
Miami, Florida, 255
Michaux, André, 73
Mirages, 95
Mississippians, 4
Mississippi River, 74, 77, 137
Missouri River, 74, 77, 93, 130, 138, 148
Mojave Desert, 177, 187
Monroe, Pres. James, 91
Morgan, Allen, 253
Mount St. Elias, Alaska, 44
Muir, John, 218

Napoleon Bonaparte, 75
Natural History of Carolina (Catesby), 28
Natchez Indians, 32-34
National Audubon Society, 246
Nelson, David, 63
Nelson, Edward, 218
Nelson's Gull, 223
Nelson's Ptarmigan, 223
Nelson's Sparrow, 223
New Harmony, Indiana, 106, 136
New Orleans, Louisiana, 30
Noctiluca, 66
Nomenclature of Color (Ridgway), 165
Nootka Sound, 67
Nordenskiold, Baron, 219
Northwest Passage, 66, 203
Norton Sound, 223
Nulato, Alaska, 212
Nuthatch, Pygmy, 157
Nuttall, Thomas, 125, 146-157

Ohio River, 1, 76, 136-137
Okhotsk, Siberia, 41, 42, 72

Omega (steamboat), 131
Oriole, Spotted-breasted, 255
Owl, Burrowing, 98, 102
Owl, Kennicott's, 216
Owl, Richardson's, 195
Owl, Screech, 242

Pacific Railroad Surveys, 163-165
Paisley, Scotland, 107
Pallas, Dr. Peter Simon, 52, 65
Papagai à tête aurore, 38
Parakeet, Carolina, 37, 122
Pawnee Indians, 94
Peale, Titian Ramsey, 92
Peale's Museum, 82, 90
Pease, Charles, 211
Pease, William, 180
Pelican, White, 78, 171-173
Percy, George, 21
Perry River marshes, 237
Peterson *Bird Guides*, 245
Peterson, Roger Tory, 245, 246
Peter the Great, 39
Pettingill, Olin Sewall, 238
Phainopepla, 176
Philosophical Society, 73
Phoebe, Black, 158
Phoebe, Say's, 96
Piasa Bird, 7
Pigeon, Band-tailed, 99
Pigeon, Passenger, 37, 168
Pig War, The, 160
Pike, Zebulon, 91, 113
Pike's Peak, 98, 100-101
Pinzon, Martin, 12
Pipes, Hopewellian, 5
Platte River, 150
Poland, J. Lloyd, 252
Portola, 20
Prairie Dog, 98, 102
Ptarmigan, White-tailed, 194
Pyramid Lake, Nevada, 171

INDEX

Quadrupeds of North America (Audubon), 128
Quail, Blue, 179
Quail, Mountain, 90
Queen Victoria, 206

Rail, Virginia, 189
Railroads, Birds and Boundaries, 159
Raven, 1
Raven Pipe, 1
Reed, Chester A., 245
Reed's *Bird Guides,* 245
Regulus, Cuvier's, 125
Resolution (ship), 65
Richardson, Dr. John, 190-204
Richardson's Grouse, 194
Richardson's Owl, 195
Ridgway, Robert, 165-173, 223
Ridgway's Sparrow, 169
Ripley (ship), 126
Robin, 68
Ross, Bernard R., 234
Ross, Sir James Clark, 196
Ross Goose, 234
Ross Gull, 196
Rozier, Ferdinand, 117, 120

Sacajawea, 81, 88
Ste. Genevieve, Missouri, 121
St. John River, Florida, 57
St. Louis, Missouri, 90, 130, 138, 147
St. Michael's, Alaska, 212, 223
St. Peter (ship), 39, 43
Salmonberry, 46
Sandpiper, Sharp-tailed, 224
Sandpiper, Spoon-billed, 224
Sandwich Islands, 66
San Juan Island, 160
Santa Maria (ship), 12, 17
Sapsucker, Red-breasted, 69
Say, Thomas, 92-106, 137
Say's Phoebe, 96

Sea Cow, 49
Sea Lion, 49
Semple, John Bonner, 238
Seton, Ernest Thompson, 237
Shannon, George, 77
Shawnee Indians, 122
Shoshone Indians, 84
Shrike, Crested, 223
Shrike, White-rumped, 84
Shufeldt's Junco, 178
Siberia, 41, 71, 205, 215
Sitgreaves, Capt. Lorenzo, 180
Smith, Capt. John, 21
Smithsonian Institution, 173, 207
Snakebird, 61
Soda Lake, 187
Solitaire, Townsend's, 156
Soper, J. Dewey, 233
Southhampton Island, 234
South Pacific, 65
Sparrow, Baird's, 134
Sparrow, Cape Sable Seaside, 251
Sparrow, Harris's, 131, 237-240
Sparrow, Lark, 94
Sparrow, Lincoln's, 128, 131
Sparrow, Ridgway's, 169
"Sparrow, Satin," 176
Sprague, Isaac, 129
Sprague's Pipit, 132
Squires, Lewis, 129, 132
Stackpole, Richard, 253
Steller, Georg Wilhelm, 39-52
Steller's Albatross, 52
Steller's Eider, 49
Steller's Jay, 46
Steller's Sea-Lion, 49
Stilts, 168
Sutton, Dr. George M., 234, 237-240, 247
Sutton's Warbler, 253
Swallow, Cliff, 98
Swans, Whistling, 123
Swift, Lt. William H., 92, 105

INDEX

Swift, Chimney, 24
Swift, White-throated, 181

Tahiti, 64
Tanager, Hepatic, 181
Tanager, Louisiana, 90
Tanner, James, 247
Telegraph Trail, 205-216
Tensas River, Louisiana, 247
Tern, Royal, 11
Thoreau, Henry David, 241
Thrasher, Sage, 151
Thrush, Gray-cheeked, 230
Thrush, Hermit, 244
Thrush, Varied, 69, 87
Townsend, John K., 125, 146
Townsend's Solitaire, 125
Tropic Bird, 11
Tundra, 218, 233
Turkey, Wild, 55
Tushepaw Indians, 86

Ulloa, 20
Unalakleet, Alaska, 212

Vancouver Island, 67, 160
Vigors, N. A., 157
Vireo, Bell's, 132
Virginia's Warbler, 183

Wake Robin (Burroughs), 243
Warbler, Grace's, 182, 184
Warbler, Kirtland, 206, 211
Warbler, Lucy's, 182, 183
Warbler, Orange-crowned, 99, 186

Warbler, Sutton's, 252
Warbler, Virginia's, 182, 183
Washington, D.C., 244
Waxell, Lieutenant, 48
Western Engineer (steamboat), 92
Western Union Telegraph, 205
Whipple, Lt. A. R., 162
Whipple Pass, 184
Wilson, Alexander, 107-118
Wilson's Petrel, 118
Wilson's Phalarope, 118
Wilson's Plover, 118
Wilson's Snipe, 118
Wilson's Thrush, 118
Woodhouse, Dr. S. W., 180
Woodhouse's Jay, 182
Wood River, Illinois, 77
Woodpecker, Black-breasted, 163
Woodpecker, Ivory-billed, 26, 114, 247-250
Woodpecker, Red-headed, 108
Woodpecker, White-headed, 163
Wrangell Island, 222
Wren, Rock, 98

Xantus, Captain John, 178
Xantus's Hummingbird, 178

Yellowstone Expedition, 91-106
Yellowstone River, 92, 132
Yellowstone (steamboat), 138
York, 84
Yukon River, 209
Yuma, Fort, 181

Zahl, Paul, 246